Portraits of Basques in the New World

The Basque Series

Portraits of Basques in the New World

EDITED BY

Richard W. Etulain and Jeronima Echeverria

University of Nevada Press, Reno & Las Vegas

Basque Series Editor: William A. Douglass

This book was published with the support of The Program for Cultural Cooperation between Spain's Ministry of Culture and United States Universities.

University of Nevada Press, Reno, Nevada 89557 USA
Copyright © 1999 by University of Nevada Press
Individual copyright notices can be found at the end of the book.
All rights reserved
Manufactured in the United States of America
Design by Carrie Nelson House
Library of Congress Cataloging-in-Publication Data
Portraits of Basques in the New World / edited by Richard W. Etulain and Jeronima Echeverria.
    p.   cm. — (The Basque series)
    Includes bibliographical references and index.
    ISBN 0-87417-332-9 (alk. paper)
    1. Basque Americans—West (U.S.)—Biography.   2. Basque Americans—West (U.S.)—History.   3. West (U.S.)—Biography.
    I. Etulain, Richard W. II. Echeverria, Jeronima, 1946– .
    III. Series.
    F596.3.B15P67   1999   99-18318
    978′.00499928—dc21   CIP
The paper used in this book meets the requirements of American National Standard for Information Sciences—Permanence of Paper for Printed Library Materials, ANSI Z39.48-1984. Binding materials were selected for strength and durability.

Frontispiece: Tomás Alcorta's sheep camp during lambing time, 1919.

FIRST PRINTING
08 07 06 05 04 03 02 01 00 99
5 4 3 2 1

To Bill Douglass,
mentor to the Basques,
and
to the memory of
Pat and Eloise Garmendia Bieter

Contents

Part III. Modern Basques

Illustrations

Preface and Acknowledgments

For several centuries, the Basques have intrigued numerous writers and travelers. Whether describing Old World Basque villages nestled in the Pyrenees Mountains between Spain and France or depicting Basque sheepherders as the "lonely sentinels" of the American West, writers have portrayed *Euskaldunak* (the Basque speakers) as one of the world's unique ethnic groups. Frequently they are labeled "mysterious," "enigmatic," or "exotic."

By the mid-twentieth century, these early interpretations of the Basques had often solidified into stereotypes. Impression piled upon impression added up to static generalizations, usually based more on tradition, tourist hype, and outright romantic nonsense than on solid, systematic, and up-to-date research. By that time, only Englishman Rodney Gallop had produced his widely circulated *A Book of the Basques* (1930), an accessible overview of Old World Basques. Meanwhile, in the United States, those interested in studying *Amerikanuak* (the Basques in the Americas) had to be satisfied with dozens of newspaper and Sunday supplement stories, scattered references in local histories, a few novels, and a handful of master's theses and doctoral dissertations. No one had yet written a substantial account of the Basques in the United States.

That situation changed dramatically in the next twenty-five years. When Robert Laxalt's novelized biography of his father, *Sweet Promised Land,* appeared in 1957, and when William A. Douglass and Jon Bilbao's monumental overview, *Amerikanuak: Basques in the New World,* was issued in 1975, general readers and scholars had two helpful sources for understanding American Basques. One book probed, in appealing narrative form, the life of an archetypal Basque sheepherder, and the other volume furnished a sweeping overview of Basque experiences over time, beginning with Old World backgrounds and reaching out to their settlements in North and South America.

Simultaneously, Jon Bilbao's multivolume bibliography *Eusko Bibliographía* (1970–), Ann Nolan Clark's moving adolescent novel *Year Walk* (1975), and the flowering of the Basque Series at the University of Nevada Press testified that imaginative and scholarly interpretations had come of age. Still, many other Basque personalities and subjects merited further attention.

This collection of biographical portraits, clearly building on these important scholarly achievements since 1950, adds new information on several notable American Basques. Moving beyond earlier stereotypes, these essays span four centuries and cover a rich variety of geographical, occupational, and gender experiences. Taken together, these life stories furnish a mosaic of Basque experiences and thereby enlarge understanding of an important American ethnic group.

The first three essays gathered here deal with early Borderland Basques. Ralph Vigil's chapter details the signal importance of Bishop Juan de Zumárraga in the sixteenth century, and Marc Simmons shows Juan de Oñate's central role in the founding of New Mexico. Next, Donald Garate assesses the significance of Juan Bautista de Anza, father and son, in expanding and protecting Spanish settlements in what is now northern Mexico. In many previous historical accounts these men are not identified as Basques, but in these discussions their ethnic identities receive full coverage.

The next several essays focus on nineteenth- and early twentieth-century experiences. Carol Hovey demonstrates how Pedro and Bernardo Altube were major players in Basque expansion from California into Nevada ranching areas in the second half of the nineteenth century. In the early decades of the new century, John B. Archabal occupied a similar position among Basques in Boise, where, as John Bieter shows, he became known as the Basque Sheep King of Idaho. Robert Boyd's photo essay portrays several Basque families who traveled from Europe to settle in the high-desert country in Oregon, Idaho, Nevada, and California.

The next four sketches trace careers of contemporary Basques who began in the sheepherding business or were closely linked to it. In a warm autobiographical piece, Rene Tihista chronicles a cycle of seasons, during his teenage years, on a Montana sheep ranch, where he lived with his family. Tihista did not remain a sheepman, and neither did Santiago "Santi" Basterrechea, whose biography by William A. Douglass shows him to be an archetypal Basque. For Lyda Martinto

Esain, the connection with hundreds of Basque sheepherders came through her work as a *hotelera*. As Jeronima Echeverria points out, Lyda Esain represents the hundreds of Basque women throughout the American West who worked long, arduous hours in Basque boardinghouses. Although Idahoan Pete Cenarrusa began his career as a rancher and sheepman, his interests soon shifted to politics, and as Patrick Bieter makes clear, Cenarrusa was a forthright champion of Basque civil rights during his long career as Idaho's secretary of state.

The final chapters examine the important cultural contributions of three other recent Basques. More than any other person, Juanita "Jay" Hormaechea was responsible for sparking renewed interest in dancing among western Basques. In her essay, Angeline Blain demonstrates how Jay Hormaechea urged and cajoled young Boise Basques into learning and performing Basque dances throughout the country. As a result of Hormaechea's teaching and leadership, the Oinkari Dancers have gained a much-deserved reputation as America's leading Basque dance group. Even more widely recognized are the writings of the best-known Basque author in the United States, Robert Laxalt. His smoothly written life story of Dominique Laxalt in *Sweet Promised Land* and his later Basque trilogy, Richard Etulain asserts, mark him as a notable writer of American ethnic literature. Finally, William A. Douglass uses the life of southern California journalist and businessman Robert Erburu as a vehicle for discussing the complex, ever-changing nature of ethnic identity. For Douglass, Erburu's search for his Basque heritage parallels similar quests by millions of Americans for their ethnic identity in a postmodern world.

As a collection, these essays provide illuminating insights into varied New World Basque experiences, especially as they played out in the greater American West. From friars, explorers, and political and military leaders to ranchers and herders and on to modern cultural figures and entrepreneurs, Basques have exhibited individualistic, shifting faces to their interpreters. Although best known as herders and ranchers, Basque Americans increasingly and persistently have left those occupations for urban work. Will Amerikanuak be able to retain their ethnic heritage in the face of occupational and geographical trends and shifts militating against the maintenance of that ethnic identity? A generation hence, another group of scholars will need to reexamine that important question. Meanwhile, this collection, coming one generation after Douglass and Bilbao's benchmark volume *Amerikanuak*, clearly attests to the long, important Basque presence in the American West. These essays likewise illustrate the growing interest among scholars, Basques and non-Basques alike, in examining important contributions of Euskaldunak to American history.

Editors of collaborative projects like this always pile up several debts. We are no exception. Jeronima Echeverria and Richard Etulain wish to thank William A. Douglass for his generous and helpful suggestions.[1] Richard Etulain is also grateful to Robert Laxalt for his help and to Jen Clark, David Key, and Cindy Tyson for preparing several parts of the manuscript. The University of New Mexico aided greatly in providing a research semester for Richard Etulain, and California State University, Fresno, granted Jeronima Echeverria a semester sabbatical.

Part I

The Basque Diaspora in the New World

1

Don Fray Juan de Zumárraga
Loyal Basque Vassal and Spanish Churchman

RALPH VIGIL

The Spanish Background

Juan de Zumárraga's childhood and youth coincided with the glorious springtime of Spain's rise to power in the Old World and the New. Born in either 1475 or 1476,[1] Zumárraga was shaped by the social and intellectual conditions of the age of Ferdinand and Isabella, the "Catholic Kings" who united Spain and began a worldwide empire. Zumárraga spoke Spanish, but his style of expression was decidedly "Bizkaian" ("Biscayan"), probably because he had not imbibed the Castilian dialect with his mother's milk.[2] He shared with other distinguished Spaniards of his time a distinct attitude toward the world. This attitude was fundamentally and inevitably religious, given the importance of the clergy as interpreters of ideology in his day. In Zumárraga's case, this was a traditional Catholic spirituality of an age still rooted in Scholastic theology. Granted his fondness for Desiderius Erasmus's evangelical humanism, Zumárraga was essentially, as Fernando Benítez writes, "a monk of the Middle Ages, to judge by the picture we have of his life."[3]

Caught in the cultural web of a nation whose kingdoms were united in the pursuit of common goals by the Defenders of the Faith, Zumárraga as friar and first bishop and archbishop of Mexico is an example of the moderate reformed clergy who believed that everyone should be given his right and due by virtue of his station in a hierarchic society. Rigidly orthodox, he was more tolerant than his friend and confessor Fray Domingo de Betanzos and less radical than Fray Bartolomé de Las Casas, the most famous defender of the Indians in the struggle over Indian labor and tribute.

The restoration of royal power in Castile brought peace and order, economic and religious reforms, the establishment of the Spanish Inquisition, increase of state revenues, the promotion of the arts, literature, and letters, and greater administrative control of the regions extending from the Basque Provinces and Navarre to Andalusia. The end of civil war in the kingdom also made possible the end of the Reconquest with the incorporation of Granada. Following the surrender of the Moors, Castilian imperialism began with the voyage of Christopher Columbus. The end of the holy war in 1492 also saw the expulsion of those Jews who would not convert to the Catholic faith. This last act joined politics and religion and sought to "impose a unity which transcended administrative, linguistic, and cultural barriers, bringing together Spaniards of all races in common furtherance of a holy mission."[4]

In their consolidation of what is today modern Spain and the beginnings of royal government in the Indies, Ferdinand and Isabella were guided by the concept that the well-ordered state cannot be divorced from religion. Royal control of the Church in Spain and America allowed the crown to nominate candidates to higher ecclesiastical offices. In her reform of the Church, Queen Isabella had a strong ally in her confessor, Francisco Jiménez de Cisernos, a member of the Observant branch of the Franciscan Order. Religious reform of the clergy in a corrupt age improved the morals and learning of the clergy, and the spiritual conquest of America would be carried out by friars, among them Franciscans like Zumárraga selected from the ranks of the lower nobility and the middle class for their learning and humanity. Faithful to the rule of poverty, the Franciscans were eager to establish a worship in the image of the primitive church of the apostolic age.[5] In addition to their religious duties, prelates like Zumárraga often served as royal officials or assisted the civil authorities in their efforts to establish a Christian commonwealth respectful of God and the king's service.

Zumárraga's Basque Identity

Most biographers of Zumárraga have focused on his episcopal career. More recently, Richard Greenleaf and the Academy of American Franciscan History have shown the close relations the bishop maintained with his family.[6] Greenleaf's book and other works and documents were used by Joxe Mallea-Olaetxe to place Zumárraga "within the framework of Basque culture and to scrutinize his words and deeds in order to reveal the 'Biscayan' rather than the 'Spaniard.'"[7]

In his treatment of Zumárraga's dealings with relatives and other Basques in Spain and Mexico, Mallea-Olaetxe examines some of the traits associated with this regional people as personified in Zumárraga. In addition to commenting on Zumárraga's work ethic, pragmatism, irony, candidness, talent for business, and administrative ability, Mallea-Olaetxe confirms Zumárraga's pride in family, his loyalty to and favoring of relatives, and his attempt, as bishop in Mexico, "to re-create his native environment through his hiring of Biscayan *mayordomos,* Basque confidants, secretaries, stonemasons and household help."[8]

Little is known about Zumárraga's family and education. His father, Juan López de Zumárraga, was the only son of Lope de Zumárraga. According to the bishop, his father "was wealthy" when he married his mother, a widow and a member of the Arrázola family of the house of Muncháraz, honorable and prosperous small proprietors of good lineage.[9]

A sister and brothers are mentioned, as is a niece who married Martín de Aranguren, the bishop's *mayordomo* in Mexico. Another relative, Manuela Gómez de Solórzano, the widow of Juan de Mendiola, stated in 1551 that fifteen years before she had gone to Mexico with her brother-in-law, the archbishop Zumárraga, "where she remains, poor and with four children." Her request for sustenance appeared just to the Royal Council of the Indies.[10] Zumárraga's heir was his nephew, an embroiderer named Sancho García Larrazábal. Sancho García and another relative, a hosier, went to Mexico with Zumárraga. Sancho García prospered in Mexico, for in 1541 Zumárraga advised his greedy nephew to examine his conscience and his present condition with his former state and the things he had concealed ("y andar a sombra de tejados").[11]

The letter of Manuela Gómez de Solórzano mentioned above would indicate that Zumárraga's half-brother was surnamed Mendiola. However, Mallea-Olaetxe states that Juan de Mendiola was a nephew of the bishop; he also notes that Zumárraga had at least one older brother, named Lope, like his grandfather.[12] In any case, it appears that his parents formed part of the middling group of respectable townsfolk of Durango, famous for its cloth in the sixteenth century and the manufacture of sword guards and other iron fittings, crossbows, hoes, axes, saws, nails, and the like. Zumárraga noted that large nails used to secure the latches on doors that faced the street sold for a high price in Mexico City.[13]

Juan López de Zumárraga and his wife, doña Teresa de Lariz, were pious folk who welcomed and lodged Franciscans passing through Durango, and the young Zumárraga's acquaintance with these friars undoubtedly influenced his decision to join the Order. Shortly before his death, Zumárraga declared that he and his nephew would continue the practice of his parents by building a hospice and infirmary for the Franciscans in the houses they had inherited from their parents and grandparents "on the street called Goyencalle."[14]

As is evident from his correspondence, Zumárraga joined the idea of Christian social service with family matters. After 1528 Zumárraga's family in Durango and the hospice he proposed to establish as a memorial to his family were his major concerns in his transatlantic affairs. As late as 1547 Zumárraga, now more than seventy years old, wrote that the Council of the Indies, scandalized by the large sum of money he had sent for the hospice in 1544 even as he pleaded poverty, had taken from him the tributes of the Indian village of Ocuituco he had held in encomienda. Moreover, Zumárraga wrote, there were those who stated that he "had a greater obligation to use such alms within my own bishopric."[15]

Zumárraga must have felt the sting of those parishioners offended by his almsgiving, for in 1541 he also questioned his use of church funds designated for the marriages of poor orphans in Mexico. After providing a dowry of one thousand ducats for his relative, the "noble orphan" María Iñiguez de Muncháraz, so that she might marry his nephew Sancho García Larrazábal, the bishop learned that Sancho García had stinted on the marriage and the purchase of houses and property for his wife by perhaps five hundred ducats. He also noted that his nephew had pilfered funds provided by Zumárraga for María's mother. Zumárraga admonished his nephew for his despicable behavior and stated that bishops should not give money intended for the poor to rich relatives.[16]

When Zumárraga entered the Franciscan Order is unknown, but he may have professed at the monastery of Aranzatzu in the ecclesiastical province of Cantabria, then under the jurisdiction of Burgos.[17] However, if the Franciscan seminary at Aranzatzu was only established in 1517 and Zumárraga met the future emperor Charles V at Abrojo for the first time in November of the same year, this seems unlikely.[18]

Whether he professed at Aranzatzu or Abrojo in the province of Concepción, his affection for Aranzatzu is evident in letters he wrote in 1547 to Francisco del Castillo, a native of Durango and father provincial at Burgos. A considerable part of the books that he had sent Castillo, including works by Erasmus, were intended for the library of the hospice at Durango when completed, and other books were to be given to the monastery of Aranzatzu.[19]

Situated some nine kilometers from the town of Oñate, the monastery of Aranzatzu dates from 1469, when tradition has it that a shepherd saw a vision of the Blessed Virgin above a hawthorn tree or shrub (*arantz*). Like other sanctuaries of Our Lady and holy places venerating particular saints, Our Lady of Aranzatzu, although known beyond the Basque provinces, would have an ardent local cult.[20]

Sacred shrines and visions of the divine were not the only signs of the wonders of the invisible world in the Basque regions. Chronicles of Our Lady of Aranzatzu narrate that the worship of the devil and witchcraft were first joined and taught in Bizkaia by a great sorcerer from Guyenne, a false preacher and apostate of the Gospel. Complaints of harm done by witches in Gipuzkoa date from 1466, and in 1500 the presence of countless heretics and devil-worshiping witches of the sierra of Amboto in Bizkaia was discovered. In the villa of Durango itself, a heretical sect similar to that of the "dishonest and evil" Fraticelli arose in 1442, led by the Franciscan friar Alonso de Mella, brother of Don Juan de Mella, bishop of Zamora.[21]

Four of the seventeen heretics of Durango condemned to death in 1500 may have been related to Zumárraga: doña María Muncháraz, Marina and Teresa Arrázola, and María Pérez Urquiaga. Zumárraga mentioned the heresy of Durango in his *Doctrina Breve* (1543–1544). Called the heresy of Amboto, or of the lay order of Franciscan sisters, it was first disseminated by Fray Alonso de Mella and thus perverted and deceived many, especially simpleminded women. Mallea-Olaetxe suggests that Zumárraga's puritanical bent and rigid orthodoxy may have been a reaction to the excesses that had taken place in Durango and the execution of his relatives as heretics.[22]

At the time that witchcraft and sorcery were being discovered and investigated in the Pyrenees, Zumárraga was acting as guardian of the monastery of Abrojo, where he apparently met Charles V for the second time, in 1527. In need of money to battle the Turks threatening Vienna, the emperor summoned the national assembly of Castile, the *Cortes,* to Valladolid. Unsuccessful in his attempt to persuade the assembled estates of the realm to vote him the service he needed, the king sent the town's representatives home at Easter and elected the monastery of Abrojo, close to Valladolid, as a retreat during Holy Week. Impressed by the austere life of the friars and Zumárraga's devotion, charity, and gravity, he shortly had Zumárraga appointed inquisitor in charge of the investigation against witches in Vizcaya.[23]

Zumárraga, whose mother tongue was Basque, chose as his fellow judge Andrés de Olmos, a very pious friar who was distinguished for his knowledge of sacred scripture and canon law and who had joined the Franciscan Order at the monastery of Valladolid. Olmos would accompany Zumárraga to Mexico, where he would master the Nahuatl, Totonac, Tepehuan, and Huastec languages and complete a comprehensive work on Indian antiquities to serve as a guide in Franciscan efforts to refute native religious beliefs.[24]

No record of the witch investigation made by Zumárraga and Olmos is available. But given Zumárraga's origins in Durango and his fluency in Basque and Olmos's disbelief in the power of witches, they were undoubtedly aware that complaints of witchcraft arose from credulity, lineage and village hatreds, and pagan traditions.[25] That no witches were found in Zumárraga's "very fair and complete" investigation is confirmed by the inquisitor Antonio de Salazar y Frías: In 1613 he noted that no person had been found guilty of witchcraft by the Inquisition in its nine investigations conducted in the Basque provinces between 1526 and 1596. The restraint of the inquisitors in these investigations contrasts greatly with the actions of judges in Basse Navarre during these years and with the trials and sentences of Basque witches and sorcerers of French Lapurdi (Labourd) and Spanish Zugarramurdi in 1609 and 1610.[26]

Unlike the magistrates who believed in witches and their powers, Zumárraga, writing in 1543, said that practices associated with witchcraft were vain and superstitious idolatry: "The concern with witchcraft or *sorguinas* said to exist in our native land and who have been condemned and burned may also be reduced to this type of idolatry." Those persons, commented Zumárraga, who made use of or believed in the efficacy of spells, charms, fortune-telling, lucky and unlucky days, divinations, and invocations to demons dishonored God by their credulity and evil intentions, acted contrary to the teachings of the holy Catholic faith, and sinned against the First Commandment.[27]

Protector of the Indians and Bishop-Elect

On December 12, 1527, Charles V nominated Zumárraga for the bishopric of Mexico. This appointment and that of the judges of the first *audiencia* of Mexico were based on the decision to remove Cortés from the governorship of New Spain. Before capturing Tenochtitlán, Cortés had used dubious legal means to renounce Diego Velázquez's governmental jurisdiction in Mexico and assume independent authority for himself in an expedition of conquest and colonization. After the collapse of the Aztec Triple Alliance, Cortés, against the crown's instructions, granted encomiendas to his soldiers, unpaid after two years with the exception of a few spoils.[28]

Despite Cortés's actions, his conquest gained him the governorship. But treasury officials were appointed to assist him and to report on his activities. As governor and captain general, Cortés began the creation of a new society on the ruins of Tenochtitlán. So that the Indians might be quickly converted to the Christian faith, he requested that Franciscan and Dominican friars of good character be placed in charge of the spiritual conquest of Mexico. Seculars should not be sent, since bishops, canons, and other dignitaries would only squander the Church's wealth "and leave entailed estates to their sons or kinsmen."[29]

In 1523 Fray Pedro de Gante, a relation of Charles V, and two other Flemings of the Franciscan Order arrived. In the following year the "Twelve Apostles," led by their superior Martín de Valencia, joined them. Friars of the Dominican Order joined in the work of conversion beginning in 1526. It would be the friars who would found and organize the Church in Mexico. As one scholar has written, "The influence of a prelate like Zumárraga upon the evangelization of the country owes less to his rank and title than to his personality and to the excellent relations he always maintained with his Order."[30]

Cortés's political downfall began when he left for Honduras in 1524 to put down the rebellion of his captain Cristóbal de Olid, who had joined the Velázquez faction. In Cortés's absence the treasury officials fell out, anarchy prevailed, and the *factor* (business manager) Gonzalo de Salazar became Mexico's first gangster dictator. Meanwhile, Cortés's many enemies sent letters to the crown accusing him of disloyalty and many crimes. On Cortés's return from Honduras in 1526, he restored order, but his rule was brief. Invited by Charles V to visit the imperial court, the conqueror left for Spain to justify his actions in Mexico as the new government for the colony was being formed.

Cortés returned to Mexico in 1530 a wealthy man but without the governorship. He continued to favor the friars as he developed his vast estate, and they and Zumárraga saw him as the Moses chosen by God to open the door through which they entered to defeat the devil and convert the Indians. In his last will and testament, dated October 11, 1547, Cortés made Zumárraga and Fray Domingo de Betanzos two of his executors in New Spain.[31]

Because unpaid Spanish troops and German mercenaries sacked Rome in 1527, relations between the emperor and Clement VII were such that approval of Zumárraga's presentation was delayed. He therefore arrived in Mexico in the company of the audiencia judges as bishop-elect with the "high-sounding" title and office of Protector of the Indians, an office first given to Bartolomé de Las Casas in 1516 and later to various bishops.

As Protector of the Indians, Zumárraga was to ensure that those in charge of Indians treated them well and instructed them in matters of the faith. This was to be done in accordance with laws enacted or to be passed for this purpose. Although he might proceed against those persons found guilty of abusing Indians or of neglecting their Christian instruction, Zumárraga's judgments could not be enforced without the support of the civil authorities.[32] As had happened to Las Casas and to other protectors of Indians after Zumárraga, local and provincial offices were monopolized by encomenderos who looked after their own interests, and any efforts in behalf of the Indians ultimately depended on the royal judges of the audiencia. In the case of Zumárraga, the chief oppressors of the Indians were judges Juan Ortiz de Matienzo and Diego Delgadillo and audiencia president Nuño Beltrán de Guzmán. Matienzo was old and greedy, and Delgadillo was young and without experience. Both judges were morally corrupt and easily controlled by Guzmán, who quickly gained control of the municipal council of Mexico City through his ally Gonzalo de Salazar.[33]

Two judges chosen for the audiencia died of pleurisy shortly after reaching Mexico. In 1529 Zumárraga wrote Charles V that he was "very sure that in what profits the peace and well-being of the land, God allowed great harm to this country with the death of these two and the life of the others [Matienzo and Delgadillo]."[34] He described Guzmán as a "greedy infernal devil who has consumed the land."[35] He also noted that the robberies, killings, extortions, whippings, and tortures of Spaniards and Indians, the enslavement of free Indians, and the taking of their women by the judges, as well as the transfer of encomiendas from the followers of Cortés to the faction of Diego

Velázquez and the allies and friends of Guzmán, had been directed by Gonzalo de Salazar.

From the time that Guzmán arrived in Pánuco and began the enslavement of free Indians in that province, Salazar had wooed him as an ally and fellow Cortés hater. After Guzmán arrived in Mexico City, he acted as the judges' adviser and sought to "totally destroy" Cortés and favor his own party. Zumárraga affirmed and offered proof to Charles V that "the root and poison of all past dissensions and tumults is the business manager Salazar, and after him the other officials of Your Majesty; currently they are Nuño de Guzmán and the judges, guided and put on their road by the said factor, wishing to favor his faction to such a degree that it is openly seen that they do nothing more than what he wants and orders, and moreover, as everyone says, it is he who rules." [36]

When the audiencia judges learned that Zumárraga, in the presence of the friars at the Franciscan monastery in Mexico City, had promised many Indian lords and nobles that he would defend them, the judges warned him under threat of severe penalties to turn a deaf ear to anything having to do with the Indians. Indian complaints concerned only the judges, they said, and claimed he had no jurisdiction since he was merely an ordinary friar—not bishop-elect, but rather a *postulado* (candidate) for this office.[37]

After exhausting peaceful means of dealing with the judges, Zumárraga publicly denounced them, and he and the friars used spiritual weapons in the conflict that followed. The judges, for their part, accused Zumárraga and the friars of having joined the Cortés faction. Some friars were assaulted, all were slandered, and two priests imprisoned by Zumárraga in the Franciscan monastery were seized; one was executed, and the other was sentenced to a hundred lashes and the loss of a foot. Zumárraga responded with an interdict of the city and excommunicated Matienzo and Delgadillo. Letters sent to the crown by the friars and Zumárraga were confiscated;[38] the letters sent by the judges charged Zumárraga with abusing his powers and claimed that the Franciscans were more covetous and passionate in their desire to command than their habits warranted.[39] Fortunately, Zumárraga's letter of August 27, 1529, to Charles V, in which he gave full details of the judges' misrule, was given to a Basque sailor at the port of Veracruz and reached the Council of the Indies.

As Zumárraga and the friars waited for a response from Spain to Zumárraga's letter, Guzmán left Mexico City on December 23, 1529, for the conquest of what would become the province of New Galicia. There he would torture, burn, enslave, and kill Indians, sowing the seeds of hatred that led to the Mixton War of 1541.[40] In 1531 Zumárraga stated before the second audiencia that he had originally declared Guzmán's war against the Indians of Jalisco unjust for various reasons. However, Zumárraga said, since the Indians of that region were infidels and idolaters who practiced heathen rites, they deserved to be attacked. The war should continue, but Guzmán should be replaced as commander by the new judges.[41]

Zumárraga and Indian Policy

As early as 1529 Zumárraga urged that friars Martín de Valencia and Domingo de Betanzos be given the office of Protector of the Indians.[42] The recommendation noted that the office lacked specific powers to settle all civil and criminal cases involving Indians and seems to indicate that the protectorship hindered Zumárraga's work as bishop. With the removal of the judges of the first audiencia in 1530, largely brought about by Zumárraga, enforcement of protective Indian legislation was vested in the second audiencia, under the presidency of the bishop of Santo Domingo, Sebastián Ramírez de Fuenleal.[43]

Under the new tribunal, whose work was praised by Zumárraga, the protector had jurisdiction in cases involving fines not to exceed fifty *pesos de oro* or ten days in jail. However, all investigations of corregidores and magistrates, officials in charge of Indians held by the crown, were to be sent to the royal judges if these agents were found guilty of abuses against the Indians. The tribunal would take into account the protector's opinion in assessing punishment of these magistrates, but it was not the crown's intention that he have any superiority over these royal agents. This decree, as noted by Lesley Byrd Simpson, effectively made Zumárraga an informant on Indian affairs to the Council of the Indies and "a spy on the encomenderos and corregidores," thus tending "to destroy the cordiality which must exist between them if any progress was to be made in the evangelization of the Indians."[44]

Both President Fuenleal and the Franciscan Order supported Zumárraga's desire to rid himself of the office of protector. Fuenleal recommended suppression of the office, suggesting that tours of inspection by the judges be made in the company of guardians or priors of the Orders. The Franciscans requested that the protectorship be placed in the audiencia.[45]

In compliance with a royal order to report on conditions in New Spain, Zumárraga left Mexico in 1532. After vindicating his actions as protector and his consecration as bishop in 1533, he was relieved of the office that had caused him so many problems before returning to Mexico in October of 1534. He now devoted his energies to the organization of the Church, social services, and education, and to the extirpation of idolatry. Zumárraga supported the reestablishment of authority by the judges and the administration of Viceroy Antonio de Mendoza, who assumed his office in 1535. Mendoza and Zumárraga proved to be good friends, agreed on Indian policy, and favored the work of the friars.

An important factor in Zumárraga's success as bishop of the Mexican diocese was his "realist" position in things concerning Indian policy and the Christian commonwealth of his day. Zumárraga defended a society characterized by social divisions in which the different orders had varied rights and privileges. In accordance with natural and divine law, every subject should enjoy the rights belonging to his station in a commonwealth of unequal classes with different functions and mutual obligations.

Zumárraga has been called "the contradiction of his time" by Fernando Benítez and "a segmented thinker not untypical of the sixteenth century" by Richard Greenleaf.[46] In fact, Zumárraga's compromise position in the struggle over Indian policy was held by "the majority of the clergy, both regular and secular," and the tensions inherent within this middle-of-the-road position are the measure by which both the objectives and standards of the colonists living off the labor and tribute of the Indians and the handful of reformers led by Bartolomé de Las Casas may be judged.[47]

Zumárraga, a man of many virtues, was not merely a bitter critic of those who mistreated Indians; he and Viceroy Mendoza furthered the work of religious and secular education begun by the friars. In addition, he distributed alms, founded the hospital del Amor de Dios for the treatment of contagious diseases, favored the development of agriculture and industry, and was instrumental in bringing the first printing press to Mexico. He paid for the printing of the first book published in the colony in 1539, a brief, bilingual catechism, and desired that the Gospels and the Epistles of Saint Paul be translated "into all the languages of the world so that not only the Indians but also other barbarous nations might read them."[48]

One cannot fault the good intentions of Zumárraga, who preferred the doctrine of Jesus Christ to the difficult and disputed precepts and doctrines of philosophers like Aristotle.[49] But when Zumárraga and the friars were forced to choose between the liberty of the Indians and the exploitation of Indian labor, they opted for "an Aristotelian world of masters and servants."[50]

Although aware of the virtual extinction of the Indians of Española by encomenderos obliged to protect, Christianize, and teach them Spanish ways, Zumárraga in 1529 recommended the perpetuity of the encomienda in Mexico. If perpetual encomiendas were assigned, he argued, the Spaniards would treat their Indians well so as to pass them on to their heirs. In addition to protecting their Indians, the encomenderos would develop their properties for the ennoblement of the land and the increase of the royal patrimony.[51]

When the crown proclaimed the New Laws of 1542–1543 and it appeared that the encomienda was doomed, Zumárraga sided with the encomenderos. In 1544 Zumárraga and Viceroy Mendoza, backed by the audiencia, the town council of Mexico City, and the religious Orders, persuaded the royal visitor Francisco Tello de Sandoval to suspend their enforcement until agents of the encomenderos might bring pressure at court for their revocation.

The New Laws, promulgated largely for the crown's own political and economic interests, also recognized Las Casas's irrefutable argument that the personal liberty of the Indians as vassals of the crown could not be reconciled with their direct subjection to Spaniards as encomienda Indians, slaves, or personal servants.[52] The Pizarro revolt in Peru and the flood of protests caused the crown to retreat and compromise. Laws against Indian slavery remained and were affirmed, but the continuation of the encomienda by right of inheritance benefited only a small group of colonists at the expense of Spain's colonial interests.[53]

Zumárraga's defense of the encomienda was based, in part at least, on his agreement with the Dominican chapter in Mexico City about the need for the institution. In their defense of the encomienda, these friars declared that "there could be no permanence in the land without rich men, and there could be no rich men without encomiendas, because all industry was carried on with Indian labor, and only those with Indians could engage in commerce."[54] His defense of the well-regulated republic was also based on his view of the Indians.

In 1531 Zumárraga and several Franciscans, including the saintly Martín de Valencia, declared that because the Indians were a meek people who acted more out of fear than virtue, they should be protected but not exalted.[55] "And what office could be more exalted for the believer of any religion than that of priest?" asks Alberto María Carreño, a profession closed to the Indians in 1539 except for minor orders before it was formalized by the First Mexican Provincial Council in 1555.[56]

Spaniards, said Zumárraga and the friars in 1531, should be obliged to treat Indians well, but in such a way that the Indians not lose their reverence and fear of the Spaniards. Indians, they said, were industrious under those who ordered them, but despite their good qualities and capabilities they had faults and were in the main addicted to drunkenness.[57]

In other endeavors, Zumárraga supported and participated in the establishment of the Colegio de Santa Cruz de Tlateloco, a Franciscan secondary school founded in 1537 for the training of a native elite and the intellectual and moral education of noble Indian youths showing aptitude for the priesthood. In the same year, he and the bishops of Tlascala and Michoacán planned to establish a primary school in Mexico City and in each bishopric for Indian boys; a convent school, large enough to accommodate a large number of Indian girls, should also be built. The girls, to be taken from their parents at the age of six or seven, would be married to the Indian boys at age twelve "because, given their character and inclination, it is advisable to marry them at a young age so that God will not be insulted by abominable offenses." [58] In 1540 Zumárraga doubted how long the Colegio of Santa Cruz would last, given the inclination of the students "more toward marriage than continence." [59]

Zumárraga's unfavorable view of Indian character was shared by other churchmen. The ecclesiastical junta of 1544, "attended by such important personages as Juan de Zumárraga, Alonso de la Vera Cruz, and Domingo de Betanzos," recorded its opposition to the New Laws "and declared that the Indians were incapable of civilization or Christianization without the tutelage of Spaniards, whether ecclesiastical or lay." [60]

Although it is true that Zumárraga, like Las Casas, opposed Indian slavery by war, purchase, or exchange and in 1536 recommended peaceful conversion of the Indians, he owned black and Indian slaves. In 1541 Zumárraga expressed his displeasure with his nephew for exchanging two of the bishop's Indian slaves in Seville for the latter's own benefit. Zumárraga freed his remaining Indian slaves on the condition that they serve him until his death.[61]

Zumárraga as Inquisitor

Between 1535 and 1543, Zumárraga acted as apostolic inquisitor for the Holy Office in Mexico. "Conservative in all things," Greenleaf asserts, the cautious Zumárraga proceeded with restraint and leniency against those accused of Judaizing.[62] In contrast, his trials of Indian heretics indicates that he regarded his work as "a necessary complement to his work in favor of the Indians."[63]

As bishop, Zumárraga wrote in 1531 that he had destroyed some five hundred temples and twenty thousand idols. As inquisitor, Zumárraga in his campaign against Indian apostates found Don Carlos, lord of Texcoco, guilty of heretical dogmatizing, sexual immorality, and undermining Spanish rule. With the approval of Viceroy Mendoza and the audiencia, Don Carlos was executed in 1539. In 1540 the Council of the Indies reprimanded him for excessive zeal in the burning of Don Carlos. It also recommended that since the Indians were new converts, still not sufficiently instructed in matters of the faith, they should be attracted to Christianity by love and kindness.[64] In 1543 Zumárraga's title of inquisitor was taken from him and given to Tello de Sandoval.

Zumárraga, "the Contradiction of His Time"

Zumárraga as a contradiction was less inconsistent than many other clerics of his time. His apparent duality arose after he left monastic life for the world, compared by Fray Martín de Valencia to a stormy sea in which great waves threaten a navigator in a small boat without oars.[65] Zumárraga reluctantly left the monastery of Abrojo to organize the "church of the secular clergy" rather than the "church of the friars," which caused some members of his Order to question whether he was any longer one of them.[66] He went from a defending protector of Indians to apostolic inquisitor to organizing bishop, all the time wanting to give up these offices for the life of an evangelizing mendicant. In 1545, at the age of seventy, he tried to give up his bishopric to go to preach the Gospel in the Philippines and go on from there to China. When the Franciscan provincial chapter and Rome refused their consent, Zumárraga remained in Mexico and was appointed archbishop in 1547.[67]

Contradictions also arose from the imperial system Zumárraga and the Franciscans defended, the crown tolerated, and the true realist Las Casas wished to totally reform. Zumárraga as moderate desired that Spaniards and Indians should be joined in Christian love based on an economic system in which perpetual grants of encomienda should be given in accordance with distributive justice recognizing distinctions between greater, intermediate, and lesser persons for the benefit of the body politic, "which is the republic, in which it is not suitable that all persons or constituent parts be equal."[68]

Charles V, the head of the body politic and more liberal than Zumárraga, directed a partial reform of the imperial colonial system but failed to free the Indians from encomienda and slavery. Gold and conversion, dual and contradictory goals, motivated the crown, and compromise was dictated by the fear the colonists would revolt in the fashion of the Pizarros. The colonial system, denounced by Las Casas as resting on an unjust foundation, continued to allow the abuses of the encomienda and the de jure slavery of Indians after it was outlawed by the New Laws. Protective Indian laws, frequently contradictory, were passed but were either ignored or imperfectly executed, because government by remote control failed to moderate royal agents filled with greed and Spanish colonials who sought to acquire wealth quickly "and thus rise to very high estates disproportionate to their persons."[69]

New systems of exploitation arose and old ones continued after the compromise of the New Laws. An example is the tribute burden first made by Zumárraga as Protector of the Indians. "He made very little inquiry into the matter, and it is said that he used to weep thereafter each time that assessment was mentioned." Given "the great frauds connected with this assessment" and those that followed, tribute increased or may have even doubled for surviving Indians in the 1560s.[70]

The final duality of Zumárraga's soul, the linking of his name with the "apparition" of the Virgin of Guadalupe of Tepeyac, is a trick played by posterity upon the dead. Originally a Creole cult denounced in 1556 by Fray Francisco de Bustamante, minister provincial of the Franciscan Order, as having "arisen without the least foundation,"[71] the cult was encouraged by Archbishop Alonso de Montúfar, who questioned Zumárraga's orthodoxy as found in the latter's *Doctrina breve* of 1544.[72]

Indians soon joined the Creoles in worshiping at the hermitage of Guadalupe where the natives had once sacrificed to the goddess Tonantzin-Cihuacóatl, the mother of the gods and the wife of the Serpent, the latter always associated in the Christian mind with "the Devil, and Satan, which deceiveth the whole world" (Rev. 12:9). In his study of the formation of Mexican national consciousness, Jacques Lafaye observes that this Creole cult eventually triumphed over the Erasmian purity of the Franciscans. In the seventeenth century, pious tradition affirmed the "apparition" of the Virgin of Guadalupe (Tepeyac) in 1531, a historically "false" date but a mythically "real" one "in the minds of its devotees."[73]

In conclusion, Juan de Zumárraga was a loyal Basque vassal of the crown and an orthodox cleric who appreciated the writings of Erasmus and Thomas More's *Utopia*. However, he did not possess the utopian mentality of the pro-Indian party led by Las Casas, which accepted the noble savage concept and cultural relativism and which called for the conversion of the Indian but without the anti-Christian encomienda and other forms of Indian subjection to the Spanish colonists. However deeply solicitous in protecting Indians from physical abuse and moral corruption by Spaniards, Zumárraga and most of his fellow Franciscans loved the Indians as children rather than as equals. But had he remained a friar, and given time, Zumárraga, basically inclined to justice and tolerance, might have arrived at the idea that under their natural lords the Aztecs had been the equals of the ancients in intelligence, ability, and achievements. His fault as inquisitor was his zealous orthodoxy and the failure to recognize that military conquest was accompanied by disease, exploitation, and the destruction of the Aztec social and religious organization.

In a world turned upside down, "degraded forms of the old polytheism combined with popular superstitions" and strange reinterpretations of Christian tradition, passed themselves off "as the spiritual heritage of the past."[74]

2

A Borderlands Basque
The Career of Don Juan de Oñate

MARC SIMMONS

In 1598 Juan de Oñate y Salazar founded the kingdom of New Mexico on the upper Rio Grande, thereby laying the foundations for the establishment of Spanish civilization in the American Southwest. His life was filled with high adventure as well as tragedy, and he left a story that even across four centuries has the power to fascinate and inspire.

Born in 1552 in Zacatecas, the bustling silver-mining center on the frontier northwest of Mexico City, the young Juan from an early age accompanied his father, Cristóbal de Oñate, on expeditions against the Chichimec Indians. Those bellicose nomads roamed the Mexican north, committing hideous massacres and destroying wagon trains that supplied the isolated settlements of pioneering Spaniards. Through participation in military campaigns against the bold enemies, the boy matured into a seasoned soldier, one well equipped to defend his own interests and those of the crown.

Heredity more than environment, however, seems to have shaped the man Juan de Oñate became. On his father's side he was a Spanish Basque, a circumstance of birth that implied much in the formation of character and behavior.

The Basques are thought to have been one of the thirty or so tribes of Iberians, speaking different languages, who far back in antiquity moved out of North Africa into Spain and spilled over the Pyrenees Mountains into France. If that is the case, then the Basques remain the only pure descendants of the ancient Iberians. This origin theory was first advanced by German scholar and natural philosopher Alexander von Humboldt in 1821.[1]

Some traits attributed to the Iberians, and recognizable among Basques of a later day, were love of freedom, fierce pride in their culture, hospitality, dogged persistence, fortitude in the face of misfortune, and plain arrogance, which manifested itself in an ill-concealed sense of superiority. That last characteristic their fellow Spaniards found galling.

One other Basque trait casts light on their behavior in the overseas colonies: That was intense devotion to family, notable among all Spaniards but nowhere more so than among the Basques. They looked upon the home as sacred and observed a strict loyalty to family members. Those who immigrated to the New World and engaged in grand enterprises were as a rule surrounded by their blood kin and in-laws.

Three small all-Basque provinces lay off the western end of the Pyrenees in north central Spain: Bizkaia, Araba, and Gipuzkoa. Further, a large Basque population extended into the neighboring kingdom of Navarre. Juan de Oñate's great-grandfather, Cristóbal Pérez de Narria, resided in the village of Oñate within the judicial district of Bergara in Gipuzkoa. Genealogical records testify to his ancient and distinguished lineage and note his status as a hidalgo, or member of the lesser nobility.[2]

It is sometimes said that his son, Juan Pérez de Narria, upon marrying, moved south across the Zadorra River to live in Gasteiz, the main city of Araba province. However, historian Donald T. Garate has recently established that Juan Pérez, in fact, continued to reside in his native Oñate.[3] There, he and his wife had three children, one of whom, Cristóbal de Oñate, became the father of Juan, the founder of New Mexico. In 1524 at age twenty, Cristóbal left his native Gasteiz for a government job in the royal treasury of Mexico City. It marked the beginning of his spectacular career.

In the viceroyalty of New Spain (colonial Mexico), Cristóbal de Oñate rose rapidly in the social, economic, and political hierarchy, partly through his own energy and ability but also through the influence of new friends in high places. A propitious marriage to doña

Catalina de Salazar, daughter of a prominent treasury official, no doubt further contributed to the ascent of his fortune.

From an early date, don Cristóbal maintained a sumptuous residence in the viceregal capital, staffed with many servants and retainers. But much of his time was spent in the countryside, where he owned stock ranches, farms, a sugar refinery, and, later, extensive mine holdings. He was often away, too, campaigning against Indians, particularly in Michoacán and in the sprawling kingdom of Nueva Galicia on the western edge of the viceroyalty.

After his appointment as lieutenant-governor of Nueva Galicia in the latter 1530s, Cristóbal de Oñate led exploratory expeditions and assisted in the establishment of new municipalities, including the city of Guadalajara. In 1540 his good friend, Governor Francisco Vásquez de Coronado, departed with a glittering company of adventurers for the far north (today's Arizona and New Mexico) to search for the fabled Seven Cities of Gold. In his absence, Oñate served as acting governor and took the lead in quelling a major Indian uprising, the Mixton War.[4]

About 1546, Cristóbal formed an association, for purposes of prospecting, with three other energetic Basques from Gipuzkoa: Juan de Tolosa, Miguel de Ibarra, and Miguel's nephew Diego de Ibarra. Within two years, they made a huge silver discovery on the frontier and established the flourishing mining city of Zacatecas. In the adjacent camp of Pánuco, Oñate, now enormously wealthy, built a large two-story house with a private chapel. Here, in 1552, his wife gave birth to twins, Juan and Cristóbal.

The twinship of New Mexico's illustrious explorer and first governor, Juan de Oñate, is an interesting detail that until recently had been overlooked by historians.[5] But now that the fact is firmly established, it indeed appears strange that one twin, Juan, spent much of his life in the public eye, whereas the other, Cristóbal, lived entirely in his shadow and left virtually no mark upon history. In truth, Juan far outshone the other three Oñate brothers as well.

In his youth, the twin Cristóbal crossed the Atlantic to attend Spain's celebrated University of Salamanca, which along with those of Paris, Oxford, and Bologna was one of the four great European universities of the Middle Ages. Coincidentally, the city of Salamanca was also the birthplace of the conquistador Coronado, in 1510.

The possibility exists that Juan de Oñate accompanied his brother to Spain and attended the same university. If such was the case, he could have met for the first time another student from Mexico, Gaspar Pérez de Villagrá, who long afterward would join the Oñate expedition as quartermaster in the colonization of New Mexico. Villagrá became the chief chronicler of the enterprise, publishing his *History of New Mexico* at Alcalá de Henares, Spain, in 1610. The work is considered the first published history on any part of the future United States and thus enjoys the status of a literary landmark.[6]

From what has been said, we can safely conclude that among the important factors molding the personality and temperament of a youthful Juan de Oñate were his Basque ancestry, the influence of a strong father, and the early challenges he faced growing up on a raw and violent mining frontier.

When the patriarch don Cristóbal de Oñate died on October 6, 1567, Juan was just fifteen years old, but like his brothers he had long since begun to assume the responsibilities of a man.[7] In time he developed a keen interest in the Oñate mines, smelters, and stamp mills in Zacatecas and became the manager of these family properties. From the riches he thereby accumulated derived the common assertion that the settlement of New Mexico in 1598 was financed by Zacatecas silver.

Coronado's much-publicized expedition northward in the years 1540 to 1542 had revealed the existence of a large sedentary Pueblo Indian population concentrated on the upper Rio Grande. But the natives' lack of any gold and silver treasure, of the kind already seized from the Aztecs, proved a major disappointment. For another generation, this land, now designated as New Mexico, was neglected by explorers and even missionaries.

By 1580 the line of Spanish settlement, containing ranches, missions, and mines, had advanced as far as southern Chihuahua, and the royal government was taking a fresh look beyond, toward the long-ignored New Mexico. Three years later King Philip II sent a decree to the viceroy of New Spain, requiring him to find a wealthy and able person willing to undertake colonization, largely at his own expense, of the land of the Pueblos.

After a string of false starts and the rejection of several other candidates, Juan de Oñate was chosen to bring the kingdom of New Mexico into being. On September 21, 1595, he met with Viceroy Luís de Velasco in Mexico City to sign a formal contract, defining his specific agreement with the crown. In it, he obligated himself to bear most of the expenses—and risks—involved in the New Mexico project.

As an immediate reward, he got the honorific title of *adelantado* and the office of governor, which carried an annual salary of six thousand ducats. The treasury also underwrote the expense of six Franciscans to minister to the settlers and convert the Indians. All in all, it was a wonderful bargain for the king, who was promised expansion of his realm, shared in any rewards that might be forthcoming, and invested very little.[8]

Oñate launched into his work with high expectations. From what he could learn about New Mexico, its mountainous landscape resembled the country farther south that had already yielded vast fortunes in silver. Therefore, he took pains to supply himself with mining tools and smelting equipment. He was, in fact, counting heavily upon making a major strike, a mineral bonanza large enough to sustain the huge expenses of his new colony.

To assist him in the difficult task ahead, Oñate selected two young Basque kinsmen who, like himself, traced their origins back to Gipuzkoa. He named Juan de Zaldívar second in command of the expedition, with the rank of *maese de campo* (field marshal), while his younger brother, Vicente de Zaldívar, received the title of *sargento mayor*. Oñate's selection of the pair, who were nephews as well as cousins, illustrates the high value placed by Basques upon family bonds.

Sometime in the late 1580s (the exact date is unknown), Oñate married Isabel de Tolosa, daughter of his father's old business partner. On her mother's side, doña Isabel's lineage led back to both Fernando Cortés and the Aztec emperor Moctezuma. Initially, the Oñates had a single son, Cristóbal, who was only eight years old when don Juan decided to take him on the march to New Mexico. In spite of his tender age, he was commissioned with the rank of lieutenant and placed under the watchful eye of Vicente de Zaldívar. A pregnant doña Isabel was left behind and after her husband's departure bore a daughter, María, who one day would marry her cousin, the very same Vicente de Zaldívar.

Owing to an assortment of obstacles and problems, Oñate and his huge caravan of soldiers, settlers, friars, servants, livestock, and wagons did not get under way until early in 1598. For more than two months, the great cavalcade crawled across arid plateaus rimmed by desolate, whale-backed mountains and struggled through patches of desert marked by Sahara-like dunes. On April 20 it struck the Rio Grande, below the future site of El Paso, where Governor Oñate camped for one week to allow his exhausted followers a rest.

Here, at the gateway to New Mexico and following an ancient tradition that derived from the Visigoths of the early Middle Ages, he conducted a formal ceremony to take possession of the land. The rite included slashing by sword the branch of a tree, tossing stones in the air, and pulling up handfuls of grass by their roots. Further, don Juan personally nailed a crucifix to a cottonwood while trumpets blared and his soldiers fired their harquebuses skyward. A royal notary duly certified the legality of these proceedings.[9]

From the El Paso Valley, the expedition began its ascent of the Rio Grande with the aim of penetrating northern New Mexico, the area in which Oñate had decided to build his first settlement and capital. Within a week, he and a smaller, select group left the slow-moving train to ride ahead and make the first contact with the Pueblo Indians. He wished to calm their fears at the approach of such a large body of strangers and also arrange for the purchase of foodstuffs.

The first Pueblo province Oñate reached was that of the Piros, many of whom fled in panic. But in one village on the west side of the Rio Grande, the inhabitants came out from behind their leader and extended a welcome. Here the Spaniards were able to purchase much-needed corn, and in gratitude they named the place Socorro, meaning "relief."

Over the next several weeks, Governor Oñate continued his advance northward. By the first week of July 1598, he had come upon a large pueblo, which he named Santo Domingo, some thirty miles above the future site of Albuquerque. Pausing for a week, he issued a call for a grand council of chiefs, and in response native leaders hurried in from neighboring towns to find out what the bearded newcomer had to say.

Don Juan, speaking through inadequate interpreters, did his best to explain that he came at the behest of the world's grandest monarch, Spain's Philip II, who wanted the Indians to become his subjects. And the Pope, head of the one true Church, wished them to gain salvation through the acceptance of baptism. This no doubt escaped the understanding of the *caciques,* as the Pueblo headmen, or chiefs, were called, but still they went down on their knees before Oñate and swore vassalage to King Philip in a formalized ceremony that, like the one earlier in El Paso, had a strong medieval flavor about it.

Leaving Santo Domingo, Oñate and his band climbed a high volcanic escarpment and emerged upon a plateau that extended to the foot of the towering Sangre de Cristo Mountains. He moved on to the Española Valley, which held several Pueblo towns where Tewa was spoken. At one of these, named San Juan Bautista in honor of the governor's own patron saint, the Spaniards received a cordial reception. The site lay on the east bank of the Rio Grande, near the junction with the Chama River, and the surrounding mountains and mesas presented a spectacular view. Here don Juan decided to establish his seat of government.

While waiting for the main caravan to catch up, he explored farther northward to Taos on the outer rim of his new kingdom, then swung eastward, visiting the magnificent Pecos pueblo that faced the plains. One of the purposes of this excursion was to seek signs of silver, for an early strike was essential to the colony's success. On the edge of the Galisteo Basin, southwest of Pecos, the Indians showed Oñate their extensive turquoise and lead mines, and nearby he found promising signs of other minerals. Samples of ore were collected for assaying.

Returning to San Juan, the governor on August 18 greeted the arrival of the wagon-cart train commanded by his nephew Juan de Zaldívar. A few days later, Oñate discovered that some of his men were plotting to mutiny and return to New Spain. The reason, as he explained in a letter to the viceroy, was that they had become angry because bars of silver were not scattered on the ground for the taking. As compensation for their disappointment, they planned to seize and carry away the docile Pueblo Indians so they could be sold as slaves in the mines.[10]

Showing strong leadership, don Juan moved quickly and forcefully to suppress the challenge to his authority. By way of diverting the settlers' attention to more productive matters, he ordered on August 23 the construction of New Mexico's first church, a missionary chapel for the San Juan Indians that would also serve the Spaniards until they could build a church for themselves. It must have been a simple structure, since it was ready for dedication and a fiesta by September 8. On that date also Oñate assigned his missionaries to their stations in the several Pueblo provinces.

Now that things seemed calm in his little capital of San Juan, the governor went exploring again, this time down to pueblos near a group of salt lakes below the Manzano Mountains. Once there he decided to go directly west in search of the Pacific coast, under the mistaken assumption that it lay within easy reach. After sending a message to Juan de Zaldívar, ordering him to bring reinforcements and meet the expedition, he started across New Mexico using an old Indian trail that passed through Acoma and Zuni pueblos.

At Acoma Oñate paused to conduct a ceremony of submission and receive gifts of food. A hostile faction within the village was prepared to attack him but was restrained by fellow tribesmen. The pueblo itself enjoyed a superb defensive position atop a soaring mesa, accessible only by a steep pathway and steps cut in the face of sheer rock. If rumblings of disaffection reached don Juan's ears, he took no notice of it. Instead he pushed on to the scenic rock of El Morro and then to Zuni, where he stopped to await his nephew's reinforcing party.

After Juan de Oñate left Acoma, the war faction there gained the upper hand. When young Zaldívar arrived shortly thereafter, he and ten of his men were lured to the mesa summit, where a host of club-swinging warriors fell upon them. All died except three soldiers, who leaped off the edge of the cliff, landed in sand dunes hundreds of feet below, and were rescued by members of the horse guard who had remained on the plain.

When the governor received word of this catastrophe, he abandoned his exploration and hastened back to San Juan, avoiding the rebellious Acoma. As he well knew, the other pueblos were watching to see what the Spanish response would be to this challenge. Should the colonists fail to punish the Acomans, a general uprising surely would follow, bringing down the newly created kingdom of New Mexico.

On December 28, 1598, the governor opened a war council that lasted for two weeks and was attended by all the soldiers and the missionaries. From open debate emerged the decision to attack and vanquish Acoma, after first giving it the opportunity to surrender.

Oñate announced his wish to conduct the campaign in person, but members of the clergy and his officers dissuaded him from that course, arguing that should the assault upon Acoma fail, he would be needed to lead the settlers in flight from the kingdom. The governor yielded and turned over command to Vicente de Zaldívar, the younger brother of the slain Juan de Zaldívar.

On the bitterly cold morning of January 12, the punitive expedition, its officers clad in full armor, rode out of San Juan. Nine days later it reached the foot of Acoma's mesa. The Indians crowded to the edge and jeered their enemies before unleashing a hail of arrows and stones. The Spaniards had come ready for a fight, and now they had one.

What followed has to be classed as one of the most astonishing episodes in the annals of North American history. Since the pueblo on its promontory formed a natural fortress, Zaldívar devised a clever strategy that offered some chance of success. Detaching a dozen men from his army of seventy-two, he led them undetected behind the mesa. While the main force launched a frontal assault, diverting the Indians' attention, the commander and his companions scaled the rear ramparts, gaining a foothold on top.

Although furiously attacked, the Spaniards held their ground and, after two small brass cannons were hauled up by rope, began to advance against the pueblo. The slaughter was appalling. Following three days of stand-up fighting, Acoma surrendered. The number of Indian casualties was estimated at six hundred to eight hundred. Incredibly, only one Spaniard died, having been struck by a stray bullet from his own side. The army looked upon these results as truly miraculous. The outcome, however, can probably be credited to a determined Basque leader and to pure Spanish brazenness.

Zaldívar returned to the Rio Grande bearing a string of captives. His uncle put the Indians on trial, and stern punishment was meted out to them. Men over age twenty-five were condemned to have one foot cut off; young men under that age, as well as all women over twelve, to twenty years of personal servitude. Further, sixty young girls were sent to convents in Mexico City, never to see their homeland again. This harsh retribution effectively cooled the spirit of resistance among the Pueblos, achieving the result Oñate had intended.[11]

The Spaniards had achieved a military victory, but they never quite recovered their balance after the Acoma episode. From that point forward, Governor Oñate's misfortunes multiplied, and although he may not have been immediately aware of it, his colonizing project slowly began to decline.

In the aftermath of his Indian troubles, don Juan sometime early in 1599 moved his people out of San Juan and across the Rio Grande to a smaller pueblo (which was either taken by the Spaniards or given to them by the Tewas). Here at San Gabriel, as the colonists named it, they could live apart and organize a formal municipality with a cabildo, or town council. This small step represented an effort by Oñate to fortify his shaky government.

By now don Juan had used up many of his own resources, as well as those of his family; and inasmuch as New Mexico had proved unproductive, he found it embarrassingly necessary to appeal to the viceroy for military support and material aid. That plea in itself alerted the royal government that all was not going well on the Rio Grande.

Owing to inevitable bureaucratic delays, a relief column, including a new contingent of soldiers, did not reach San Gabriel before Christmas Eve in 1600. Until then, the governor had not dared go on lengthy expeditions without a strong garrison to leave behind to defend his capital. But the arrival of the reinforcements freed him to resume exploring the far frontiers of his kingdom.

A series of minor problems delayed Oñate's departure until June 1601. His destination was Quivira, that wispy land of legend and supposed riches on the high plains, centering on the modern state of Kansas. Coronado had gone there sixty years earlier and uncovered nothing of interest, but still the aura of mystery remained, or at least enough of it to lure Oñate back. In desperate need of some accomplishment that might buttress his New Mexico project and impress the viceroy and king, he gambled and headed east with seventy soldiers, servants, carts, and artillery.

Once more luck deserted don Juan. A long ramble beneath the glaring prairie sun produced only a fierce two-hour battle with Quiviran Indians and no sign of any wealth. As he retraced his trail to San Gabriel, after an absence of five months, he may have composed a little speech to explain to his grumbling colonists this latest setback. If so, he never got to deliver it because upon arrival, he found his capital nearly abandoned.

The majority of the colonists, soldiers, and missionaries, taking advantage of the opportunity, had packed up their meager possessions and fled to New Spain. Their dissatisfaction with Oñate's stern rule and with the poverty of New Mexico prompted the desertion.

In spite of this crowning blow, the governor clung to the hope that with the few loyal subjects remaining to him he could somehow resurrect the battered framework of his enterprise. First he sent Vicente de Zaldívar to Mexico and on to Spain in a bid to raise new money and recruits. Then late in 1604, he resumed his old plan to find the seacoast, which had been interrupted at the time of the Acoma uprising.

A new trip across central Arizona to the head of the Gulf of California yielded no profitable results. Rumored pearl fisheries failed to materialize, and the coast proved much farther away than expected, too far to be of any benefit to New Mexico. With this final reversal, Governor Oñate's last bit of optimism evaporated.

For several years the Spanish Crown had been unable to decide what to do about its troublesome and profitless kingdom on the Rio Grande. The first reports sent back by Oñate had been highly encouraging, but when no silver was found and the impediments to farming and ranching became evident, economic reality forced the conclusion that New Mexico would need the support of the king's treasury to survive.

His majesty's advisers, in fact, recommended withdrawal of the colonists and relinquishment of the outpost on New Spain's northern rim. Before that drastic step could be taken, however, word came from missionaries in New Mexico that the Pueblo Indians were beginning to respond to their overtures and that eight thousand had been converted and baptized. As chief patron of the Spanish Catholic Church, the king was delighted with the news.

Therefore, he ordered that New Mexico be transformed from a proprietary colony, governed by a private contractor, to a royal one, managed and funded directly by the crown. That meant, of course, the end of Oñate's governorship and the conclusion of his dream.

A royal decree removing him reached Mexico City in the summer of 1607. But don Juan had already submitted his resignation. In accepting it, the viceroy instructed him to remain in New Mexico until a replacement could be found and sent northward. The new royal governor, Pedro de Peralta, did not arrive in San Gabriel until late 1609, at which point don Juan, his son Cristóbal, and his nephew Vicente left for Mexico City. Their departure ended Juan de Oñate's frontier adventure.[12]

The stresses associated with the experience had seriously undermined don Juan's health, and he appears to have remained in the viceregal capital for some time to recover. But by 1613 he was back at his old home at Pánuco outside Zacatecas, where he discovered that in his long absence the family mines had been seriously neglected. He quickly brought them back into full production and within a brief time restored his personal fortune. That disproves the claim sometimes made that the losses he suffered in New Mexico left don Juan permanently impoverished.

Another serious problem was not so easily resolved. The deserters who had fled New Mexico in 1601 had leveled serious charges of misconduct against their former governor, and even though their testimony could not be fully credited, it was sufficient to launch the start of an official inquiry. Once Oñate was back in Mexico City, the judicial proceedings escalated. To the original indictment was added the charge that he had used excessive force in putting down the Acoma rebellion.

Brought to trial in 1614, Oñate was exonerated on most points but was convicted on several of the more serious, including the mishandling of the Acoma affair, adultery, unjustly hanging two Indian captives, and executing two of his officers. The viceroy sentenced him to perpetual exile from New Mexico and to a four-year exile from Mexico City and ordered him to pay a fine of six thousand Castilian ducats. Those penalties don Juan could easily bear, but not the stain to his reputation. Claiming innocence, he would spend the remainder of his life attempting to remove the cloud that had settled upon his family name.

The first of his formal appeals to the king, seeking a reopening of his case, was filed in 1617. Three years later, when his wife, doña Isabel, died, he still had received no positive response. Her death, however, left Oñate free to travel to Spain and press his case in person before the government. Once established in Madrid, he began submitting petitions in a single-minded quest for exoneration.

In 1623 the king partially relented by granting the return of the six thousand ducats he had been fined. Oñate eagerly seized upon that as vindication. It appears he was also brought back into the good graces of his monarch: He was offered the important post of mining inspector for all of Spain, a position for which he was well qualified. In this capacity, don Juan traveled throughout the length of the peninsula.

About June 3, 1626, while on inspection at the mining center of Guadalcanal in southern Spain, Juan de Oñate died suddenly. He left instructions that his remains be taken to Madrid and entombed in the chapel of the Colegio Imperial, a Jesuit institution. So ended the life of a remarkable Basque who always did his duty, as he saw it.[13]

From what has been said about Oñate's career, at least those fifteen years of it closely identified with the Spanish kingdom of New Mexico, a casual reader might assume that the man was a failure and his efforts and resources largely wasted. That was not how don Juan saw his life, nor has history defined it in that way. Through perspective granted by time, we can acknowledge that Oñate achieved much that was significant and enduring.

First, as the founder of New Mexico, he established a province that one day would become the main anchor of Spanish power along a fifteen-hundred-mile frontier stretching from the Texas Gulf Coast to California. New evidence also suggests that he had a hand in the founding of Santa Fe, which became the capital after his departure for Mexico City.[14] Moreover, Oñate was a road blazer. During his initial trip in 1598, he marked out the Camino Real, or Royal Highway, from the mining settlements of Chihuahua to upper New Mexico. Finally, he ought to be accorded honors as the father of the ranching and mining industries in the western United States, owing to his introduction of livestock and his mineral exploration. Many other figures in history have been remembered for far less.

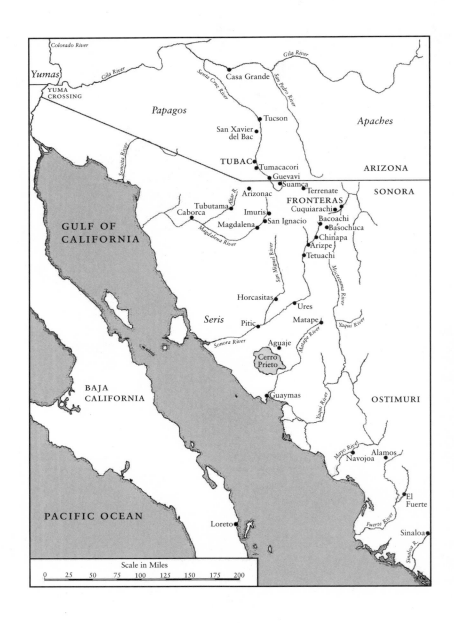

Colorado River

Gila River

Yumas

YUMA
CROSSING

Gila River

Santa Cruz River

Casa Grande

San Pedro River

Papagos

Tucson

San Xavier
del Bac

Apaches

TUBAC

ARIZONA

Tumacacori

Guevavi

Suamca

Terrenate

SONORA

Sonota River

Arizonac

FRONTERAS

Cuquiarachi

Tubutama

Altar R.

Imuris

Magdalena

Caborca

San Ignacio

Bacoachi

Basochuca

Magdalena River

Chinapa

Arizpe

Tetuachi

GULF OF
CALIFORNIA

San Miguel River

Moctezuma River

Horcasitas

Ures

Seris

Pitic

Matape

Yaqui River

Sonora River

Aguaje

Matape River

Cerro
Prieto

BAJA
CALIFORNIA

Guaymas

OSTIMURI

Yaqui River

Mayo River

Alamos

Navojoa

El
Fuerte

PACIFIC OCEAN

Loreto

Fuerte River

Sinaloa

Sinaloa R.

Scale in Miles

0   25   50   75   100   125   150   175   200

3

Anza
A Basque Legacy on New Spain's Northern Frontier

DONALD T. GARATE

On May 9, 1740, the frontier of New Spain stood in transition. Juan Bautista de Anza lay dead on the desert floor east of Santa María de Suamca Mission in northern Sonora, the victim of an Apache ambush. To the Apaches, his violent death was undoubtedly considered a fitting and just end to the life of a cavalry officer who had severely curbed their activities. For nearly fifteen years as *capitán vitalicio* (captain for life) of the royal presidio of Fronteras, Anza and his cavalry soldiers had exacted swift retribution on the Apaches for raids on the missions and communities of Sonora.

Now, in one sudden, shocking moment, that era was ended. A fellow Basque, Captain José Díaz del Carpio, and his soldiers of the presidio at Janos, Chihuahua, went in pursuit of the raiders. Thirteen Apaches were killed and fourteen captured, but it did not bring the beloved captain back to life. Besides, they were probably not the Apaches who had committed the crime, which kept the door open for further retribution and depredation as the vicious cycle went on and on.[1]

Meanwhile, another fellow Basque and close friend of Juan Bautista de Anza, Agustín de Vildósola, *sargento mayor* of the Sonora militias, was on a forced march to help put down an Indian rebellion in Sinaloa. His decisive actions against the Yaquis in the south were soon rewarded with an appointment as governor of Sonora and Sinaloa. Although Sonora's Basque community would rejoice in that appointment, it would not bring their beloved protector and benefactor back from the grave either. Sonora went into mourning, as did Captain Anza's young family.

The name *Anza,* which in the Basque language refers to the dwarf elder–spotted foothills of Navarre, had been known on the northern frontier of New Spain for nearly thirty years in 1740. Another thirty years would elapse before fame would come again to the name. This time it would be known throughout not only Sonora but all of New Spain. The man who had just been killed by Apaches had a four-year-old son, also named Juan Bautista, who would grow to become one of the most dynamic frontier soldiers, explorers, colonizers, and statesmen in the history of the American continent. Both father and son were renowned in their own day for their accomplishments on an extremely hostile and explosive frontier. Both have largely been forgotten by succeeding generations, which have tended to ignore Spanish colonial history in both the United States and Mexico. The following, in chronological order, is the story of both Juan Bautistas de Anza.

Juan Bautista de Anza, senior, arrived in New Spain, probably in Culiacán, Sinaloa, at the age of nineteen from the province of Gipuzkoa, Spain. He was born in the town of Hernani to Antonio Anza and Lucia Sasoeta on June 29, 1693. It was most likely his connection with the many representatives of the Sasoeta family in Culiacán that brought him to the Sonora-Sinaloa region in 1712.

The Anza family had resided in Hernani for several generations, having migrated from Navarre, via Irun, Gipuzkoa. Antonio owned and operated the town *botika* (pharmacy) and was involved in real estate and money lending. He also served on the town council and was mayor for a term. The Sasoetas were even more prominent and well-to-do and had provided a substantial dowry when Lucia and Antonio were married. Lucia's older brother was the vicar of the local parish.

The Anzas and Sasoetas shared business connections and family relationships touching every walk of life in the little town. Even more important, those associations reached into a network in the various towns and villages of the surrounding area. Friendships, business associations, and family ties, either through direct blood relationship or marriage, in the neighboring communities of Irun, Oiartzun, Errenteria, Usurbil, and Donostia would prove invaluable to Juan Bautista de Anza and his posterity on the faraway frontiers of New Spain for many years to come.

Hernani was set back a few miles from the Atlantic Ocean and tucked into vibrant green foothills that quickly rose up into rugged mountains called Franco Mendiak. The village had only two streets—one was Kale Nagusia, or Main Street, and the other, Kardaberatz, or Thistle Street. The most imposing structure in the town plaza was the huge stone church, called San Juan Bautista, with its public clock built into the bell tower. Here the infant Juan Bautista Anza was baptized by his uncle, Domingo Sasoeta, the vicar. Other buildings surrounding the plaza were the town hall, a slaughterhouse and butcher shop, and a women's prison adjacent to the town hall. The Anza botika stood a few hundred feet away on Kale Nagusia.

Although small, Hernani was a crossroads on the pilgrimage routes to Compostela and the well-known Basque sanctuaries of Aranzatzu and Ziortza. On the edge of town the road crossed the Urumea River on its way north to the port of Donostia a few miles away. Going south, the road climbed quickly into the mountains, destined for Tolosa, Oñati, and Aranzatzu. Many travelers from northern Spain who were destined for the *Indias* funneled south to Cádiz through Hernani. The Anza botika, established four years before Juan Bautista was born, was a thriving business by the time he was old enough to remember, doing business with locals and outsiders alike. The boy must have grown up hearing adventurous stories of travelers on their way to or from faraway places.[2]

Unfortunately, little is known of Anza's journey to New Spain. Equally unknown are the events of his childhood beyond what can be surmised from later circumstances. Certainly his parents provided him with an education that involved learning Spanish so he could be taught to read and write, since Basque was virtually an unwritten language at this time. Meticulous practice with quill pens made for a beautiful handwriting and signature, but his grammar was that of one writing in an acquired language.

The first known instance of Anza's intricate signature in the New World is dated January 22, 1718, wherein he was a cosigner of a frontier decree banning knives and machetes in the *real de minas* (royal mining camp), called Nuestra Señora de Guadalupe de Aguaje, in Sonora. Although he appears to have been financially successful in the six years he had been in Nueva España, this newly established silver-mining boomtown, where he had been living for three of those years, was antithetic in every way to the tranquil community he had left behind on the other side of the world.

Far from the lush, green countryside and mild climate of his native country, Aguaje was situated in the harsh, rugged basin-and-range country of the Sonoran Desert in the intense heat of near-sea-level elevation. The plants and animals of this region were spiny, prickly, poisonous, dismal, and sparse compared with the flora and fauna of Gipuzkoa's mountains. Aguaje was a hasty assortment of miner's shacks and tents, strikingly different from the durable stone houses of the Basque Country. Like most boomtowns, it was destined for abandonment. Aguaje's demise, however, was not so much because the silver played out but because of difficulties between the Spanish and the Seri Indians.

At that moment, however, the problem was not the Seris. They were at peace with the Spaniards in 1718. The dilemma that Aguaje faced was the influx of swindlers, thieves, and other riffraff that such communities tend to draw. Horse and mule herds were being stolen. Cattle were being killed or driven off. Brutal quarrels took place daily, and stabbings were commonplace. The mines at Aguaje were owned by three Basques—Martín de Ibarburu, Francisco de Aldamiz, and Juan Bautista de Anza. Anza also owned one of the ten stores in town. These and the other businessmen in the village needed some way to protect their interests.

Thus, when Antonio Bezerra Nieto, captain of the presidio at Janos, arrived on the scene in Aguaje as a military inspector for the governor of Nueva Vizcaya, he swiftly dictated the decree banning knives and machetes. Anza boldly signed as a witness. Stiff fines were to be imposed on those of Spanish citizenship, increasing in amount with the number of offenses. The money would be used to build a jail. For "mulatos, negroes, coyotes, mestizos, and Indians,"[3] punishment ranged (depending on repetition of the crime) from fifteen days with one's head in the stocks, to fifty lashes at the stake, to six months of hard labor at the newly established presidio at Santa Rosa de Corodéguachi in northern Sonora, on New Spain's frontier.

This is probably the first time Anza and Bezerra Nieto had met. It was the beginning of an important relationship. Anza made other lasting acquaintances in this remote and harsh community, especially among the Basques, which would benefit him in his New World career.[4]

Within a year, silver was discovered in the north at a place called Tetuachi. In the Opata Indian country, this verdant gorge on the Sonora River lay beneath the Sierra San Antonio on the west and the Sierra Las Palomas on the east. It is unknown who first discovered the silver, but the first miners on the scene in 1719 were five Basques—Francisco Barcelon, José Goicoechea, Antonio Miranda, Juan Berroeta, and Juan Anza. The soon-to-be real de minas was appropriately given the patron's name of Nuestra Señora de Arantzazu. No other name could define a location as being of Basque origin more than this one. It would not be surprising to learn that either Anza or Goicoechea named it. Although the latter was several years Anza's senior, he, too, came from Hernani, just down the mountain from the original Aranzatzu.

Other miners and fortune seekers soon rushed to the scene, and Tetuachi became Sonora's newest boomtown. Men of other ethnic backgrounds were brought to work the mines, but all the mine owners were Basque. Led by Juan Bautista de Anza they soon found themselves embroiled in a controversy with their Spanish countrymen, especially with Gregorio Álvarez Tuñón.

Alcalde mayor (lieutenant governor) of Sonora, "Don Gregorio" was also captain of the presidio at Corodéguachi, popularly called Fronteras because the *Caballería de las Fronteras* (the Cavalry of the Frontier) was stationed there. The calvary's duty was to protect the citizenry from the frequent Apache raids that were threatening to destroy Sonora. Captain Álvarez Tuñón, however, was too busy pursuing his own interests to spend much time on the campaign. Politically ambitious and morally corrupt, Alvarez Tuñón forced his soldiers to work in his mines and on his ranch properties. He even collected pay for soldiers who had been dead for years. A few of his countrymen courageously contested him; but under Anza's leadership, the Basques (known in those years as Vizcaínos) came out in mass in vehement opposition to him. Don Gregorio made it clear that he would "not rest until he had run all of the Vizcaínos out of Sonora."

The first major conflict came in January 1720, when the Basques of Tetuachi disputed the political appointment of Joaquín de Rivera to the office of lieutenant to the *justicia mayor* (chief justice). They claimed he was the son of a *mulata* (black woman) and did not possess the necessary nobility to hold such an office. Anza, by this time, was lieutenant of all the militia units in Sonora. His own nobility as a native Vizcaíno was secure. Just two years before, his father had gone through the detailed process of obtaining a *prueba de nobleza* (proof of nobility) for two of his sons—Juan Felipe, who was living in Cádiz, and Juan Bautista. The document guaranteed that they could be "admitted to all honorable occupations of peace and of war, as all other noblemen, without prejudice in the Royal Patrimony with exclusive rights of possession." [5]

The authorities, in proving that Rivera's mother was not a mulata, also succeeded in showing that he was of illegitimate birth, which was nearly as restrictive. When Rivera's appointment went through anyway, Anza led a group of thirty-four armed men into Motepore, where the inauguration was to take place. The protestors shouted their opposition and demanded that Rivera step down immediately. The day was saved by the vicar, who arrived on the scene and managed to persuade Rivera to step down in the interest of peace and harmony.

Álvarez Tuñón, however, fought to maintain the appointment and sent a letter to Manuel San Juan de Santa Cruz, the Basque governor of Nueva Vizcaya. His dispatch screamed foul play. In reaction, the Vizcaínos met to organize their opposition to Rivera. It was illegal for anyone but the alcalde mayor to call such a meeting. Anza was accused of being the "principal cause of the controversy" because of a "blind passion" he had against Rivera. Allegedly, Rivera had wronged Pedro de Alday, one of Anza's Vizcaíno cohorts at Tetuachi. In the opening remarks of his letter, Álvarez Tuñón claimed, "It being my first obligation to report the state of this Province to Your Honor, I am obligated to notify you of the miserable condition of five of its subjects, and especially a boy of little more than twenty-five years called Juan Bautista de Anza." [6]

In the end Rivera was not reinstated, but the controversy with Don Gregorio continued. Anza was appointed inspector of mines for Sonora but soon left Tetuachi and took up residence at the Janos presidio. It is not known from the archives which came first, Anza's appointment by Captain Bezerra Nieto as *alférez* (second lieutenant) of the presidio or his infatuation with the captain's daughter. Regardless, Juan Bautista de Anza and María Rosa Bezerra Nieto were married by April 1722.

Because of Seri, Pima, and Yaqui Indian uprisings and incessant Apache raids on this frontier, records are far from complete, and it is impossible to determine the exact number of children the marriage produced. Of Anza's six known children, only two can be unquestionably documented as having been born at Janos—Francisco on January 17, 1725, and María Margarita on June 29, 1727. Two other daughters, María Manuela and María Gertrudis, were probably born at Janos, but their birth records have yet to be located. Either of these could be older or younger than Francisco and María Margarita, but both were probably younger.

Under the tutelage of his father-in-law, a veteran of the reconquest of New Mexico after the Pueblo Revolt of 1680, Anza gained the reputation of "Apache fighter" while serving at Janos. He was quickly promoted to lieutenant and led a number of far-reaching campaigns against the marauding Indians in what is today northern Sonora and Chihuahua and southern Arizona and New Mexico. He also continued to be active in the struggle to oust Álvarez Tuñón from Fronteras, whose territory he tried to protect from the Apaches in don Gregorio's absence, which was most of the time. On more than one occasion Anza delivered pack strings of food and supplies to the starving families of the Fronteras soldiers who were being forced to work in don Gregorio's mines or on his ranch at Jamaica.

The turmoil finally came to a head when Álvarez Tuñón, at a secret meeting, attempted to drum up sufficient support to get the Jesuit missionaries ousted from the region. Anza, like most Basques of the day, was an ardent supporter of the Jesuits. Living at Janos, he was too far removed from the conflict to again be accused of leading the opposition. This time, his old friend and companion from his days at Aguaje, Martín de Ibarburu, who called himself *El Anciano de la Soledad* in reference to his Soledad Mine at Aguaje, led the resistance. A large group of Sonorans, the majority of whom were Vizcaínos, joined in the clamor to rid the area of don Gregorio and his intrigues forever.

Although it took a few years to see action, the uproar did not fall on deaf ears. Brigadier Pedro de Rivera was sent north from Mexico City to investigate. After talking with the Fronteras soldiers and other members of the community, he put Álvarez Tuñón under house arrest and ordered his removal to Mexico City to stand trial on charges of misconduct and misuse of the king's funds. Don Gregorio managed to cheat justice by dying at the last minute, however. Ironically, Juan Bautista de Anza was appointed executor of his estate, and in 1726 he was appointed commander of Fronteras in Álvarez Tuñón's place. Later, Felipe V, king of Spain, made him "captain for life."

Morale quickly picked up in Sonora when Juan Bautista de Anza set about doing what he was hired to do. The calvary at Fronteras now retaliated immediately against Apache raids. Led by their fearless and energetic captain, the soldiers campaigned far northward into the mountains of the Chiricahua and the Gila River. Anza invited those Apaches not responsible for the depredations to live in accord with the Spanish and mission Indian communities. Soon he was known both as an Apache fighter and as a peacemaker. Settlers began to feel safer in their highly volatile communities. Anza also worked with the Pima Indians, who were striving to adapt to the new way of life the Spanish had introduced. Furthermore, he supported and cooperated with the Jesuit missionaries as none of his predecessors had done. Things looked better for Spanish colonists in Sonora than perhaps they ever had.

Nevertheless, Fronteras, like Aguaje, was strikingly different from everything Anza had known in his childhood. Its isolated location made it vulnerable on every side from countless enemies. This windswept, gray desert was so far removed from the ocean that few inhabitants ever saw it or possibly even knew it existed. The Fronteras River, an intermittent, brackish, meandering stream, was a dry wash most of the year. There was, however, a clear, flowing spring at Corodéguachi, the original site of an ancient Opata village.

The presidio was built on a rocky promontory about a mile northwest of the spring, where the captain's house and adjacent guardhouse sat on the point of a hill overlooking the valley. Behind the guardhouse and surrounding the primary plaza were the soldiers' living quarters and a chapel, where Mass was celebrated. At the foot of the hill, below the captain's house, a small village of adobe houses had sprung up. In the distance, a flour mill was the only remaining building at the site of the original Corodéguachi.

Captain Anza's relatively small, one-story adobe residence was strikingly different from the massive, three-story rock house in which he had grown up; but to his frontier family, who had known nothing different, it was not unusual. Anza undoubtedly had to make adjustments to the frontier life and Indian customs. His children, however, grew up playing and associating with Indians and mixed-bloods of all types in a culture vastly different from the one he had left behind.

Although the Basque Country was far away, Anza maintained an association with the Old World. His letters home traveled slowly via Mexico City to Vera Cruz, where they were placed on a ship bound for Cádiz. There his merchant brother, Juan Felipe, sent them to their final destination. With good fortune, a reply could be expected within the year. It was through this primitive mail service that the captain learned of his mother's death in 1735 and his father's in 1737. It was also via the mail that he and other native sons of Hernani living in the Indies were asked for contributions to help with the costs of repair work on the cemetery, church roof, and courtyard of the San Juan Bautista

Parish back home. Acquaintances and family ties were maintained through the mail, and arrangements were made for Anza's first cousin, Pedro Felipe de Anza of Donostia, to come to New Spain and take up residence with his family in Sonora.

At least two children were born to the Anzas while they lived at Fronteras. Josefa Gregoria was born on March 30, 1732, and baptized the same day in the little presidial chapel on the hill by Carlos de Roxas, Jesuit missionary at the Opata mission of Cuquiárachi eight miles away. Agustín de Vildósola, a fellow Basque and close friend of the family, was her godfather. Juan Bautista de Anza, the second, was born at Fronteras but taken to Cuquiárachi to be baptized, also by Father Roxas, on July 7, 1736. His godfather was his first cousin once removed, Pedro Felipe de Anza.

Although communication with his home country was sporadic at best, there was little time to get homesick or bored. Besides having innumerable duties as a presidial captain and a father, Anza maintained mines at Aguaje, Tetuachi, and Basochuca. He also owned and operated the San Mateo and Guevavi ranches in the San Luís Valley of the Pimería Alta.[7]

Keeping the peace and watching out for the king's interests in this explosive district, however, was his most arduous task, requiring constant vigilance and continuous decisive action. The Apaches were the ever-present threat, traveling at night so their dust could not be seen. They attacked in small raiding parties that would take flight rapidly and disperse almost instantaneously. "It is not possible," Anza lamented, "with the forces under my command to guard against the damages which have been done and which may be done in so vast a province where the inhabitants fear destruction from such cruel and troublesome enemies. Certainly it is very difficult to foresee where they will go to vent their fury, whereby they could be forestalled." [8]

Anza was also concerned that his soldiers were spread far too thin to carry out all that was expected of them. He had no sooner taken command of the Fronteras presidio than he was ordered to go on a forced march with his soldiers to put down an uprising of the Pimas Bajos, or lower Pima Indians, south of his old home at Aguaje. As he put it, "Neither has there been a lack of restlessness among the inhabitants of the Pimería Alta." [9]

Sonora's frontier was tumultuous in many ways, but the civic and military leaders cooperated with each other and worked together during this era, in part, no doubt, because all the principals were old-country Basques. The governor of Nueva Vizcaya, Ignacio de Barrutia, was a native of Bergara, Gipuzkoa. The alcalde mayor of the Sonora district, Cavalry Captain Gabriel Prudhom Butron y Mujica, was Basque, even though he held a number of prestigious titles from other countries in Europe. The captain of the only presidio in Sonora at this time, Juan Bautista de Anza was, of course, from Hernani, Gipuzkoa. And the sargento mayor of all the militia troops in Sonora, Agustín de Vildósola, was from Billaro, Bizkaia. Even Viceroy Juan Antonio de Vizarrón y Eguiarreta had roots in the Donostia region of Gipuzkoa near the Anzas' ancestral home.

An example of this New World Basque cooperation occurred in 1729, when the Seris on the coastal plains of central Sonora rebelled, burning houses, destroying property, and killing Spanish settlers. To inflict any kind of punishment on them, Captain Anza's entire garrison would be required. Sergeant Major Vildósola sent militia troops to his aid and kept a wary eye on the northern settlements while the presidial soldiers were fighting on Tiburón Island in the Gulf of California, where the Indians had fled. Alcalde Mayor Butron y Mujica also sent Yaqui auxiliaries and saw to it that the Jesuit missions sent food, supplies, and Pima reserves. Even Father Campos at San Ignacio, who had gotten old, grumpy, and senile in his nearly forty years' service in the Pimería Alta, was persuaded to provide auxiliaries from his fiercely guarded flock. Anza ferried the men, supplies, and horses across the gulf in boats and stormed Tiburón Island. In his own words, he "was able to carry out some punishment which caused them fear and was not a small accomplishment." [10]

Any time the captain's attention was not being diverted by some crisis in the south, there was more than enough to do in maintaining order in the north. Although Captain Bezerra Nieto was probably not of Basque descent, he was Anza's father-in-law, and they worked together extremely well in trying to establish the king's policy of peace through "Christian charity and kindness." Once, a few days after Anza sent a "pack train of horses loaded with food, coarse blankets, and knives" from Fronteras to the Apaches, along with their women and children whom he had captured a few days before, the Apaches sent a large band of their people into Janos to make peace. Bezerra Nieto tried to persuade them to live peacefully by offering them food and other gifts. Although the situation probably seemed more hopeful than ever before, Apache raiders killed a mission Indian in Cumpas shortly afterward. Those who had come in peace fled in fear, and hostilities resumed. Bezerra Nieto, a widower for ten years, died shortly thereafter, on May 1, 1733.[11]

The year 1736 was probably the most momentous in Anza's life. Even though there were no major Indian uprisings or conflicts, other events proved consequential. That spring Father Campos finally succumbed to senility or his own assimilation into the Pima culture. When church superiors tried to remove him from his post at San Ignacio for unrepentant insubordination, he rallied his loyal Pimas and refused to budge. Some of his fellow Jesuit priests attempted to reason with him, but he fled north to Ímuris and surrounded himself with devoted Indians and Spanish settlers agitating for a confrontation. Despite a strong desire that no harm come to Father Campos, an armed rebellion seemed imminent.

Juan Bautista de Anza was notified, and though he was sick in bed, he got up and rode to San Ignacio with a company of soldiers. When Campos learned the soldiers were approaching Ímuris he sent an emissary to inform Anza that he had repented of his scandalous behavior and was ready to obey his superiors. Hearing this news, the captain changed the course of his march and traveled to Remedios to speak with Father Ignacio Keller. On "bended knee" Anza begged that Campos be allowed to go home with him, where he and his wife would care for the old man. Permission was granted, and back at Ímuris, Anza persuaded Campos, who had accomplished so much in the Pimería Alta, to retire peacefully. An explosive situation had been averted.

Because of his actions in this incident and the many other kindnesses Anza had shown in support of the Jesuit missionaries, he was "admitted as a brother into the Holy Company of Jesus." Since present-day Jesuits have no such "third order," they deny that such a thing could have happened. How legitimate this action was or how much authority Anza's new title carried are questions that perhaps cannot be answered. Whatever the particulars of the case, Anza was deeply honored by the recognition. Although he claimed the main reason the Jesuits bestowed this singular honor upon him was because he was a Vizcaíno, he also recognized that the reverend fathers deeply appreciated the "great affection" he professed and the "tie of friendship" he had maintained with them since childhood. The Jesuits recognized the benefit of entrusting old and feeble priests, no longer able to carry out their duties, to the gentle care of the captain and his wife, whom they loved as much as they did her husband.[12]

In the summer, shortly after this incident, the final addition to the Anza family, the captain's namesake, was born. Father Campos died a few months later, and young Juan Bautista would not remember him. He did, however, grow up with the stories of his father's compassion for the old man and his great love for the Jesuit missionaries. This was one of many legacies left to young Juan Bautista by his father, whom he would also remember dimly, if at all.

Later that fall, one of the most curious events ever to befall the Pimería Alta occurred. Many unanswered questions remain about the drama, which left its mark on the area now known as Arizona. Juan Bautista de Anza, senior, was involved in this famous *planchas de plata* (slabs of silver) incident almost from the very beginning.

At that time, Anza was not only capitán vitalicio at Fronteras but also chief justice for the district of Sonora. On November 13, 1736, while performing his judicial duties in the town of Bacanuche, he heard about the sensational silver discovery near the *realito* (small mining camp) of Agua Caliente. More than a hundred miles away in north central Sonora, the rugged, oak brush–covered mountain country near the headwaters of the Altar River was untamed and sparsely populated, but word of the astounding discovery spread like wildfire. Unearthed by a Yaqui Indian called Antonio, this was no typical silver vein. Incredibly massive balls and sheets of the precious metal were found either on or slightly below the surface of the ground, inspiring the name "planchas de plata." People soon flocked to the area.

Anza, as the king's representative in Sonora, was charged with investigating the situation to ensure that the king would receive his fair share of tax money from any mining activity. He rode over the mountain to Chinapa, where he spent several days sending and receiving letters in an attempt to solve the first problem: Was the discovery a treasure, buried there by an ancient Indian people, a clandestine smelting operation, or a virgin vein of silver? Anza consulted three Jesuit legal authorities as to how to proceed. They agreed that he should first ride over and inspect the situation. If the silver had been placed there by Indians or was a covert smelter, everything would belong to the king. If it was a natural vein, mining claims would be laid out, and the king would get a fifth of the production.

Anza arrived at the site of the discovery on November 20 and named it San Antonio de Padua. The *real* of Agua Caliente was several miles down the canyon. The only closer settlement was a ranch, called Arizona. In all probability this Basque name (which means "the good oak") referred to an oak tree growing there.[13] Arizona was what the Spaniards called a *puesto* (place). A handful of vaqueros lived there, the same as they do today. The puesto did not have the status of a real, nor was it even a large ranch; but because of the silver rush nearby, its name became engraved in history. In 1912, 176 years later, the forty-eighth state admitted into the United States of America was named Arizona, even though the original puesto with that name is in Mexico, fifteen miles south of the international border.

Anza set about organizing the developing chaos. He divided the area into claims, but once the original slabs were removed there was no more silver to be found and the site was abandoned. Anza and his deputy justice in Agua Caliente, a fellow Basque named Bernardo Urrea, interviewed everyone who had anything to do with the discovery. Anza sent out a decree that all the silver was to be confiscated until it could be determined how much belonged to the king. Rounding up the silver proved a difficult task. The largest chunk weighed more than a ton and a number of pieces weighed several hundred pounds each. They had been chopped and sawed into manageable pieces, many of which had already gone into trade around Sonora. Merchants as far away as Arizpe were unhappy when forced to return silver they had taken in trade for goods already consumed.

Debate over the origin and ownership of the nearly pure silver raged for years. Repercussions were felt as far away as Mexico City and Madrid. By the time the lawyers and politicians had sorted everything out, Anza was dead.[14]

On January 14, 1737, Anza petitioned Viceroy Vizarrón y Eguiarreta, another Vizcaíno, to open a land route to Alta California. Although Spain had a long-standing interest in settling Alta California, maintaining a supply route through inhospitable Baja California had proven virtually impossible. A supply route by sea was even more difficult because of the south-flowing currents and prevailing winds. A route from Sonora was necessary to populate California, and Juan Bautista de Anza wanted to discover it. Unfortunately, he would be dead before the opportunity came.[15]

The last major service Anza was able to provide the king occurred in the summer of 1737 when the Pimas Bajos and Guaymas Indians became restless. A smallpox epidemic was decimating several of their villages in southern Sonora when a Guaymas Indian of about forty-five years of age, Agustín Ascuhul, claimed to have been visited by Montezuma, the Indian god. According to Ascuhul, Montezuma had named him *arisivi* (prophet), and he was going to raise ancient warriors from the dead to gloriously drive the Spaniards from their presence once and for all.

Agustín, or Arisivi, as the Indians began to call him, built a throne and a house of palm fronds on the rocks above the surf near the village of Guaymas. Inside he placed a basket lined with cotton on which rested an image of Montezuma. Indians from as far as two hundred miles away abandoned their villages and traveled to Guaymas with their livestock to make offerings to this god and prophet. All of southern Sonora was becoming disrupted, and insurrection appeared imminent.

Anza rode south with twenty-two of his soldiers. Seven more soldiers from the Sinaloa presidio joined them on the Seri frontier. At Tecoripa they picked up Father Felipe Segesser and twelve Basque militiamen, financed by Agustín de Vildósola. Joining the company at Aguaje was an old acquaintance, Francisco de Aldamiz. Two years Anza's senior and a native of Gauteguiz de Arteaga in Bizkaia, Francisco was still mining at Aguaje and was Anza's deputy justice in that district.

Arriving at the coast, the soldiers found four thousand to five thousand Indians at Arisivi's sanctuary, where there was singing and dancing and sacrificing of animals in all-night ceremonies. Although the soldiers were greatly outnumbered, they apprehended Arisivi and transported him back to Guaymas. There, on June 1, 1737, after Father Segesser administered the sacrament of repentance, the soldiers hung Arisivi by the neck from a high palm tree. The Indians quickly dispersed without a shot being fired.

As a result of Anza's decisive actions with such a small force, the king issued a royal *cédula* on July 13, 1739, thanking Anza for his many services to the crown. Anza never saw the royal cédula, since he was ambushed and killed by Apaches before it arrived on the frontier.[16]

His young family was thrown into a quandary. They could no longer live in the captain's house at Fronteras. Francisco Anza was barely fifteen years old and Juan Bautista, the second, was not yet four. Probably all four daughters were still at home, leaving Anza's widow with many mouths to feed. Over the next few years they lived on various holdings the captain had left them. They lived at Basochuca for awhile, then settled permanently on the Divisadero Ranch on the Santa Cruz River. Although Anza's holdings were fairly extensive, this period was economically and emotionally difficult for his family.

Francisco de Anza married Victoria Carrasco. Little is known about her beyond the record of her death at Buenavista on October 2, 1763. Whether the marriage produced any children is unknown. Francisco continued in ranching and was always at his younger brother's side after the latter became a presidial captain.

María Margarita may have been the first of the Anza children to move away from home. She and Manuel Esteban Tato were married at least as early as 1745. The only thing known of María Manuela de Anza is that she was godmother for one of the Tato children in Basochuca in 1749. There is some evidence that María Gertrudis may have been married to Ignacio Díaz del Carpio, a frontier soldier and son of the presidial captain who pursued the Apaches who killed her father. Gregoria married Gabriel de Vildósola, an old-country Basque from Elexabeitia, Bizkaia, on February 1, 1747, at the church in Basochuca.

The details of the life of Juan Bautista de Anza, the second, up to age sixteen are obscure. One legend says he was educated by the Jesuits; another, in a military school in Mexico City or Guadalajara. Tradition dictates that his godfather, Pedro Anza, would have been a part of any decision about young Juan Bautista's education. Although Pedro Anza eventually ended up in Mexico City in partnership with the Basque mining magnate José de Laborda, he appears to have been in Pitic during his godson's formative years. Perhaps young Juan Bautista obtained his education there. His footsteps seem to have followed his father's from his very first days. Although his handwriting is clear, his grammar and sentence structure are not that of a native Spanish speaker, leading one to believe that he might have spent his early years with his godfather, speaking Basque as his first language.

He may also have been absent from the Pimería Alta when the infamous Pima rebellion erupted in December 1751, but his family was definitely there, living on the Divisadero ranch. Gabriel Vildósola and Gregoria Anza, who was five months pregnant with their first child, lived on the adjoining Santa Barbara Ranch. Gabriel sent her back to Basochuca for safety, and with four men in his employ, he rode south to San Ignacio and offered his services to the governor to help end the hostilities.

A 1783 *hoja de servicio* (service record) indicates that Anza began his military career as a volunteer in December 1752, exactly one year after the beginning of the rebellion. Since the hoja de servicio was compiled thirty years after the fact and since much of the military action during the uprising took place in the early months of 1752, it seems likely that the record is incorrect and that Anza actually joined the militia in December 1751, rather than in December 1752. If so, he was probably one of the four who went into military service with his brother-in-law at the beginning of the rebellion and, at age fifteen, would have been with the first troops to reconnoiter the Pimas' positions. He would have participated in the campaign led by fellow Basque José Díaz del Carpio, then stationed at Terrenate, and would have been with the group of soldiers led by Vildósola and assigned to find a location for a new presidio. The site decided upon was Tubac, where Anza eventually served as captain for seventeen years.[17]

Because of Vildósola's exemplary service during the Pima rebellion, he was appointed captain of the royal presidio of Fronteras in 1754. Anza accompanied him as a *cadete* and quickly rose to the rank of lieutenant in 1755. In slightly more than four years as a lieutenant, he gained a reputation as an Apache fighter, as had his father. Under Vildósola, Anza commanded five general actions against the hostile Indian tribe. His detachments killed forty of the enemy, took two hundred captive, and reclaimed more than five hundred stolen cattle.

On one occasion Anza was ordered to take up a position in the rugged, unfriendly Sierra de Chiricahua, where a large band of Apache raiders were camped. With a number of presidial soldiers and ten loyal Indians, he attacked the Apaches at least six times, finally forcing their retreat from the mountains and capturing, "by [his] own hand, the enemy captain." Anza was wounded in one of these engagements, one of two times that he was injured in skirmishes with the Apaches during his career.

Conditions in Sonora had worsened since his father's days, and Lieutenant Anza was soon ordered by Sonora's Basque governor, Juan de Mendoza, to help suppress a burgeoning Seri insurrection in the south. He took part in five separate campaigns against the Seris under the command of Mendoza, but it was becoming obvious that the war was being lost. During the years from 1755 to 1760, ranches, villages, and mining camps were being deserted under mounting pressure from Indian raiders. The town of Aguaje, where the Anza family still had mining interests, was one of many settlements that were totally abandoned.

In September 1759 Juan Tomás de Belderrain, the first captain of the Tubac presidio and a fellow Vizcaíno, was wounded by a Seri arrow while fighting on Tiburón Island. Belderrain's injury was not extremely serious, but because the Seris poisoned their arrow points he died a few weeks later at the mission of Guevavi. In December Governor Mendoza appointed Juan Bautista de Anza, the second, to take his place. The following summer the governor himself was struck in the throat by a Seri arrow and died some days later.[18]

These were trying times. Expanding Apache and Seri depredations and sporadic Pima unrest seemed to be driving Sonora to the brink of destruction. People flocked to the safety of larger settlements or left the province entirely. Never had the prospects for peace and safety seemed so dismal. For a new generation, another Juan Bautista de Anza arose to the occasion. Although many others came up through the ranks at the same time, Anza played a significant role in nearly every battle and campaign waged on any of Sonora's frontiers.

During those years, his life appears to have been one continuous horseback-mounted Indian campaign across the "great Southwest," or what the Mexicans call the "great Northwest." He did take time, however, for other, more personal experiences. Anza's aging mother moved with him to Tubac in the beginning months of 1760, and he was at her funeral Mass at Mission Guevavi on October 14, 1760. The widow of twenty years had died of natural causes. She was laid to rest beneath the church's altar steps, beside Captain Belderrain, whose body had been placed there just one year previously.[19]

Anza, like all Spanish soldiers, needed the permission of his commanding officer before he could marry. Governor Mendoza, who had taken a deep interest in the young officer, was now dead, and Bernardo de Urrea, captain of the presidio of Altar, had been appointed interim governor. On June 1, 1761, Anza's petition for marriage was sent to him, a fellow Vizcaíno and longtime friend of the family. With it went several letters of support and recommendation from friends of the family, including one from the aging Father Segesser, who, like Governor Urrea, not only was a friend of the young officer but had been his father's friend for many years.

Like the other writers, Father Segesser stated that the deceased governor had expressed on several occasions that he hoped Anza would marry. The priest even pointed out that Mendoza had hoped Anza would marry a specific girl. That young lady had married another man, however, so Father Segesser could see no reason why the deceased governor would not want Anza to marry the girl he was proposing to take as his bride. Governor Urrea, seeing no reason to oppose the marriage, granted permission for the ceremony and dispatched the marriage license from his residence at San Miguel de Horcasitas on June 8.

Juan Bautista de Anza and Ana María Pérez Serrano were married in the imposing Nuestra Señora de la Asunción Cathedral in Arizpe on June 24, 1761. Carlos de Roxas, an old friend of the family who had baptized the groom twenty-five years earlier, performed the ceremony.[20] The Pérez Serrano family were longtime Basque residents of Arizpe and old acquaintances of the Anzas. In fact their fathers had been neighbors at Tetuachi before either of the newlyweds was born.

Juan and Ana's marriage was childless, undoubtedly to their great sadness. Anza's older brother, Francisco, whose first wife died a few years later, married Ana María's sister, María Teresa Pérez Serrano. They also moved to Tubac, probably for the protection that the presidio provided, but Francisco continued to operate the family ranches and did not join the military. Their marriage produced two daughters, both born in Tubac—María Rosa in 1772 and Ana María in 1775.[21]

Clearly, Juan Bautista de Anza never seemed to have time for relaxation or reflection on his problems. His marriage in Arizpe took place only after he had returned from a concerted campaign against the Seris, executed in conjunction with Gabriel de Vildósola. A year later they were on a joint maneuver in the north, chasing Apaches on the Gila River. In the autumn of 1762, all the presidial captains and a large percentage of their cavalry were back down in the Seri country trying to curtail the spreading unrest there.

These captains of the northern frontier were forced to spend more and more time in the rugged Cerro Prieto, a range of mountains surrounded by the merciless desert floor south of Pitic. The Seris would hole up there after a raid. For Anza, their insurrection meant riding more than two hundred miles to participate in military actions against them. Invariably, once he was at the Cerro Prieto, an Apache raid would occur in the north, and he and his men would be needed elsewhere in his jurisdiction. They would gallop back to defend Tubac, or maybe a hundred miles beyond, to track Apaches across the Gila River Basin. When the Apache problem was secured, he and his soldiers would lope back to the Cerro Prieto as the cycle continued.

By 1767 the situation was so grim in the south that the king ordered regulars sent in from Spain and Mexico City to help crush the incessant Seri uprising. A huge barracks complex was built at Guaymas to house the soldiers coming in by sea. Detachments from all presidios in Sonora and Sinaloa were required to participate in the effort. In addition, mission populations and their surrounding communities in the north were gearing up to provide auxiliary soldiers and supplies.

First, however, a royal decree sent out in secret on February 27, 1767, sealed with the king's own stamp, superseded everything. Shrouded in mystery, it stunned and dismayed the populace, leaving the frontier reeling in a state of bewilderment. The king had decided the Jesuits were conspiring to overthrow him, and he ordered that they be arrested and sent to Spain, where they would be imprisoned.

The governor of Sonora sent orders, dated July 14, 1767, to Anza by special courier. Anza's old friend Bernardo Urrea, captain at Altar, in the company of a few soldiers, delivered the orders to Anza at Tubac. The information in the *pliego sellado* (sealed packet) was not to be read until July 23. When he opened it, Anza learned that he had been ordered to the rectorship of the Sonora River. There, on July 25, he was to arrest all the Jesuit priests and march them to Mátape, where presidial captains responsible for other rectorates would also be arriving with their prisoners. Once all the priests from the north were assembled at Mátape, José Vildósola, nephew of Gabriel, would transport them to the new military barracks at Guaymas. From there they would begin their long journey to prison and exile.

The expulsion was met by a wide range of reactions. Certainly the enemies of the Jesuits exulted in seeing them marched away on foot in complete humiliation. The Basques, however, generally held the Jesuits in high regard, and a large majority of presidial captains were Basque. The aging Bernardo de Urrea, ordered to arrest the missionaries in the Altar and Santa Cruz River Valleys, broke down emotionally as he escorted his captives to Mátape and had to leave the rest of the journey to his junior officers.

For Juan Bautista de Anza, the decree was especially painful. His father had been a Jesuit "brother." In fact, his family, openly professing their love for the Jesuits, took in aging priests to care for them in their final hours. Jesuits had supplied at least a part of Anza's education, and some of them must have replaced the father figure he never had. To compound his anguish, the rectorate where he was assigned included some of his family's most beloved priests. The aging Father Roxas, for example, who had officiated at Anza's baptism as well as his marriage ceremony, was serving at Arizpe. Father Nicolas de Perera, nearly seventy-one years old and in ill health, was at Aconchi. Perera had been with Anza's father as he convinced Father Campos to leave Ímuris. Although the orders allowed sick or aging priests who could not travel to be left behind and taken at a later date, Father Perera begged to go with his brothers. So Anza had a reed stretcher made, and the aging priest was carried all the way to Mátape between pack mules.

The emotional agony of Anza, who was torn between his love for the Jesuits and his duty as a soldier of the king, can hardly be overemphasized. In a moving letter to Governor Pineda he described the people crying as the soldiers and arrested priests trudged through each village. It had been "very inconvenient" for him, Anza confided, because he had "had no premonition or foresight regarding the expulsion." He begged the governor's "support . . . in sending into exile some very forlorn and dejected men." In his original order, Governor Pineda had advised Anza that he should "acquaint . . . [himself] with the royal resolution in deep meditation and in the presence of the spirit." Then, he ordered, "you shall perform this duty without excusing yourself with the anguish you will feel in giving evident proof of your loyalty." Despite the distress he was feeling, Anza stoically performed his duty.

After delivering his arrested missionaries at Mátape on August 17, Anza immediately turned back north. Probably in part to rid himself of a nightmare, he immersed himself fully in the work at hand. Food and supplies had to be gathered and guarded at the missions. No priests were available now to take care of such things, and a year would pass before Franciscan priests replaced the Jesuits. Horses, mules, and other livestock had to be obtained and auxiliaries and support personnel recruited. The great Seri war was about to begin.[22]

After taking part in a brief Apache campaign in September, Anza was back at Pitic, helping prepare for the massive invasion being planned. In late February 1768 he was sent in command of sixty soldiers to reconnoiter the waters in the various canyons leading up into the heart of the Cerro Prieto. In the craggy and jagged ravine called Cara Pintada, Anza determined where and how many horses and men could be watered. He and his soldiers rode the few miles east to examine the springs at Aguaje, where his father had started mining so many years before. He noted with sadness that the mines were caving in because of rotting timbers. Inspecting other watering places as they went, Anza and his men rode south to Guaymas and on to the presidio of Buenavista in Sinaloa. There he met with Governor Pineda and General Domingo Elizondo, an old-country Basque in command of all the troops.[23]

Although many small campaigns were fought in the Cerro Prieto and vicinity, and the presidial soldiers continued to travel many miles to perform their duties in that region and to defend the north, the first all-out invasion was not staged until October 1769. By that time, the heavyset Governor Pineda had suffered a stroke and was unable to participate, but all the other officers, including Anza, were ready with several hundred soldiers. Because of difficulties traveling in the rocky, mountainous terrain and communicating across the craggy canyons, this campaign, like all other concerted attacks staged in the Cerro Prieto, had limited success. Over the next few years, however, the Spaniards applied sufficient steady pressure and killed enough unfortunate Seris and Pimas Bajos in alliance with them to declare the war won and go home.

After the first all-out attack and a subsequent meeting of the officers with José de Galvéz, minister of the Indies, Anza was sent with a detachment of soldiers to attack an encampment of Seris in the high country. Under heavy fire, Anza and his soldiers routed the Seri camp, killing seventeen. Moving slowly across the rugged terrain, the soldiers were mopping up on foot as the sun was setting. As Anza neared a small grove of trees, three Seris stepped out and fired arrows at him. One arrow struck a glancing blow across his face, causing his cheek to bleed profusely. As the Indians fled, Anza fired a shot from his pistol, injuring one of his opponents. This was the second time he had been wounded by the Seris. Although most men died when wounded by the poison-tipped Seri arrows, Anza was more fortunate and survived.[24]

After the Seri War finally dragged to a close, Juan Bautista de Anza renewed the petition to the viceroy that his father had made thirty-five years earlier. He requested that with the aid of a few soldiers from Tubac, he be allowed to find and open a road between Sonora and Alta California. Permission was slow in coming, but Anza and twenty-one soldiers, five mule packers, a carpenter, an interpreter, two personal servants, a courier, an Indian guide, and two Franciscan priests finally left Tubac for this purpose on January 8, 1774. Because Apaches had stolen the reserve horses of Anza's command a few days before, the expedition turned south to the Altar Valley in search of more mounts, then west across what is known today as the Camino del Diablo (road of the devil) and on to the confluence of the Gila and Colorado Rivers. There they made friends with Chief Palma and his band of Yuma Indians.

After crossing the Colorado, Anza's company experienced some severe difficulties in what is now Baja California, but after regrouping and sending most of the men and livestock back to the Yuma village, the remaining explorers quickly crossed the mountains, reaching the newly established Mission San Gabriel on the evening of March 22, 1774. There Anza dispatched his courier to Mexico City with the news of their arrival. One of the Franciscans, Father Garcés, was sent to San Diego to try to obtain more horses. Father Díaz rested at San Gabriel while the captain and a few soldiers made a hard ride north to the new presidio of Monterey. Upon leaving Monterey, Anza and his men rode all the way back to Tubac without fresh horses, for San Diego had been unable to supply any.

Anza spent that summer commanding the forces at the presidio of Terrenate, but in the fall he traveled to Mexico City to make his favorable report. This time he rode, not as a captain, but as a lieutenant colonel, an advancement the king had granted when news of Anza's success in locating a route to California reached Spain. That December he received the commission to take thirty families to colonize the newly discovered San Francisco Bay, which the Spaniards called the Puerto or Río de San Francisco.

Over the years, wealthy Basque bankers, financiers, and monopolists in Mexico City, including Manuel de Aldaco, Ambrosio de Meave, Francisco de Fagoaga, and Juan José de Echeveste, financed Anza's activities as a presidial captain, mineowner, and rancher. They had lent him money to finance the exploratory expedition to California, and they now backed this colonizing effort, as did the powerful Basque politicians in Mexico. Domingo de Arangoiti, Francisco de Gamboa, José de Areche, Antonio de Villaurrutia, among others, including Viceroy Antonio María Bucareli y Ursua, whose mother was Basque, supported Anza fully in this endeavor.

Lieutenant Colonel Anza arrived in Culiacán, Sinaloa, from Mexico City with a large mule train laden with supplies and began recruiting families on March 25, 1775. On March 10, 1776, he delivered his recruits safely to the presidio of Monterey in Alta California. On March 28, he and expedition chaplain Father Pedro Font, seventeen soldiers, and his lieutenant, José Joaquín Moraga, were the first Europeans to stand on the San Francisco side of what we call the Golden Gate. There they erected a cross and claimed the magnificent bay for Carlos III, king of Spain.

At the moment Juan Bautista stood at the Golden Gate, his sister, Gregoria, and her family were making final preparations in Mexico City for passage back to the Basque Country. Perhaps as they crossed Sonora in opposite directions they met and said their last good-byes, for they never saw each other again. Gregoria, the last of that generation of Anzas to die, passed away peacefully in the village of Billaro, Bizkaia, and was buried in Elexabeitia on May 3, 1800.

The epic colonizing journey that Juan Bautista de Anza led to California is unrivaled in the history of the North American continent. With roughly a hundred soldiers, vaqueros, mule packers, scribes, personal assistants, three priests, and various other servants and workers, Anza safely conducted two hundred recruits to California. They had no wagons. Everyone rode horseback. Including horses, beef cattle, and mules, more than a thousand head of livestock accompanied them.

The expedition spent the summer in Horcasitas, the capital of Sonora, training the men as soldiers for the Apache country ahead, gathering supplies, and waiting for the fall rains. The final gathering point was at Tubac. When it departed on October 23, 1775, the group numbered approximately 300; 92 were twelve years old or younger and 125 were eighteen or younger. Four babies were born at Horcasitas, two while the expedition was traveling between Culiacán and Tubac, and three between Tubac and San Gabriel. All nine lived to see California.

Although disease struck the town of Horcasitas while the expedition was there, killing three recruits, only one person died en route to San Francisco Bay: Manuela Piñuelas died in childbirth on the evening October 23, 1775, as the result of complications from a breach delivery. During the journey, a number of animals died from the harsh desert conditions or freezing winter weather in the mountains. It is to Commander Anza's credit that the expedition succeeded beyond anything that could have been imagined.[25]

The career of Juan Bautista de Anza was far from over. When he rode back south to Mexico City, he learned that he had been appointed commander of all the troops in Sonora. Anza had been in Horcasitas for less than a year, carrying out that commission, when the king appointed him governor of New Mexico on May 19, 1777. He traveled first to Chihuahua, where he met with Teodoro de Croix, *comandante general de las Provincias Internas* (commander general of the internal provinces), and other high-ranking officials, including his predecessor in Santa Fe, a Vizcaíno from the province of Navarre, Fermín de Mendinueta. There the officials in attendance devised a plan to bring the Apaches under control by using soldiers from Nueva Vizcaya, Nuevo México, El Paso, and Sonora to surround and crush them. The plan called for Anza to open a supply route between Santa Fe, New Mexico, and Arizpe, Sonora, seat of government for the Provincias Internas.

When Anza arrived in Santa Fe, however, he found New Mexico being torn apart by Comanches. Anza sent a dispatch to Commander Croix requesting that he be allowed to solve that problem first. Permission was granted, and Anza left Santa Fe on August 15, 1779, in pursuit of Chief Cuerno Verde. With 800 men and 2,500 horses, riding much of the time during moonlit nights to escape detection by the enemy, Anza headed north through the high country of present-day

Colorado, crossing and recrossing the Arkansas River before ambushing and killing the infamous Comanche chief. The governor was back in Santa Fe on September 10, having killed or captured many of the enemy leaders. He then started the process of negotiating the longest-standing peace treaty ever signed with the Comanche nation.

Before setting out to find a route to Arizpe, Anza again obtained a postponement from Croix in order to alleviate a problem in the Hopi country. The Hopis had not had rain for several years and were starving. Anza brought to Santa Fe those who were willing to relocate, settling them among the Pueblos. The next summer Anza himself made a trip to the land of the Hopis. Although he was unable to befriend all factions of the Hopis, his policies in carrying out the king's edict to treat the Indians with kindness were exemplary and pathbreaking.

Finally, on November 9, 1780, the governor left Santa Fe with 151 men, including 38 Indians. Captain José de Vildósola, commander at Las Nutrias, where the presidio of Terrenate had been moved, was to meet the Santa Fe contingent somewhere near the present-day border between New Mexico and Arizona, but the two detachments never saw each other. So Anza pushed on past Las Nutrias and arrived in Arizpe on December 18.

By the time he returned to Santa Fe, Anza had covered eleven hundred miles, a round trip nearly twice the length of either the Comanche or Hopi expeditions and one-fifth the distance traveled on the colonizing expedition to California. Calculating from existing documents for the years between 1754 and 1788, it is known that Anza rode at least thirty thousand miles on horseback. The unrecorded distances he covered in the course of everyday activity might push the total to sixty thousand miles or more.

Juan Bautista de Anza was promoted to full colonel on February 19, 1782. Things began to sour for him the following year, however, when Felipe de Neve was appointed to take Croix's place as commander general of the Provincias Internas. Neve, governor of California during the colonizing expedition, attempted to discredit Anza, even ordering him to quit taking credit for having discovered the route to Alta California. Although their disagreements were many and varied, Neve was not the first "Californian" to exhibit jealousy that Anza, not he, was given the commission to colonize the San Francisco Bay. During his colonizing expedition, Anza had experienced troubles with Fernando de Rivera y Moncada, commander of the California troops, for the same reason.

Neve died after only one year in office, and things improved somewhat under José Antonio Rengal, but it was the appointment of Jacobo

Ugarte y Loyola, an old-country Basque, as commander general in 1786 that finally led to Anza's being absolved of all Neve's charges. By that time, however, Anza had petitioned the king to be relieved of his governorship. His brother, Francisco, had died, so Juan was helping raise his two small nieces, whom he loved as daughters. In addition, his health was failing. For the first time in his life, Anza asked for an easier assignment.[26]

Finally relieved of his governorship in 1787, he returned to Arizpe as commander of all troops in Sonora. Later he was made commander of the presidio of Tucson. He inspected the troops there on September 7, 1788, in what was probably his last official act. He died in Arizpe at midnight on December 19. He was buried the next day beneath the floor of the side chapel of Nuestra Señora de Loreto just a few feet from where he had been married twenty-seven years earlier in this ancient Jesuit church. Sadly, Anza had sent his wife, her sister, and his two beloved nieces to Horcasitas the previous week, so they were not there when he died and were unable to attend the funeral Mass.[27]

Still, he left his family a monumental legacy that would only gain in significance with each passing generation—a heritage that belonged to all of Sonora, the Southwest, and even North America, the Basque Country, and Spain. Indeed, the Anza heritage truly belongs to the world. That legacy, however, has been largely ignored and nearly forgotten for two reasons. First, we live in a society, whether in the United States or Mexico, that largely ignores, and even denies, the importance of the Spanish colonial period in the history of our nations. Second, even among Spanish colonial historians, ethnicity and cultural differences among "Spaniards" have been almost universally overlooked.

The Anzas were Basque. They knew it, and everyone they dealt with knew it. They used their heritage to their advantage and some of their non-Basque neighbors complained about it. They played an active part in a vast Basque network, centered in Mexico City, that permeated all aspects of life and reached into the farthest corners of the frontier. With the help of that network and through their own abilities and ingenuity they created a relatively prosperous and comfortable life for themselves and their families. Because of their political and military involvement in community and regional affairs, they helped improve the lot of all their "Spanish" neighbors. In so doing, they were prime movers in forging the outcome of history across an immense expanse of the North American continent.

Juan Bautista de Anza, the father, was among the earliest pioneer explorers and colonizers to push north and establish a Spanish presence in the formidable Sonoran desert in the early years of the eighteenth century. He and his fellow Basques were among the first to develop the livestock and silver mining industries in northern Sonora and southern Arizona. Fiercely loyal to the "two majesties," God and king, Anza was always perceived as a leader, fighting to maintain and uphold that Spanish community against nearly inconceivable odds, including Native American opposition from without and corruption and infighting from within. As captain of the royal presidio of Santa Rosa de Corodéguachi, he was a scourge to belligerent native factions, while striving to expand the mission system as a means of promoting peaceful assimilation of native nations into Spanish society.

Because of the father's early death while carrying out his duties as a soldier, it was left to the younger Juan Bautista de Anza to continue the fight to maintain Spain's precarious foothold in the north by protecting and expanding existing missions, communities, and supply lines. Although best remembered for making his father's dream of a supply route to California a reality and shepherding three hundred people and a thousand head of livestock across eighteen hundred miles of wilderness to establish San Francisco, one of the best-known cities in the United States, many of his other contributions are just as impressive.

Like his father, Juan Bautista, the second, was deeply loyal to his God and country. Despite opposition from his fellow Spaniards, he instituted sweeping economic, political, and military reforms, while serving as the governor of New Mexico, that strengthened the province and brought peace with the Indians. His dealings with the native populations, especially the Comanche and Hopi, during his governorship were and are exemplary. The Apache and Seri wars of earlier years would probably have had different outcomes had Anza not been on the frontier. To the casual reader, unfamiliar with the times, both father and son might appear to have been avid Indian killers. Actually, they were two of New Spain's foremost advocates of peace through negotiation and friendship. Although they lived in a society based on castes, it is impossible to detect in the actions of either the slightest hint of prejudice.

When the history of the Spanish colonial period on the North American continent is finally told without prejudice and its contributions to the well-being of modern society are examined for their true value, the name Juan Bautista de Anza, the father as well as the son, will take its place among the names of other distinguished world figures.

4

Pedro and Bernardo Altube
Basque Brothers of California and Nevada

CAROL W. HOVEY

The lives of Don Pedro and Don Bernardo de Altube spanned four-score years and three continents. From the Pyrenees of their birth, the brothers emigrated to South America, following older brothers to the pampas of Argentina. In 1849, Pedro left the pampas, bound for the gold mines of California. Pedro sent for Bernardo a year later. After years of running cattle and dairy operations throughout California, in the finest tradition of the American West, Pedro and Bernardo established the rancho of their dreams—the renowned Spanish Ranch in northeastern Nevada.

Pedro de Altube Idigoras was born April 27, 1827, in the *baserri* (farmstead) Zugastegi, in Oñate, Gipuzkoa, Spain. As the second son of the second marriage of both his parents, he held a position in the Altube family lineage that was neither auspicious nor ill-fated. It could have been predicted, in fact, that when Pedro came of age, he would emigrate to a foreign shore to seek his fortune, because the majority of boys from Oñati and the neighboring Basque villages and towns snuggled in the valleys of the Pyrenees did so during the nineteenth century.

For at least six generations preceding Pedro and Bernardo, the Altube line thrived as *etxejaun* (head of household) of Zugastegi. Pedro and Bernardo's father, Joaquín de Altube Balenzategi, married late in life, waiting until the arrival of the nineteenth century before beginning a family of his own. Joaquín married Josefa Ursula Lazkanoiturburu Aiardi of Oñate in 1808, and they had four sons and a daughter before Josefa died in 1821.[1] Joaquín was left with three sons, aged ten, eight, and six (their firstborn son had died young), and a baby daughter. As was the custom, Joaquín did not remain unattached for long. Just four months after Josefa's death, he contracted marriage with a young widow from nearby Aretxabaleta who had a family of her own.

When Joaquín remarried he chose a bride who had not been born and raised in Oñate, the first time that had happened in two centuries of direct-line descendants. He married Micæla Idigoras Eraña on November 7, 1821, and they added to their already large, combined family: Félix in 1822, Maria Josefa in 1825, Pedro in 1827, and Fernando in 1831. In all probability, more children would have followed, but on November 8, 1831, Joaquín died. Micæla was left a widow again, this time to raise the four children from her first marriage, the four from Joaquín's first marriage, and their own four—the youngest of whom, Fernando, was only five months old. At his father's death, Pedro was almost five years old.

During the next ten years, the family survived and prospered. José Miguel, the oldest surviving son of Joaquín and Josefa, assumed his responsibilities as *etxekojauna* (head of household). Two years later, in 1833, he married his stepsister, Micæla's daughter, Gregoria Uribe-Echeverria Idigoras. Over the next several years, the remaining sons of the family began to establish themselves independently. Gregoria's brothers had been the first to emigrate to Montevideo. Then José Miguel's three younger brothers followed suit. Santiago left for Buenos Aires in 1840 and was followed in 1842 by Miguel and Félix.[2]

In 1845 money for Pedro's voyage was guaranteed by José Miguel, the collateral a mortgage on the family property in Oñate.[3] The eighteen-year-old Pedro soon was aboard the *Irurac-Bat,* sailing away from his homeland port of Bilbao. In 1848 the fifth Altube brother, Fernando, emigrated to Argentina. Pedro worked with his brothers for three years and learned the skills that served him later in his own cattle, dairy, and ranching operations. In 1848 the electrifying news of the discovery of gold in California reached Buenos Aires. Pedro, along with a group of his friends, decided to try his luck in the gold fields. Fernando arrived in Buenos Aires as Pedro was preparing to leave. At eighteen, he had to stay behind with his older brothers' families (all except José Miguel had immigrated to Buenos Aires) with the understanding that if Pedro was successful, he could send for Fernando; if not, he would return to join his brothers in Buenos Aires.

With a group of at least thirty-five Basques, Pedro crossed the continent on horseback, instead of taking the longer and more dangerous sea route out of Buenos Aires and around Cape Horn. The group arrived at Valparaíso, Chile, and sailed from there to San Francisco.

The legend of Pedro Altube began to take shape around this time. Several anecdotal references name Pedro Altube as one of the first Basques in the American West. One account says that "the first two Basques, Pedro Altube and Segundo Ugariza (known as 'Sendo'), arrived at San Francisco in 1850. They were sailors on a whaling boat." [4] It is more probable, however, that Pedro arrived with the Basques who shipped out from Valparaiso about 1848.[5] Certainly Pedro's temperament would have demanded that the journey be made without delay. His youthful enthusiasm whetted by the lure of gold would have made inaction intolerable. By whatever means he arrived in the gold fields, Pedro made the trip as quickly as was humanly possible.

In joining the rush for gold in California in 1849, Pedro was like many other young men who saw themselves as adventurers, wanted to live dangerously, believed unquestioningly in their own good fortune, and would give all they had for the chance to make it big overnight. At age twenty-two, Pedro compensated for his lack of years with youthful exuberance, a strong body, and an imposing stature. He also loved drinking and gambling. These habits led to the downfall of many gold seekers, since indulgence in either often led to being swindled repeatedly or even murdered. Pedro, however, came through unscathed and richer than ever.

Pedro was an extroverted individual who did not hesitate to greet those he met along the way with "Hello, son-of-a-bitch, my friend! Stop and have a drink with me." [6] Pedro's talents during his years in Argentina had been used in the hide-and-tallow trade on one brother's rancho. With his skills as an expert vaquero, Pedro epitomized the flamboyant and colorful figures who so often caught the eye of the more mundane gold seekers in the California placers. Pedro also valued good horses, considering them to be a partner in adventure. The details of Pedro's years in the gold fields are lost forever, but much can be pieced together of his probable endeavors and the rigors he suffered.[7]

From San Francisco, prospectors were forced to choose between the northern mines above Sacramento or the southern mines via Stockton. Gold seekers from the United States usually headed for the northern mines, while "foreigners" were more likely to mine the San Joaquin Basin and Tulares. Since there was a large Basque contingent mining at Sonora by late 1849, it is probable that Pedro was among their number.[8]

Although mail delivery from California was at best erratic, Pedro was able to establish himself and send for Fernando in little over a year. An indication of his success was the money for Fernando's passage and the gold to be invested in property and managed by Félix in Buenos Aires. The land purchase was recorded in 1851, and although Pedro was the landowner, he never returned to Argentina.[9] Fernando made his arrangements, applying for a passport to California on December 13, 1850. In the process, he also changed his name from Fernando to Bernardo. Bernardo disembarked in the port of San Francisco to meet Pedro in the spring of 1851.[10]

During the first ten years Pedro and Bernardo were in California they amassed a small fortune. These two young men probably would not have accumulated such a large sum of money working for their brothers in Argentina. If they had been able to prosper as well in Argentina, they would not have left so quickly for California upon learning of the Gold Rush. By the time Pedro sent for Bernardo, he was convinced that California was the key to riches. After a season in the mining camps, an astute businessman would have quickly ascertained that the adventurers who took the most out of the area, with the exception of those who made a lucky strike, were not miners but traders. Quite possibly Pedro had succeeded in mining gold, perhaps had even more luck in gambling—since that ever was a passion—and then saw a way to multiply his stake many times over by supplying cattle to the miners and the booming population of San Francisco.[11]

The Gold Rush created an enormous, expanding demand for beef, raising the price per head to unheard-of rates. The long-established custom of slaughtering cattle solely for hides and tallow quickly gave way to the more profitable business of selling the stock for beef. Thus began, in the early days of the Gold Rush, the practice of driving large herds of cattle on hoof from Southern California to northern markets. A full month was required to move a herd from the southern ranchos near Los Angeles to San Francisco. Several methods were used to make cattle delivery profitable to the investor. According to one source, "Some southern rancheros leased grazing rights in the vicinity of San Jose, Sacramento, or San Francisco Bay, where the stock fattened after the long drive; other owners sold direct to cattle buyers who came down in large numbers from the north either to purchase on their own account or to serve as agents for butcher shops and meat dealers in the larger cities."[12] The period of high profits on cattle began in 1849 and continued on an upward spiral for almost seven years. As early as 1855, however, a number of factors contributed to a sharp, relatively sudden decline in cattle prices.

Recognizing their own "gold mine," Pedro, Bernardo, and a group of Basque companions went into the business of cattle buying. They purchased herds of cattle in Los Angeles County, ran them up the San Joaquin Valley, and fattened them at Santa Nella. Then they drove the herds either east to the Calaveras mining camps or north into the San Jose mining camps, selling the cattle for almost double their purchase price. In an interview on November 23, 1930, a few weeks before his death, José Antonio Aguila talked about the group of Basques who lived at Sentinella (Santa Nella) in the 1850s.[13] José Antonio remembered Pedro and Bernardo Altube, Juan Chico (Little John Indart), Juan Grande (Big John Etcheverry), Joaquín Bolado, and Sanjurjo, who all ran cattle from around 1851 to at least 1856. Rather than running their herds up the coastal trail along El Camino Real, they drove cattle along El Camino Viejo.

Rancho Sentinella, where Pedro set up headquarters, was essentially "an Indian aguaje about fifty yards to the north of El Camino Viejo, where the Old Spanish Trail crossed El Arroyo de San Luis Gonzaga."[14] The partners built an adobe house; a spring at its front and larger springs rising from the creek at the back of the adobe made a comfortable base for their cattle operations. There was also an orchard. All this land was open when the Basques arrived; nobody had proved title to it. To the west of the rancho was the Pacheco-owned San Luis cattle camp, an important station because of its ever-present water for cattle being driven north along El Camino Viejo or east through the Pacheco holdings to the gold mines. The Basques would drive their cattle into San Luis Camp when the water went down and the feed dried up around Santa Nella. Of course, as José Antonio Aguila relates, this was not without its price. During one particularly dry year, Juan Indart was forced to pay $1,500 for the privilege of watering and feeding his cattle.[15]

From Rancho Sentinella, the partners ran cattle both north and east. Several Basques, including the Altubes, ran butcher shops in Calaveras County. It was a very lucrative practice. Descendants of the Garat-Indart families tell of how the partners would trail cattle up to Angel's Camp to sell for meat and divide the money earned so each man would carry only a "small amount," returning to Santa Nella by separate routes. These precautions were taken to safeguard against all their money being stolen by Joaquín Murieta's gang after a successful drive.[16]

In the mid-1850s, when the partners began going in different directions, Rancho Sentinella remained the headquarters for Juan Indart and Juan Etcheverry, who established a partnership with a third Basque, Salvador Itsague, and a Spaniard, Segui Murrietta. The realigning of partners seems to have occurred shortly after Pedro Altube married Marie Ihitzague and settled in San Mateo. What was more natural than for Pedro to set up in business his new brother-in-law, Salvador? [17]

When Pedro and Bernardo quit running cattle around Santa Nella about 1855, they moved to San Mateo and established a dairy on the hill in Palo Alto where Stanford University now stands. While Pedro lived there his legend expanded. Pedro was nicknamed "Palo Alto," or "tall pole." He was indeed a tall stick of a man, standing a full six feet eight inches. In later years, some claimed that the town had been named after Pedro Altube, rather than the other way around.[18] Pedro himself would have set the record straight, leaving just a hint that he was far too modest to say otherwise.

While in California, the Altube brothers maintained ties with the Arrambide brothers, the Garats, Bernardo Ohaco, Antonio Harispuru, and Bernardo Yparre, all shipmates or fellow Basques from Buenos Aires.[19] Bernardo Altube and Juan Baptiste Arrambide were among a group of eighty ethnic Basques who emigrated from Buenos Aires around 1850. Tradition demanded that when Basques immigrated to new lands the first group established a support system for followers. For example, Juan Miguel Aguirre established the famed Basque Hotel of San Francisco as early as 1851, greeting new arrivals in their own language, orienting them to their new surroundings, and helping them settle in a new country. This pattern replicated the similar support system in Buenos Aires that provided employment and funneled a continuing supply of help to Basque-owned concerns, a system that the Altubes themselves had benefited from when they arrived from Spain. In the 1850s and 1860s, the Altube brothers were partners with other Basque immigrants in several cattle and dairy operations spread throughout California's central valley and coastal areas. As this first generation of Basques turned from gold mining to other occupations, many sent for their families from the Basque region and from South America, just as Pedro did when he sent for Bernardo.

A fairly substantial Basque community lived in California by the mid-1850s, and a large percentage of this group remained there. For many Basques, San Francisco provided a home base, especially for those living in the outlying, less-populated areas of California. Many Basque families returned to San Francisco for landmark occasions such as baptisms, marriages, and burials, which were ceremoniously recognized in the church. The Saint Francis Xavier Church served the needs of the Catholic French and Spanish-speaking population during San Francisco's early years. Traveling priests ministered to their wide-spread flock.

During the 1850s and 1860s in California, the economic conditions affecting the Basques underwent significant changes, which were divided into four relatively even periods. The first phase—between their arrival in the gold fields in 1848 to 1850 and the sudden decline in the demand for beef "on the hoof" around 1855—saw the Altubes and their partners scouting out a new land of opportunity. By the mid-1850s the original group of Basques running cattle at Santa Nella had begun to diversify its business operations. In partnership with each other, a subgroup of partners was designated to spearhead different ventures. Indart and Etcheverry remained at Santa Nella; in 1855, the Altubes and Arrambide moved up to San Mateo to run dairy operations.

The years 1855 to 1860 framed a second phase as the Altubes and fellow Basques in the cattle industry shifted from hide-and-tallow methods to raising cattle for beef production, requiring a fundamental change in the breeding and feeding of stock. Not only was new stock introduced for its beef, but dairy cows and sheep made their appearance. Since the dairy business undertaken by the Altube brothers in the mid-1850s apparently did not fulfill their expectations, they explored other business options, deciding in fact to return to selling cattle. Bernardo Altube, Arrambide, Bernardo Ohaco, and the Garats began running cattle on rangeland at the northern end of the San Joaquin Valley in mid-1857. In that year, the estate of Etienne Garat purchased a half-share in the Rancho Cañada de los Vaqueros land grant, paid off the mortgage, and transferred the estate to the Basque partners.[20] The Basques gave their name to the grant, known locally as "the Basco" or "the Vasco" since the 1850s. The Altubes and their partners retained their San Mateo residence until late 1859. The tax records for San Mateo County that year show that Pedro Altube and Juan Bautista Arrambide both had assets of $4,500. Pedro owned ten horses and three hundred head of Spanish cattle; Arrambide had five horses and the same number of cattle.[21]

From 1860 to 1864, the stock-raising system in California continued to change as it faced tremendous challenges. Conflicting interests between farmers and sheepmen heightened as the demand for wool during the Civil War created an impetus for raising sheep. Increased competition from superior stock driven in from Texas and the Midwest, along with the introduction of new products, forced California ranchers to make range improvements and change the composition of their herds. To complicate matters, lack of feed and water caused massive cattle deaths in the harsh winter of 1859–1860 and the drought of 1863–1864.

Pedro and Bernardo had a thriving cattle operation established on Rancho Cañada de los Vaqueros by 1860. In the 1860 census, Bernardo's household included his French-Basque wife, Marie Recarte Altube; infant daughter, Gracieuse; Juan Baptiste Arrambide; three members of the Ohaco family; and four other persons of French, Spanish, and Native American descent.[22] Of their 8,880 acres, only 5 were improved. The remaining acreage was used to graze 1,280 head of stock cattle and 50 horses worth $17,750. The use of the rancho was divided between the Sunol brothers and the Basques, who each owned half. The free-range system was problematic, however, since the owners feuded over grazing rights.[23] Other Basque friends and associates with whom the Altubes did business also bought several parcels of land in the northern end of the valley. These properties were located in the general vicinity of Livermore (just south of Rancho Cañada de los Vaqueros), which was a strategic, "central" location for pooling the cattle that were run up from the south (and later from the east) and for fattening the herds before selling them in San Francisco.[24]

Additionally, the Altubes expanded their ties with Basques still in the gold country. Bernardo, his family, and his partners Juan Baptiste Arrambide and Bernardo Ohaco invested in ranchland in Calaveras County for running cattle and in butcher shops in Vallecitos and Angel's Camp. Records of land transactions from the 1850s through the 1870s indicate that other Basques who operated extensively in the gold country in the 1860s included Indart and Etcheverry (who owned butcher shops), the Abadie brothers, Juan Miguel Aguirre, Miguel Goldarecena, Salvador Ihitzague, Juan Iribarre, Thomas Ithuralde, Jean Ochoa, and Juan Oxaby.[25] The Altubes continued to supply cattle from their central valley holdings to their Vallecitos-based butcher shop being run by Juan Bautista Arrambide until 1868.[26]

In 1860, Pedro and his family moved down to Santa Barbara County with partners Bernardo Yparre and Antonio Harispuru and his wife, Marie Amestoy. They established business ties with Basques already there: Ulpiano Indart (from Spain via Mexico), and the Joaquín Ormart and José Maria Andonegui families (from Spain via Buenos Aires).[27] Four miserable years of ruinous winters heralded by torrential rains the winter of 1860, which gave way to a devastating drought spanning the next three seasonal cycles, became even more intolerable by a grasshopper infestation and smallpox epidemic. The drought broke in late 1863 with drenching downpours and a massive snowpack that melted and created a run-off, which flooded California's central basin. When flooding in the San Joaquin Valley ended in 1864, the entire valley was carpeted with luxurious pasturage. Many ranchers were forced to sell out during these hard years, and ultimately even more sold out because everything they owned had been washed away by the floods. To add insult to injury, the cattle that had survived the disastrous weather grew fat and sleek, and resulted in a glut of beef on the market and plunging stock values. Those more fortunate took this opportunity to buy up the available properties, since real estate values were severely depressed. Some land was selling for as little as eleven cents an acre.[28] The Basques, trying to recoup their losses and build up their herds, began buying property throughout the central valley.

Business operations in San Mateo and Santa Barbara were dissolved following these disastrous years, and the stock-raising and butcher-shop interests in Contra Costa and Calaveras Counties were placed in the capable hands of Altube partners, who remained to oversee their operations. The Altube brothers decided to consolidate business by running their own wholesale slaughterhouse in San Francisco and raising stock on various ranch holdings to provide a constant supply of beef. Financial arrangements for the Altube operations were made by Buenaventura Dolheguy of San Francisco. Dolheguy brokered the land transactions when Pedro Altube divested himself of his interest in the Santa Barbara ranchos. Dolheguy also bought out J. B. Arrambide/ B. Altube et al. in October 1863, transferring the property to Louis Peres & Co. (Louis Peres and Pedro Altube) in April 1864.[29] Pedro Altube and Louis Peres were equal partners in the business of buying and selling beef and joint owners of Rancho Cañada de los Vaqueros, and were listed as wholesale butchers in San Francisco by 1866.[30] Bernardo Altube remained primarily involved in supplying cattle from their various ranch holdings and was never a partner in Louis Peres & Co.

The final half-decade leading to 1870 cemented the need for a whole new approach to ranching operations. From all accounts, the Altube brothers moved to Mendota, just above the Garat/Arrambide head-quarters. Trying to rebuild and expand in central California, however, turned out to be a bad idea. The reason was Henry Miller and his Miller and Lux empire. In the San Joaquin Valley north of Bakersfield, the Miller and Lux empire had been steadily expanding since 1858. Not even the flood and drought years had slowed its growth. Henry Miller began his land acquisition with a purchase of 8,835 acres at Santa Rita from Henry Hildreth and quickly added land along the San Joaquin River that comprised one-fourth of the old Rancho Sanjon de Santa Rita.[31] By the time Miller retired, Miller and Lux had purchased three-fourths of present-day Madera and Merced Counties, holdings that encompassed everything north of the San Joaquin River from its eastern curvature at Mendota to the confluence of the Merced and San Joaquin Rivers just below Modesto.[32] These lands, however, probably made up only about one-third of Miller's total holding. As Joe Arbu-rua observed, "When Miller bought the H-H and started to spread, it was the beginning of the end for the three Basques"[33]—that is, Indart at Santa Nella, Altube at Mendota, and Garat at White's Bridge.

Henry Miller had a habit of "pushing his neighbors considerable," to put it plainly.[34] He claimed all of the water flowing over his land for his exclusive use under riparian law. Miller was obsessed with the con-trol of land and water rights. Miller's covetousness is illustrated in a conflict with Juan Miguel Arburua in 1877. Pablo Loinaz, Pedro Al-tube's brother-in-law, had an artesian well at Berenda, which Arburua rented from him. When Juan Miguel began to fence in the well, Miller paid him a quick visit. Fencing the well would keep out Miller's cattle, so he told Arburua that if the fence came down, Arburua could feed his sheep anywhere on Miller's surrounding property.[35]

By 1870 the first generation of Basques was ready to leave the San Joaquin Valley. Bernardo Altube moved his family to San Jose in 1868, where Pedro and his family were already living, so that the brothers could reassess their options. Juan Garat was being pressured by Miller to sell out. Garat apparently had been on the verge of selling but had backed out—twice. Finally, Miller forced the issue by charging in-creasingly exorbitant rates to water the cattle during the drought years, and payment for the property was exchanged at Gilroy.[36] Indart also held out for about the same length of time, but after a bad year, he and Etcheverry sold to Miller and moved their operations to San Benito County.[37]

With their departure, the exodus of the original group of Basques who had been running cattle through the San Joaquin Valley for almost two decades was complete. Their connection with the valley was not broken completely, however, for as they left, a new group of Basques began to arrive—mostly friends and relatives of the Basques who had just departed. When the Altubes moved, for example, they did not sell the Mendota property. Instead, through a series of deed recordings, the property was leased and managed by Pablo Loinaz. The Altubes had bought out Loinaz in 1863 and hired him as their bookkeeper, a job he kept for the next twelve years. When Pedro's sister-in-law Catalina Ihitzague married Loinaz in 1875, the property was reconveyed to the newlyweds as a wedding present with the understanding the Loinazes would manage the property for the Altubes.[38] Pedro, his wife, and their daughters visited the Loinaz family two or three times a year, perhaps as much for business as for family reasons. All in all, it becomes very evident that even though the Altube/Altube, Garat/Arrambide, and Indart/Etcheverry families transferred their business interests elsewhere, they were still tied irrevocably to the San Joaquin Valley.

Henry Miller's penchant for land acquisition may have appeared to be motivated by pure greed and his pressure tactics barely short of offensive, but he was a man who accomplished his dream. Pedro Altube and Henry Miller were competitive associates in their ranching concerns, cattle raising, and slaughterhouses, even socializing with each other's families. The Altubes and Garats, who had long collaborated on business interests, were aware of the impact of Miller's business practices on their own ranching concerns. They watched and took note. By 1869, when the transcontinental railroad opened new frontiers to settlers, a new wave of Basques came to America, and the first generation of Basques again moved in new directions. After two decades in America, the Altubes had sampled what their new land had to offer and decided how to best fulfill their dreams. As they acquired their herds and drove them over the Sierra Nevada, they took with them lessons well learned. Miller had his land agent Overfelt purchase parcels of land to build his extensive holdings; Garat had Arrambide acquire property in the same way, and Pedro followed suit with Bernardo. They were also careful to establish water rights. The Altubes, for example, controlled large areas of rangeland by simply buying the properties containing the water supply for the entire area and claiming the water rights.

Pedro and Bernardo moved to San Jose and then to San Francisco to help reorganize their investments. During this period, which was a transition to firmer financial standing, they took preliminary steps toward establishing sufficient backing to consolidate their cattle onto one large ranch at a then-undetermined location. By 1869, the stage was set. Pedro and Bernardo's families were settled in comparative comfort in San Francisco. Louis Peres, Pedro's business partner, managed the Altubes' slaughterhouses, freeing Pedro and Bernardo to find a place to establish the enormous rancho of their dreams. To restock their herds of cattle, they went to Mexico. In one season, they acquired two thousand head of cattle and fifty Mexican horses and moved them as far as Los Angeles by late 1870, where they wintered. The Los Angeles County tax assessor valued the stock at just under $25,000.[39] While their cattle wintered in Los Angeles, Pedro and Bernardo returned to San Francisco to be with their families and oversee their interests in Butchertown, where their slaughterhouses were located.

Basques often initiated individual business enterprises in the company of other Basques. In the spring of 1870 the Altube brothers moved their herd up central California, through the San Joaquin Valley, over the Sierra Nevada, and into the rangeland beyond Reno, Nevada. Trailing a band of sixteen thousand sheep directly behind the Altube herds, Juan Miguel Arburua capitalized on a business venture of his own. Since 1870 was a notoriously bad year for ranchers, Arburua purchased all of his neighbor's sheep. The following spring he drove the sheep back down and sold them for a handsome profit to the same neighbor.[40] Also following the Altubes, the Garat outfit crossed the Sierra Nevada in late 1870 and wintered at Fernley. They worked their herds across the northern valleys of Nevada for another season, again trailing the Altube herds. The Garats arrived on the upper end of the South Fork of the Owyhee River by early 1872 and established their YP Ranch that year above the Altube holdings.[41] Exploring the vast expanse of the northern Nevada open range, the Altubes had finally found the land they were searching for in the ranges of northeastern Nevada. By the spring of 1872, they had settled in Independence Valley above Elko and founded the Spanish Ranch, the rancho of their dreams.

By 1875, the ranch was prospering, and Pedro was heavily involved in the forced transition of the Butchertown slaughterhouses to New Butchertown, a less-populated area where the operations would not be so offensive to city residents. The relocation, though begun on paper in 1870, was not near completion until the mid-1870s.[42] For nearly fifteen years Louis Peres & Co. was in business, with Louis Peres handling the administrative end of the business while Pedro concentrated on supplying the livestock for the slaughterhouses. Louis Peres operated the company's office at 526 Merchant Street, where he also resided, until at least 1874.[43] During the first few years Louis Peres & Co. was in business, the Altubes herded their cattle up from the San Joaquin Valley, using the same trails as Henry Miller, and ferried the cattle across to the cattle wharf and into Butchertown. By the early 1870s, however, the Altube cattle were also coming in by rail from Elko, where they had been trailed from the Spanish Ranch.

Pedro and Bernardo established the headquarters of the Spanish Ranch in Independence Valley. Even though the Spanish Ranch depended on supplies and business deals with the nearest town, Tuscarora, and the nearest rail line in Elko, the ranch itself was the private domain of the Altube brothers. The brothers loved the land in northeastern Nevada and purchased property and acquired land patents until they owned thousands of acres. Pedro Altube could rightfully claim, "This morning I leave my *rancho* house, I ride all day. Tonight I make camp on my *rancho*." [44]

Piece by piece the Altubes put together their gigantic ranch. In June 1873 the Altubes and Louis Peres bought 640 acres in Independence Valley for $1,000.[45] They also purchased Hogles Ranch, finally paying off the mortgage in 1884, making Hogle Field the base of the Spanish Ranch. In 1874, the year the paved road between Tuscarora and Elko was completed, there was a tremendous winter loss of sheep and cattle. Many small-scale ranchers sold out and moved on, and the Altubes bought up as much as they could. This was a busy time as the Altubes built up and expanded their ranch. They hired Shoshone Indians to build their original bunkhouses and corrals, and they added to their herd (most of which had perished the past winter) by trailing in more cattle from the Fresno area and down from Idaho.[46] In addition, they astutely gathered sagebrush to sell to Tuscarora miners, who burned tons of it to run their machinery. Other local ranches participated in this lucrative business, earning $2.50 a cord upon delivery.[47]

The major land acquisition began during 1878, with the Spanish Ranch eventually covering more than one-third of Independence Valley. At that time the ownership of the ranch was split into three equal shares: Louis Peres & Co., Bernardo Altube, and Pierre Dupuy. By 1880, Pedro bought out Dupuy, and he and Louis Peres dissolved their partnership.[48] This dissolution included the San Francisco slaughterhouses (Pedro did not sell the company property until 1904 but leased his lots to other butchers), the Rancho Cañada de los Vaqueros property, and Peres's share in Pedro's one-third of the Spanish Ranch.[49] The ranch was now wholly owned by Pedro and Bernardo, with Bernardo controlling one-third interest and Pedro retaining two-thirds.

The Altubes also followed the usual practice of having numerous friends and family members buy property in small parcels and then sell them to the ranch. Many of these transactions occurred during the next decade. Not only were properties purchased outright, but thousands of acres of land patents were filed, again by diverse family members and friends. Juan Bautista Arrambide took parallel actions as general partner and buyer for Juan Garat of the neighboring YP Ranch in the late 1880s. In August 1889 Pedro and Bernardo officially filed a claim to all water rights over the entire Independence Valley, and in May 1905 they claimed the water rights for improvement purposes throughout Bull Run Basin. Of course, these water rights had been claimed earlier, during the acquisition of surrounding land since 1873.[50] The practice of having associates buy land parcels as individuals and then transfer title to a larger company clearly circumvented the spirit if not the letter of the homestead laws. Following the model used so successfully by Henry Miller in acquiring hundreds of thousands of acres, the Altubes and Garats fell into the same pattern, again using lessons learned during their years in the central San Joaquin Valley.

The Spanish Ranch, like most large outfits, was a working ranch with few amenities. Centered in Hogle Field, the ranch was composed of a large bunkhouse, corrals, a stable, and a storage building for supplies. The first bunkhouse built by the Shoshone Indians resembled (in pictures) an old Basque farmhouse. It burned down many years later and was replaced with a one-story, ranch-style building. The storage building, at first glance, resembles a jail. Its thick walls and iron-barred windows protected valuable supplies from the elements as well as light-fingered passersby.

There was no house on the ranch, however, because no family members lived there year-round. When Pedro and Bernardo came up in the spring and summer, they rented a room at a boardinghouse or hotel in Tuscarora and rode to the ranch whenever they wanted. Both Altubes brought their families with them for several weeks at a time, with wives and children residing comfortably in town and participating in ranch activities as they wished. Pedro's daughters were avid horsewomen, and Bernardo's sons were expected to be expert riders and cattlemen. The most exciting time of year was the roundup, when the entire family joined in the myriad activities.

The Altubes enjoyed the advantages of having Tuscarora close to ranch headquarters, but the Garats were not so fortunate. Their ranch, until the second generation of Garats, consisted primarily of men. The Garat and Arrambide families and the Altubes maintained family households in San Francisco. The men usually spent several months each year on their ranches, coming off the range in the winters and leaving their foremen in exclusive charge.

Having cattle on these enormous ranches was like having cash reserves on hand. To the Altubes, the Garats, and all other large outfits, land was acquired, collected, and possibly traded for more land, but never sold. Land was a permanent investment. The cattle they ran on that land, however, was another matter entirely. They were viewed more as a speculative investment, a stock that experienced good years and bad years. As a valuable and essential commodity, the cattle were bred to be butchered for beef, with ranchers always trying to improve the bloodlines of their herds and weed out inferior cattle.

Understandably, the Altubes were protective of their investment, and their cattle were considered among the best. "Mr. Pedro Altube, better known as Palo Alto, has an extensive ranch in Independence Valley with some 20-25,000 head of cattle and it may be mentioned that the steers raised in that valley, especially on Mr. Altube's ranch[,] bring a better price in the market than those from any other part of the country," stated rancher Henry Brown in 1884.[51] Naturally, other ranchers had their own methods for improving their stock. Sometimes, however, since cattle were run on open range and mixed freely with other brands, it was better if their imported bloodlines were not "too different." A case in point: "The Altube Range joined the Squaw Valley Range of the Nevada Livestock Co., an English outfit that was managed by a man named Parkinson, whose center of operations was Golconda. The English outfit imported Black Angus bulls. For some reason, black cattle were considered inferior and very undesirable by western cattlemen and the Altube outfit were not about to make any exceptions. The Spanish Ranch buckaroos castrated the Black Angus bulls and it nearly started a war between England and Spain according to one report."[52]

Pedro and Bernardo built up a thriving cattle kingdom despite constant losses during the harsh winters for close to two decades. But the disastrous winter of 1886–1887 wiped out years of work. Snows were so severe that cattle that could not be reached either froze or starved to death. The Altubes attempted to save their cattle by shipping hay from California, but that effort proved futile.[53] Their herd was destroyed. In

fact, every outfit operating in the Nevada ranges that winter was devastated by the disaster. The catastrophe spelled the end of the range
practices that had been in place for decades and hastened the fencing
of the open range. It meant severe financial retrenching for all; for
some, it was the end of their ranching operation entirely.

By 1887 the Altube brothers were entering their sixties. Although
starting over must have seemed particularly difficult, Pedro's characteristic determination convinced Bernardo it was worth the effort. As
Pedro promised, "God took away from us, but God will give it back
to us. We will do better the second time and in a few years we will
be worth a million pesos."[54] They did just that. They sold property,
tapped financial sources in California, borrowed from the Henderson
Bank in Elko, and built another herd, starting with fifteen hundred
head purchased and trailed down from Idaho. Slowly and persistently
over the next dozen years, even going to the extreme of living on the
ranch between 1898 and 1900, the Altubes recouped and even exceeded their original stake.[55] By then their holdings had become the
Palo Alto Land and Livestock Co., and their 73,656 acres ran the entire Independence Valley and Bull Run Basin, ranging approximately
thirty-five miles long and five to ten miles wide. The Spanish Ranch
bordered the ranges of an English outfit based on Squaw Valley Range
to the west, the Garats' YP Ranch on the northwest, the Duck Valley
Shoshone Indian Reservation straight north, and smaller ranches east
of the Jack Creek land and south to below the Taylor Canyon Horse
Ranch.

Family ties are extremely important to the Basques, and they were
nurtured despite the obstacles placed by distance and the requirements
of raising families and running businesses. When Pedro made periodic
visits to oversee his various business properties and investments, the
family would sometimes travel with him to renew ties with friends and
family seen only rarely.[56] The interconnections among many of these
Basque families may be intricate and difficult to pinpoint, but family
loyalties are fully demonstrated nonetheless.

The Altubes were closely related to a number of other California
Basque families. Pedro's wife, Marie Ihitzague, was chaperoned by the
Señora Idiart, née Juanita Iribarren Arrambide, when she traveled to
San Francisco to marry Pedro in 1853.[57] The Altubes are related to the
Idiarts both by marriage and by family ties in Spain and Argentina. Pe-
dro and Marie's nephew, Peter Loinaz Ihitzague, married Emilie Idiart
Iribarren, daughter of Marie's chaperone, Juanita Idiart.[58] Ties with
the family are reflected in the Idiart family album, which contains pho-

tos of the Altube daughters Grace, Elena, and Lucretia taken at the time of their confirmations in the 1880s.[59] Pedro's brother-in-law, Salvador Ihitzague, maintained an interest in the Santa Nella partnership until 1864, when he thought he could do better working in the Almaden mines. When he did not do as well as he expected, he worked on the Altube holdings in Santa Barbara County until they were sold in 1866. Once again, a brother-in-law could certainly count on being given a job.[60]

As evidenced by the ranching and business interests they shared, the Altubes, Garats, Ormarts, and Aguirres were close friends; their ties appear to have been strong from the earliest years. Investigation of available church records reveals several marriage ties that reinforced their familial affection. They served as godparents for each other's children, and overlapping friendships also bound them closer to each other. San Francisco church records document that these Basque families witnessed for each other at many baptisms and marriages. The Altubes appear on entries between 1857 and 1861 and again from after 1868 through the early 1900s.[61]

One of the Altubes' closest associates and friends was Juan Garat. Two of their early Basque partners from the Santa Nella and Rancho Cañada de los Vaqueros days married Garat daughters: Juan Bautista Arrambide (a full sixteen years older than his young bride) married Grace Garat in 1865, and Jose Aurrecoechea wedded Carolina Garat in 1879. In 1895 John B. Garat married Matilda Indart, daughter of Juan Indart, and they lived on the Garat YP Ranch in Nevada.[62] All of these men and their families were involved in business and social relationships together for the rest of their lives.

The Altubes and Ormarts had ties back to Buenos Aires, which they renewed when Pedro and Marie moved to Santa Ynez, outside Santa Barbara, in 1860. Mission records document they became godparents for each others' children, and their families grew closer as the years passed. The Altubes had seven daughters: Amelia, born 1855, Marie, born 1857, and Grace, born 1859, in San Mateo; Elena, born 1862, and Honorina, born 1863, in Santa Ynez; Lucretia, born 1870, and Amelia, born 1872, in San Francisco. The first Amelia and the infant Honorina had died in Santa Ynez by 1865. In late 1887, at age seventeen, Lucretia died of tuberculosis.[63] The two middle surviving daughters grew up and married two Ormart sons: Grace married Joaquín in early 1887; Elena married Miguel in 1889.[64]

Juan Miguel Aguirre's Basque Hotel, the earliest in San Francisco, and years later Bernardo's San Francisco Hotel Bernard served as orientation points for thousands of Basques first setting foot on American shores. Reassured by a sense of home and belonging, a shared drink, a challenging handball game, a bargain reached in the native tongue, and the camaraderie of fellow Basques, the newly arrived immigrants found purpose and protection in these Basque boardinghouses as they set out to seek their fortunes. Just as often, the hotel owner found employment for the new arrivals or greeted relatives sent for by Basques who wanted to support their families and share opportunities. Frequently, these Basques found employment on the Altube and Garat spreads in Nevada, in the San Joaquin Valley, or on their other properties supplying cattle to the San Francisco slaughterhouses. The networking among Basque ranchers provided many an opportunity for work with cattle or sheep. Basques quickly gained a reputation for being hard-working, dedicated, and honest laborers, and many non-Basque ranchers who valued these traits also hired the Basque men.[65]

A genial, easygoing man, Bernardo was well-suited to riding the range and managing day-to-day activities at the ranch, but he was also very sociable. His other business interests included running his Hotel Bernard, which he modeled on Aguirre's establishment. For most of the 1870s Bernardo's family maintained their San Francisco residence at 1414 Kearney Street. In 1878 they moved to 1508 Powell Street, a few blocks from Aguirre's Basque Hotel and the Spanish Church (Nuestra Señora de Guadalupe Church). Bernardo and Marie lived on Powell Street, in the heart of San Francisco's thriving Basque community, for the next decade—ten years that saw the growth of Jules and Felix into mature young men. In 1881, Bernardo leased for the family residence one of three properties Juan Miguel Aguirre owned in the 1300 block of Powell Street. Aguirre had established his Basque Hotel at 1312 Powell Street some fifteen years before, in 1866.[66] Bernardo's family moved into 1316 Powell; the Aguirres moved next door, to 1314 Powell, three years later, in 1884. In addition, one of the Garat sons, Peter S. Garat, and his wife, Silveria Goldarecena, moved a block away on Powell Street that same year.[67] Silveria's older brother, Odel, was a well-known and successful San Francisco lawyer. The Altubes consulted Odel about legal matters, and he had also invested in Nevada property that was later transferred to the Spanish Ranch.[68] The bond between the Altubes and the Aguirres was cemented further in later years when Bernardo and Marie's niece married the Aguirres' oldest son. This niece's family, the Harriagues, were related to the Garat family dating back to either France or Buenos Aires—with children being born or married during the 1850s.[69]

There were also strong financial ties among these Basques, and the Altubes sometimes lent funds to help out their friends. Juan Miguel Arburua was the nephew of Juan Miguel Aguirre. Arburua's wife, Josefa, was the niece of Aguirre's wife, Maria Martina Leboyen.[70] Arburua purchased some of his central valley property from Pedro Aguirre, the Aguirres' son. In 1884, Juan Miguel Arburua had the opportunity to purchase his ranch outright from the leaseholder. He had just returned from an extended visit to Spain and had no funds readily available. He needed $40,000. As the family tells it: "The loan was procured from the Altubes without so much as the scratch of a pen. After all, the Altubes were Basque also, and among the Basques their word was their bond. It was considered an insult for one Basque to ask another to sign a note."[71]

During 1868 and 1869, as both Altube families established themselves in San Francisco, they wrote to Spain and sent pictures that were passed from family to family back home. Correspondence with family members in Spain, France, and Buenos Aires appears to have been fairly infrequent during the ten to fifteen years the Altube families were settling themselves in California. After that, they wrote more frequently—especially after Pedro and Bernardo established permanent residences in San Francisco by 1870. It seems that the families tried to write to each other at least once a year, usually around Christmas.[72] Ceferino Aguirre, the youngest son of the Altubes' sister Maria Josefa, immigrated to their care in 1871, and a picture was sent home in later correspondence showing Ceferino as a young caballero.[73]

Bernardo and Marie had six children. Their three little girls—Gracieuse, born 1860, Emilie, born 1861, and Lucretia (Joaquín's twin), born 1868—all died very young. Sadly, a few weeks after his seventh birthday in 1875, Joaquín died too.[74] At the time of Joaquín's death, Juan Garat was traveling back to France, so Bernardo sent a letter in his care to give to the Altube family living in exile in Bayonne during the Carlist War. The letter said that their son had "died of a very serious illness [he] could not overcome. Now [we have] only the other two sons left [Jules and Felix] and hope that the Grace of God will keep them strong."[75] The letter also mentions the possibility that the brothers might visit one another someday, a common thread in all their correspondence. A proposed trip to Spain in 1877, which was postponed for one more year, never happened. Santiago, the only brother left in Spain, died in 1878.[76]

Pedro, as partner in Louis Peres & Co., was responsible for maintaining the butcher shops and business connections in San Francisco.

By 1869, Pedro's family residence was at 9 Dikeman Place, near Butchertown. This address gave Pedro convenient access to the company offices while he was in the city. In 1875, when his Louis Peres & Co. business office and slaughterhouses relocated to New Butchertown, the family moved south of Market Street, to 23 Oak Grove. The Altubes kept this address until the birth of their first grandchild, Marie Viola Gesvret, in 1882. Their oldest daughter, Mary, had married a Frenchman, Eugene Gesvret, in 1881, and the birth of their only child left Mary in precarious health.[77] The two households remained combined at 4 Burritt Street until "baby" Viola was nine years old.[78] Although the merger of the households could have been a crowded and awkward situation, in fact it may not have been that difficult. It appears that there was much visiting between Pedro's and Bernardo's residences, especially with all the business matters that the two brothers shared. In addition, for several months of the year—from late spring through fall to the first snows—the men in the family (Pedro, Bernardo, Jules, Felix, and Eugene as their bookkeeper) always traveled to and from the ranch. Quite often in the summer, when other matters did not interfere, all family members stayed in Tuscarora for weeks at a time.

During the 1870s and 1880s, Pedro and Bernardo raised and educated their families. Both men came to love America and all it represented—possibilities were endless and dreams could come true. Pedro and Bernardo dreamed not only of material wealth—represented graphically by the land they owned—but also of sufficient wealth to share with their daughters and their sons. The family came first. Church and education were also extremely important to the Altubes. Pedro and Marie's daughters were well educated. They attended the French School in San Francisco, spoke French fluently, and were accomplished musicians. They studied music with Santiago Arrillaga, organist for the Spanish Church. Although she never actively pursued a career as a concert pianist, Grace was proficient enough to have become one. Pedro also insisted that Marie (fluent in French) become fluent in English and learn to read and write. He hired a tutor expressly for her benefit. Pedro learned to speak English but never to read or write it. He wanted the benefits of such knowledge, however, so he hired a man to read to him every winter evening from texts on various subjects, such as history, the classics, or the sciences, as well as from sources that covered current events.[79] During the 1880s, Pedro became a member of the Spanish Benevolence Society, the only organization he ever joined. Founded in 1877, one of its first presidents was Ramon

Aguirre (son of Juan Miguel), and later officers included Santiago Arrillaga, Jose Noriega, Juan Miguel Aguirre, and Orel Goldarecena.[80]

Bernardo and Marie also expected their sons to do well. Jules and
Felix spent their winters at academies, acquiring a solid education.
They were also musicians like their cousins (Pedro's daughters). Felix's
serenading skills on the violin gained him quite a reputation with the
young ladies. Bernardo was fluent in English and Spanish, as Marie
was in French. Most of the correspondence to families in Europe and
Buenos Aires came from Bernardo and Marie. The Altube daughters
and sons loved the ranch and were proficient equestrians. Jules, in particular, appreciated a good horse, raced horses at any provocation, and
kept fine stock in the stables. Pedro and Bernardo were spectacular riders and passed this love and ability on to their children during the
many summers the families spent at the ranch.[81]

At the beginning of twentieth century, Pedro slowly began to transfer the day-to-day operations of the ranch to his nephew and son-
in-law Jules. Pedro's youngest daughter, Amelia, and Bernardo's oldest son, Jules, had married in 1896. Both families had been delighted
by the marriage.[82] By this time the Palo Alto Land & Livestock Co.,
which consolidated all the Altube holdings into one giant operation,
was producing enormous wealth. In addition to the ranch itself, the
company owned the Thompson, the Taylor, and the IL Ranches, and
their range extended over thousands of acres.[83] They not only ran cattle
and kept stables of horses (some for racing), but also ran sheep. This
new investment had been made in retaliation against John G. Taylor,
whose bands of sheep had earlier trespassed on the Altube cattle range.
About 1900, the Altubes decided to fight sheep with sheep and in the
process became a sheep and cattle ranch by 1902.[84]

After living at the ranch for almost three years, the Altubes decided
to build a palatial home at 2821 Jackson Street, in the Pacific Heights
district of San Francisco. Their neighbors included Henry E. Huntington, president of Southern Pacific Railroad, and H. H. Bancroft, the
noted publisher and historian. Acquired in 1901, the property was put
in the hands of their daughter, Grace Ormart, until Pedro and Marie
took up residence in early 1902.[85] The Altube home was known as the
family mansion. A beautiful four-story Victorian edifice with twenty-
one rooms, its basement contained a large wine cellar as well as several
rooms for the live-in help. On the first floor was an enormous drawing
room; bedrooms were on the upper floors. At the time, the property
equaled half a city block, and the spacious house was surrounded by
beautifully landscaped gardens.[86]

Pedro and Bernardo should have been able to enjoy a life of ease and luxury after their years of unending labor and hardship. Management of the Spanish Ranch was in the capable hands of Jules, although Pedro was loath to give up all control. Extroverted and irascible, he was not temperamentally suited for retirement; patience and long-suffering were not his strengths. He continued his lifelong habit of carrying a flask of whiskey in an inside pocket, subjecting any person met along the way to a friendly cussing and a demanding invitation to have a drink.[87] As a trade-off, the new family home in San Francisco did allow Pedro to indulge in his favorite pastimes of poker playing, drinking, and entertaining friends on a larger scale than ever before. Both Pedro and Marie were in their seventies and enjoyed good health. Poker games were a common evening's entertainment. The Altubes were generous and contributed substantial amounts to their home parish, the Spanish Church. Pedro and Bernardo were also delighted at the birth of their namesakes, twin grandsons, to Jules and Amelia in May 1905.[88] Pedro's death suddenly and unexpectedly only a few months later shocked the family terribly. Pedro was felled by a stroke on August 8, 1905, and died at home. After a funeral service at the Spanish Church, he was interred in the family vault in Holy Cross Cemetery. The impact of his death was shattering.

Settling Pedro's estate meant the end of the Spanish Ranch as once envisioned by the two brothers. Under the terms of his will, Pedro bequeathed his entire estate to his wife, Marie, to dispose of as she desired. His two-thirds of the Spanish Ranch could be sold after a period of five years if it were to her advantage.[89] In the months following Pedro's death, the estate was settled and probate proceeded smoothly, allowing Marie to manage the family's affairs comfortably. When all the holdings of the Palo Alto Land & Livestock Co. were purchased by H. G. Humphrey and Moffat Company in November 1907, the deed filled seven enormous ledger pages of small type and required two additional multipaged deed entries to correct the original entry in order to transfer ownership of almost 74,000 acres. From the sale of the Spanish Ranch, Marie Altube was paid $150,000 and Bernardo Altube received $75,000. In all the Altubes received $225,000 at 5 percent interest.[90]

These small glimpses into the lives of Pedro and Bernardo provide insight into their interests and passions. As brothers and partners, Pedro and Bernardo were an extremely successful team, enhancing each other's strengths and minimizing their shortcomings. In California, the Altubes were not considered prestigious men of blue-blood social stature, but they were part of a flourishing Basque community and a large French and Spanish population. They did claim prominence among their peers. They had no desire for fame or recognition on the larger political, commercial, or social planes. In Nevada, too, the Altubes remained uninvolved in associations related to their business interests. They never joined the National Cattleman's Association or had their P-Bench Brand recorded in the National Brand Book, which was unusual for cattlemen with such enormous holdings. Once Pedro and Bernardo stepped onto their vast domain, however, they were given the respect accorded kings. This respect grew out of their ability to endure and master the challenges confronting them, which were no respecters of status and prestige but tested each individual's limits equally. So if in retrospect Pedro and Bernardo seem a bit rough hewn and larger than life, it is because they were able to maintain an edge when less fortunate and tenacious men sold out and moved on. Their empire was carved out of land, and land is what afforded them their sense of self-worth and well-being.

Even before his death, Pedro Altube had attained the status of a legend, and some have accorded him the title "Father of the Basques of the American West." That he succeeded enormously in the non-Basque world is without question. In fact, numerous documents record his business and financial successes. Other honors have come more recently. In 1962, he was voted Nevada's representative into the National Cowboy Hall of Fame. In 1985, he was inducted into the Society of Basque Studies in America Hall of Fame. Alongside the almost legendary proportion of Pedro's life in America was his strong allegiance to his Basque heritage. Repeatedly, Pedro and his brother Bernardo channeled the majority of their business and social activities through Basque communities they helped establish or expand. Pedro also valued his Basque ties, much as he valued his land acquisitions. Both were invaluable resources and permanent investments: acquired, cultivated, profited from, and never discarded. In business affairs, his perspective was not of callous greed or manipulation but of the shrewd investor and benevolent caretaker. Altogether, he epitomized the Basque who emigrated, embraced the unfamiliar, and made it his own. In the end, he left a heritage rich in the traditions of his ancestors as well as one enriched by the treasures discovered and claimed in a new land.

Part II

Immigration and Assimilation

5

John B. Archabal (1873–1945)
A Portrait of an Immigrant Success Story

JOHN BIETER

"You've got to be good at something in this world," Dan Archabal remembers his father saying. John Archabal followed his own advice. In
a rags-to-riches story, Archabal survived the sinking of his ship on the
way to America, and by the time of his death in 1945 he had become
one of the most prominent sheepmen in the West. His hard work, ability, wise choices, and good fortune made him a model of the Basque-
American immigrant success story. In the process, he established himself as one of the leaders of the Basque community in Idaho while being
accepted by the broader American community. As is true with most
relatively obscure immigrants, John Archabal and his early years are
not easy to trace, but his story provides insight into the forces that
shaped the lives of early Basque newcomers to the Pacific Northwest.

Juan Bautista Achabal entered the United States in 1893, at age
twenty. Born to Martin Achabal and Ventura Rementeria on June 24,
1873, Juan was raised just outside the village of Ispaster, Bizkaia, in
the heart of the Basque region. Achabal came from the area that most
other Basque immigrants were from, and he fits the profile of the typical Basque immigrant of the time: a male of agrarian background with
little or (as in Achabal's case) no education who came to the United

States to make money and planned to return to the Basque Country. Although Achabal had two brothers who had emigrated to South America, Idaho was the next destination of opportunity when it was his turn to leave. His older brother lent him money to make the trip, but he almost did not arrive.

While en route to New York, the Atlantic steamer on which Juan Achabal traveled sank, killing twenty-five of its passengers. The remaining five hundred to six hundred passengers, including Achabal, were loaded onto another vessel. After thirty-six days at sea, they finally landed in Galveston, Texas. Achabal had lost his luggage, but since he wisely traveled with a money belt, he still had enough money to pay for passage to San Francisco. There, he borrowed money from a friend. The two traveled to Boise, arriving in that city on November 18, 1893. Achabal was among the first members of a small Basque colony that began to form shortly after Idaho was granted statehood.

For the next five months Achabal labored as a ranch hand for Billy Howell, earning his board in the first three months and drawing wages during the next two. Even though few Basque immigrants were experienced herders, their agrarian backgrounds, coupled with a strong work ethic and a succeed-at-all-costs attitude, served them well. They quickly earned a reputation as outstanding sheepherders. It was a dirty, smelly job nobody else wanted, requiring long periods of intense loneliness broken only by visits from a camp tender or unexpected strangers. Nevertheless, sheepherding did not require a knowledge of English and provided an opportunity for Basques to be financially successful. By and large Basques excelled, and Juan Achabal did so even more.[1]

In 1894, Achabal went to work for W. C. "Bill" Cleveland as a herder in the Big Smokey Valley. Three years later he was foreman, and within the next year he bought half of the business. Achabal worked hard, had a knack for the sheep business, and displayed a frugality, all of which allowed him to get ahead. When others, for example, threw their dirty, bloody overalls away after lambing, Achabal would gather and wash them, saving the cost of new clothes. In fact, in one of his first years of herding, his expenses were only $50. He also knew how to work the best deals for himself, including the securing of prime pasturage. The story is told that when rival bands neared a town, Achabal made sure that alcohol was available for those herders; while they drank, he pushed on to the greenest grass.

Not long after he became a sheepman, Achabal began operating with partners, parceling out sheep on shares. He was the first to use this arrangement in Idaho. Under this system, the herder did not get paid for his work but instead took part ownership of the band. Since they were part owners, the herders had greater incentive to take care of the sheep and bring in the fattest lambs. Achabal gained from the arrangement, too, because his sheep received special care. He used this system throughout his career in the sheep business, and it was a key ingredient in his success.[2]

Achabal and other Basques entered the United States in the midst of the Spanish-American conflict. With little or no understanding of the differences between Basque and Spanish, many Americans questioned the immigrants' loyalty. Additionally, a negative image of Basque herders emerged, even though they had gained a reputation as excellent herders. Many perceived Basques as transients who used the land for their own good and then took their money back to the Basque Country. The culmination of this vitriolic attitude appeared in a 1909 article in the *Caldwell (Idaho) Tribune*, which described Basques as "filthy, treacherous and meddlesome"; "unless something [was] done," these "Bascos" would make "life impossible for the white man." Although there is no record of blatant prejudice aimed at Achabal, this background frames the threatening context in which he operated.[3]

Achabal's next actions proved he did not fit this negative stereotype. His marriage in 1901 and his declaration of intent to become a U.S. citizen in 1903 signaled that he was no transient herder intending to take his money and run. The decision to stay in their new country was among the most important choices immigrants had to make. Achabal was one of only a dozen Basques who filed for citizenship between 1888 and 1903, an act that indicated Achabal, unlike many others, ruled out returning to the Basque Country.

In 1901 Achabal married Benedicta "Bene" Aldecoa Urrusuno, a resident of Idaho but a native of Natxitua, Bizkaia, located a few kilometers from Achabal's home village. Like most Basques of his generation, Achabal married someone of Basque descent, and it was undoubtedly the sheep business that brought them together. Benedicta had arrived in the United States in 1898, and in the years before their marriage she cooked in a sheep camp. After their marriage, they moved to Boise and established their base there. In 1904, their oldest daughter, Hazel, was born.

With his new wife and citizenship came a new surname, or at least a different spelling of it. For many immigrants, a name change is part of becoming a U.S. citizen. The change may symbolize America's mark on the immigrant, disclosing the immigrant's desire to shed the old and take on the new. It can also symbolize a change of identity: Estaquio became Ed, Uriaguerica became Uria, and Juan Achabal became John Archabal. Some names were altered by immigration officers, some by immigrants themselves in an effort to make their names easier for Americans to pronounce. Archabal added the *r* for the latter reason.

A shift in Archabal's financial status coincided with his name change. By the early 1900s Archabal had become general manager of a large sheep company with a dozen partners working for him. Named My Sheep Camp, the outfit was headquartered at Blacks Creek. Building on his experience as a sheepherder, he had risen to a position in which his acumen was readily apparent. Observers were struck with his ability to accurately estimate the price of a stack of hay by pacing the sides and then throwing a tape over the top. He had no formal education, but his aptitude for calculating the number of bales of hay, the size of a band of sheep, and the prices of various types of wool was astonishing.[4]

Archabal's decision to stay in the sheep business set him apart from many other Basque immigrants who used sheepherding as a start but escaped the loneliness of the hills and secured another job as soon as they could. Especially for those who had married and chosen to stay in the United States, sheepherding was too transient. They looked for a more permanent occupation, one closer to town. In the Boise area, for example, a number of Basques began working in the stone quarries, as loggers, or in town as barbers or shoe repairmen. Others, with their wives and families, opened up boardinghouses to meet herders' needs for temporary housing.

It was a good time for a hard-working sheepman. Long before Idaho became a state in 1890, sheep had flourished on the semiarid land, much of which was unsuitable for other animals. In 1893, when Archabal arrived, there were 867,000 sheep in the new state. By the turn of the century there were more than two million. Land was available and the demand for mutton, lamb, and wool was extremely high —a combination that allowed the sheep industry in Idaho to play a major role in the state's economy. Since Archabal was one of the earliest Basques to arrive in Idaho, he was well positioned to meet the demands for these products that resulted from World War I. He prospered during this time and bought out Bill Cleveland's half of the sheep outfit, where he had started as a herder in 1894.[5]

With his growing financial strength, Archabal became a major employer of Basque immigrants. From the 1920s to the 1940s, Archabal regularly employed sixty to ninety men, twice as many during lambing time, and he was known as a very demanding but fair boss. Employee lists contain hundreds of names of immigrants who got their first job with Juan Archabal. He also paid the fare for many Basques, including his own relatives, to travel from the Basque Country to the United States.[6]

Archabal's financial success gave him considerable stature within the Basque community and made him an unofficial representative of the Basques in the greater Boise area. This prestige is evidenced by his inclusion in books written at the time. Archabal is portrayed in Sol Silen's 1917 book, *Los Vascos en el Oeste*, and he appears in James H. Hawley's *History of Idaho* (1920). Additionally, Archabal's status is indicated by his serving, along with former governors Hawley and Moses Alexander and other prominent members of the community, as an honorary pallbearer at Bishop Daniel M. Gorman's funeral in 1927.[7]

Archabal and his wife lived at 218 E. Idaho Street. The large home eventually accommodated their six children—Hazel, John Jr., Matilda, Fidel, Juanita, and Dan—and their helpers, who lived in the basement. The home also doubled as Archabal's headquarters, and a section of the porch served as his office. Complete with its own private entrance, a rolltop desk, and leather couch and chairs, the office gave Archabal a place to entertain visitors and business partners at home.

While John ran the business, Benedicta oversaw all the household duties and raised their family. Old World born and raised, Bene assumed the traditional role of wife and mother. With the aid of helpers from the Basque Country, she cooked, cleaned, and ran an immaculate and well-ordered household in a day when women were acutely aware of how these things were to be done. She was known as a quiet woman who always dressed nicely and held the busy home together. The Archabals' work was constant and demanding, but it enabled them to afford Oriental rugs, a large refrigerator, a separate sewing and ironing room, and furnishings most people of the time could not buy.[8]

The Archabals were also able to afford a good education for their children. They sent Hazel and John Jr. to Spain to be educated, a privilege that few children of Basque immigrants enjoyed. However, they also made sure their children knew the value of hard work. When one of the daughters wanted a piano, John agreed to purchase one with the stipulation that she would pay part of the cost with money she earned. When John Jr. planned his return from Spain, he wanted to show off a bit for those who would greet him at the train depot. But when John Jr. landed in New York, a wire from his father told him to stop in

Chicago and bring some lambs with him. So instead of arriving at the station as an elegantly dressed student, he got off in his work clothes. "I think, he think he pretty smart," Archabal said. Commenting on this incident years later, Archabal's daughter-in-law said, "He was a psychologist without his knowing what the word was."[9]

Although the Archabals had more money than other Basque immigrant families, many patterns of their lives were similar. The parents always spoke Basque with each other and the oldest children, but the longer the family lived in the United States and the more they came in contact with American society, the more often English was used. Because of his business contacts, John was forced to learn and use English more than was Bene, who spent most of her time at home. In fact, as early as the 1900 census, Archabal qualified for a "yes" under "Speaks English." As the children matured, they spoke English more frequently and Basque less often. Basque remained the conversational language between John and Bene and Basques of their generation, but much less so among their children.[10]

Like many herders who fell out of the practice when they came to America, Archabal did not attend Mass on Sundays. But his wife and many other Basques were devoted Catholics. When the Basque community decided to build a Basque chapel, Archabal was one of the major donors, and he made sure the plate was passed before his herders went to the hills. Through the community's efforts, the Church of the Good Shepherd, possibly the only Basque chapel in the United States, was dedicated on March 2, 1919. When Bishop Edward Kelly, reportedly encouraging a unified American Catholic Church, closed the ethnic parish as a Basque church in 1928, Archabal was very upset, and the Church lost one of its supporters.

Even though he was not a churchgoer, Archabal was a charitable man. He regularly contributed to the Red Cross, the YMCA, the Associated Charities, and the Salvation Army. He also pledged at least $50,000 in Liberty Bonds and War Savings Stamps during World War I. Many stories are told about his private assistance to families and others in need.[11]

The Prohibition movement was a curiosity to Basque immigrants. Because most Basques drank alcoholic beverages in the old country and continued that practice in the United States, many Basque boardinghouses served bootleg liquor to attract and retain their customers. Archabal, however, never drank, although he may have given the appearance that he did. "Ezin da mozkortu" (He cannot get drunk), people often said about Archabal. Before going to a dance, Archabal would fill a whiskey flask with tea and place it in his back pocket. When his friends began to drink, John would pull out his tea and drink along with them.[12]

Attitudes toward immigrants were changing in the United States. Most Americans once had been confident about absorbing and assimilating other people without being significantly altered themselves. By the turn of the century, however, many Americans began to think that too many immigrants were arriving too rapidly in the United States and that their differences were too pronounced for them to be assimilated without great social costs. World War I also made more Americans conscious of race and ethnicity, fueling another anti-foreigner movement. The postwar red scare heightened this panicky xenophobia and culminated in the passage, in 1924, of the National Origins Law, also known as the Johnson-Reed Act. The law restricted immigration by annually limiting the number of immigrants from any nation to 2 percent of that group's population in the United States as determined in the 1890 census. This legislation drastically reduced the number of Basques that could legally enter the United States and increased the status of people like Archabal, who could provide opportunities for those able to make it into the country.

Although Archabal had made Idaho his home, he and Benedicta returned to the Basque Country for a visit in 1925. He went in true American style. According to a local newspaper article, the Archabals, accompanied by a secretary, went first by train to Detroit, where they bought a new automobile. They drove the car to New York and had it shipped to Southampton. After arriving in England, they drove through London to Dover, shipped the car across the English Channel to France, and drove south to the Basque Country. They spent the summer visiting friends and family. One can imagine the attention the Archabals' car drew in a countryside where donkeys and oxen were still the norm. Later, relatives told stories of large banquets that Archabal hosted and of children following his car, running beside it, helping to polish it. Undoubtedly such experiences inspired young, dream-filled minds and kept the immigration chain intact.[13]

In October 1925 Archabal returned home to an expanding sheep business. Four years later, he incorporated the Wood Creek Live Stock, formalizing a purchase he had made nearly ten years earlier. Following the partnership arrangements typical of most of Archabal's business undertakings, "Big Joe" Urquidi was foreman and part owner of the outfit based in Grandview and running sheep in the Chimney Creek area. In 1931 Archabal incorporated the Jump Creek Sheep Company;

three years later he bought the Homedale Jump Creek Ranch, then the Homedale Ranch on the Snake River. In these years, he ran sheep in the Owyhees and near the Mckay Springs in Oregon.[14]

Meanwhile, the Archabals continued the patterns of family life at their home on Idaho Street. On Friday nights at Merino Pool Hall, Archabal loved to play cards with friends. If he was not at Merino, he sometimes went to the Lyric theater to watch cowboy or "bronco" movies, as Archabal called them. Like many other Basques, Archabal also enjoyed boxing, often going to the old fairgrounds to watch the bouts. Once, even though they had to travel over backcountry dirt roads to get there, Archabal and his friends drove to Reno to watch Paulino Uzkudun, a Basque boxer, challenge Max Schmelling in a heavyweight championship bout.

After his herding days, Archabal always wore suit pants and vests with white shirts, neatly pressed by the Chinese laundry, and a little click wallet. Archabal maintained his routine and was known to be generous to those who served him well. One day, for example, when he went to get his usual haircut from Howard "Shorty" Paulsen, Shorty was lamenting that he would never be able to own a big black car like Archabal's. John replied, "Shorty, if you give me and my boys a haircut whenever we need them, then I'll give you that car." And he did.[15]

Another perspective on Archabal comes from an American neighbor, Charles Hummel, who grew up across from Archabal's glassed-in porch office. In the summer days when the windows were open, Charles heard all about the business. "They did not even need the phone [they spoke so loudly] when they called down to Salt Lake City to do business with the buyers," he recalled. They found the Archabals to be very hospitable: "Most every year, usually around Easter, they would send over a leg of lamb with one of the kids after Mrs. Archabal had prepared it." Hummel also remembered playing over at the house as a boy. "They had a huge garage, which they had converted from a stable. There they stored all the bed rolls and saddles, with the very distinct smell of sagebrush and sheep. Archabal was always friendly to us kids when we were over there." [16]

Through the years many of the Archabal children worked in their father's sheep business or married others who worked with sheep. Hazel married a New York Basque, Zenon Yzaguirre, who became Archabal's right-hand man. John Jr. worked with his father. Fidel, the middle son, became a wool buyer in Boston. Even Dan, the youngest son, worked in the sheep business after he returned from military service in World War II.

Some of the Archabal children married Basques; others did not, though Archabal did not seem to mind. John Jr.'s wife, Marjorie Archabal, remembered the Christmas Eve meals at which thirty gathered for dinner, all the men on one side of the table, the women on the other, with Archabal at the head and his wife on his right. For days, women prepared the tongue, tripe, codfish, and other delicacies for the huge feast. Since the conversation was mostly in Basque, Marjorie found it difficult to follow, but she still felt included in the family. She remembered trying to learn how to cook Basque dishes, but Benedicta would correct her: "Johnny an American now. Johnny eat American food."

Other relatives savored the celebratory picnics Archabal hosted on the weekend closest to June 24, the feast day of his saint, San Juan. The fun-filled affair required the women to travel to the ranch days earlier to prepare all the food. Picnickers would sing, dance, and celebrate with all of the vigor of an Old World village festival but carried out in their New World setting.

Without doubt, the sheep business gave Archabal his notoriety, but his most lasting cultural accomplishment might be a charity dance that he helped establish. In the early years, immigrants formed mutual aid societies to help each other through difficult times. Yet as often happened in Basque communities, an inability to work together toward a common goal meant two organizations formed where one would have been sufficient. Over time, this division became more pronounced as these organizations attracted members who used the same banks, gathered at the same functions, and even sponsored their own affairs.

In Boise's Basque district, December was a time for celebration: Not only was it the Christmas holiday, but herders were in town before the lambing season began. The boardinghouses were full and alive with dancing and celebrating. In 1929, Boise's two mutual aid organizations, Socorros Mutuos and La Fraternidad Vasca Americana, decided to sponsor dances and picked the same night for their festivities. Not surprising, neither wanted to yield to the other. Archabal, one of the founders of Socorros Mutuos, convinced La Fraternidad Vasca Americana to hold one dance and to give all the money to charity. With that agreement, the Sheepherder's Ball was born in Boise and became the pattern for similar dances throughout the valley.[17]

Although not a dancer himself, Archabal was the key organizer of an annual social event that attracted large crowds and raised substantial amounts of money. To attend, men were required to wear Levi's and women cotton dresses; entrance was limited to Basques and their guests. At the dance a lamb was auctioned, with the proceeds going to charities primarily in the Boise community. Years later, most Basques are out of the sheep business, but the ball continues as a reminder of the past, a core function of the American-Basque cultural calendar.[18]

The first ball was organized before the Great Depression and the Taylor Grazing Act. These two events meant difficult times for many Basque immigrants and even the end for others. Archabal's son Dan remembered hearing his father pace the floor all night in the bedroom above his room. Money was tight, and borrowing from the bank to keep his business together worried the sheepman. He even had to bluff to gain needed funding.

Archabal spent a lot of time and did most of his banking at First Security Bank. The manager, Lynn Driscoll, told Archabal that the bank might not be able to lend him more money. Archabal retorted, "I've got somebody at Idaho First National who will give me the money." The bluff worked. Driscoll responded, "Old Bulldog, get over here." He got the loan. Although Archabal experienced tense times, he weathered these difficult years better than most Americans.

The Taylor Grazing Act, passed in 1934, also meant disaster for some Basque immigrants and herders. The bill closed the open ranges to herders who did not own or lease land, thereby edging the itinerant herder off the range. The legislation demanded a much larger commitment for Basques, closing the opportunities many had earlier enjoyed. The new provisions adversely affected most Basques; but because Archabal was well established in the sheep business and had purchased and leased acreage before the bill was enacted, he was not greatly harmed by the changes.

The Sheepherder's Ball continued in the 1930s, and the list of beneficiaries provides insight into Archabal and the early Basque immigrant group. Most of the money from the ball was given to local charities—the Red Cross, the Children's Home, the Boise Unemployment Fund, St. Alphonsus and St. Luke's Hospitals—but one year's collection went to the Basque Relief Committee during the Spanish Civil War. This occasion apparently was one of the few times that the Basques in the United States, as a group, formally sent aid back to the Basque Country, an exception to the general approach of noninvolvement in political matters back home.

The Spanish Civil War presented the Basques with difficult and awkward choices. Bizkaia, the home province of most Boise Basques, and Gipuzkoa established an autonomous government and fought with the Spanish Republic against Franco, their common enemy. In the United States, the press and the American Catholic Church hierarchy painted Franco and his forces as the foes of godless Communism. Thus, Basques feared being labeled Communists as they continued to support family and friends in the Basque Country.

Although a man as wealthy as Archabal was in a position to influence politics at home and abroad, he largely stayed out of the fray. In December 1937 an official delegation of the Basque government came to the United States, traveling to Boise to provide information and raise money for the Basque war effort. There are pictures of the delegation eating at Archabal's house.[19] However, there is no evidence of any large or lasting contributions to the Basque war cause.

Generally, the loyalty of Archabal and most other Basques in Boise was to their families in the old country, not to nationalistic ideas introduced in the cities after the majority of immigrants had left for the United States. Skeptical of where their contributions might go, the Boise Basques felt much more comfortable with later efforts to aid refugees by helping buy one thousand blankets for Basque women prisoners in Spain.[20]

Such practical, humanitarian actions reveal the desire of Basques to support fellow Basques while remaining loyal Americans. In April of 1940 the Independent Order of Spanish-Basque Speaking People of Idaho incorporated, with John Archabal as one of its key organizers. Formed by boardinghouse owners and other leading sheepmen, this organization included statewide representation from Basque communities, including Mountain Home and Shoshone and stretching as far away as Pocatello. According to the Articles of Incorporation, the organization was designed to "promote Americanizm [sic]." It would "encourage and aid all alien members desirous of becoming citizens of the United States of America by Naturalization to Citizenship." In addition, Spanish editions of the Constitution of the United States and a manual of the Daughters of the American Revolution were available to help in the naturalization process. Archabal's participation illustrated his leadership in the Basque community, and this organization showed that the Basques wanted to prove themselves as good Americans.[21]

In Idaho politics, Archabal favored the Republican Party, although never in such a way as to alienate any Democratic wool-buyers. Dan Archabal remembers Senator William Borah and prominent businessmen coming to the Archabals' house to court their father for contributions to the Republicans. Perhaps what Archabal liked most about politics was betting on elections. He would check the latest returns and spend many hours determining local sentiment, and then place a sizable wager on the electoral outcome. Some claim that one year Archabal hired a soapbox orator to extol the virtues of a candidate while Archabal walked unnoticed through the crowd, checking its reaction to the speaker.

Archabal bet on politics and played the stock market, but he always kept his mind focused on his sheep business. He even missed the wedding of John Jr. because the date conflicted with a crucial time of the sheep-business cycle. He paid attention to detail, always looking for new and less expensive ways of operating. In 1934 he began trucking lambs to market, one of the first sheepmen in the nation to do so. His lambs also set a new state record for the highest average weight per animal, evidence of his good business practices. The same year he formed Mendiola and Company, a joint partnership with his son John and John Mendiola. They headquartered at Central Cove near Marsing and ran sheep in the Boise Basin, in the Owyhees, and as far away as McDermitt, Nevada. By the 1930s Archabal was one of the largest operators in the Northwest, with holdings and ranches in five counties and from 80,000 to 100,000 sheep.

While war was waged in his native country during the 1930s, his adopted homeland became involved in its own combat in the 1940s. World War II provided American Basques with another opportunity to demonstrate their loyalty to the United States. They bought bonds, joined the armed forces, and volunteered in other ways to support the war. Archabal was at the head of many of these efforts. An Idaho newspaper headline in early 1945, "Largest Colony Outside Spain Helps With War Effort," emphasized the loyalty of the Basques to the American cause and supplied evidence of their support. The article explained how young Basque women worked as United Service Organization hostesses and nurses' aids in hospitals, while others sewed and rolled bandages for the Red Cross. In addition, hundreds of Basques were serving in the armed forces, including Archabal's son Dan. Basque men too old for service formed a civil defense unit, the Basque Company of Ada County Volunteers, led by Archabal's son-in-law Zenon Yzaguirre. With members of his family involved with the war at all different levels, Archabal also did what he could. He led a War Bond drive in which Basques pledged to buy a million dollars, a very large sum in those days. Archabal himself was the drive's greatest contributor.[22]

Archabal bought bonds, but he also made sure his business survived. During the years of gasoline rationing, Archabal only qualified for small amounts of fuel because he did not own a pickup truck. So he instructed a worker to take the trunk hatch off his car and add two side boards and a back board. Then C. C. Anderson, a friend on the rationing board, concluded, "Why, you've got yourself a pickup." Archabal got all the gas he needed. On another occasion, he was unable to find tires and let others know of his need. Soon after, a local dealer approached Archabal saying, "I hear you need some tires." Not knowing what to expect from the man, Archabal nodded and waited. The man hesitated, and Archabal grimaced at what the man might charge. "Can I get some lambs from you?" Archabal sighed and grinned, "How many do you want?" Later, he was taken to the attic of the man's house, which was filled with tires. Again, Archabal was able to secure all he needed. Although a war was on and Archabal helped with the effort, he did whatever it took to ensure his businesses did not suffer.[23]

When the war ended, Boiseans were ready to celebrate. The Sheepherder's Ball of 1945 was organized to welcome those returning from service and remember those the Japanese captured on Wake Island, where they had gone as civilian workers during the war. Nonetheless, the directors thought seriously about canceling the ball. John Archabal had died just a few months before. At the age of seventy-two, Archabal passed away at home after a relatively short bout with throat cancer. A local newspaper article described the funeral, noting that hundreds of Basques and Americans from throughout the American West packed into Saint John's Cathedral for the funeral mass. Both of Ada County's district courts also closed until 2 P.M. in honor of this event.[24]

Sheepherding in the American West provided many Basques with an opportunity unavailable to them in the Basque Country. In turn, they supplied a much-needed labor force in an industry that attracted few Americans. Both groups benefited. Basques made the United States their home, without fully giving up their ethnic identity. Archabal's generation established the Basques in the West. Despite a few negative instances, Basques established an excellent reputation that later generations have enjoyed. John Archabal's life models what the Basque immigrant generation accomplished.

Although John Archabal was by no means the only Basque in Idaho who succeeded in the sheep business, his outfit was the largest. In the agrarian Basque culture, hard work is the characteristic that provides real social prestige and position. Moreover, the values of hard work, loyalty, and thriftiness were also esteemed by the broader Idaho community, and Archabal's demonstration of these traits led to his acceptance and respect in that sphere as well. Like other immigrants, Archabal made decisions based on the issues and dilemmas his generation faced in Idaho and the West. The many decisions they faced included whether to stay in America, where to place their loyalty during wars, and to what extent they would take on American ways. Archabal's prominent position in Idaho accentuates the choices he made.

In 1945 plans for the winter festival continued. Zenon Yzaguirre, Sheepherder's Ball director, said at the time: "We are holding the 16th annual event in Mr. Archabal's memory and we will plan our program along the lines of those which he directed."[25]

6

Basque Families

ROBERT BOYD

From Homeland to High Desert

For more than five centuries, Basques have sought their fortune and future beyond their homeland. The small family farms in the Pyrenees foothills and fishing villages on the Bay of Biscay offered limited opportunities for young people not destined to inherit the family business or land holdings. They went to sea as mariners in the Spanish fleets of exploration and conquest. They sailed the North Atlantic Ocean in whaling vessels and established settlements on the distant shores of Newfoundland. Basque soldiers, priests, colonists, and colonial officials helped establish Spain's empire in South America, Mexico, Cuba, and the Philippines.

Wherever Basque immigrants settled, they used their ability to adapt to whatever opportunities were at hand. They took up work far different from the occupations of their homeland while maintaining their ethnic identity in the new land. Among the immigrants and their succeeding generations, family played a critical role in continuing the customs and values of the Basque Country, as the newcomers struggled with new surroundings and occupations.

Basques first came to the intermountain West in the 1870s. Some were earlier immigrants who had come to California at the time of the

1849 Gold Rush. Many of these Basque pioneers in the West found success as stockmen, raising sheep and cattle to sell to mining communities. By the 1870s agriculture had replaced mining and stock raising as the dominant industry in California, and restrictive grazing laws compelled many stockmen to search for rangeland beyond the Sierra. Basque stockmen offered opportunities to younger friends and relatives in the Basque Country to immigrate and take up sheepherding. Although it was a harsh and lonely life, it was the principal work available to young Basque immigrants coming of age in the late nineteenth century. A frugal sheepherder, enduring five or six years of this life, could hope to return home with enough savings to purchase a business or property or stay in the region as a sheepman. For the young women of the Basque Country, this opportunity to immigrate came with the invitation to join family members in the region or to work as domestic help for Basque families. Many also found jobs in the boardinghouses that were the centers of Basque community life in high-desert towns.

This photographic essay chronicles the experience of several Basque families in the high-desert country of eastern California, Nevada, southeastern Oregon, and southern Idaho. These photographs, ranging from images of relatives left behind in the Basque Country to scenes of daily life and work in the new land, do more than chronicle the lives of the Alcorta, Eiguren, Pedroarena, Lekumberry, and Barrutia families. They show the typical experiences of the immigrant generation, a history shared by scores of contemporary Basque families in the region.

Tomás and Maria Dominga Alcorta of McDermitt, Nevada

Tomás Alcorta came to Nevada as a seventeen-year-old immigrant in 1907 to join his brother Saturino in McDermitt, Nevada. This was an era of prosperity for Great Basin sheepmen, who were signing on hundreds of young men from the Basque Country as herders. Several years of herding on the Oregon-Nevada border and careful saving enabled Tomás to start his own sheep outfit. As a man of property, he could afford to begin a family. In December 1917 Tomás Alcorta and Maria Dominga Ansotegui were married at Saint John's Cathedral in Boise, Idaho. Maria Dominga had come to McDermitt, Nevada, in 1912 to join family from Ibarrangelu, Bizkaia, Spain. For almost thirty years, Tomás and Maria Dominga lived in this region.

The couple experienced success in the sheep business until they were devastated by the financial disaster of the Great Depression. Nevertheless, their family grew as Tomás went back to herding for other sheepmen. During these difficult years he also worked as a stonemason. A stone cellar built by Tomás for sheepman John Mentaberry to hide the family's wine-making operation during Prohibition still exists on the family ranch. Alcorta's initials and the date 1930 are still clearly visible on the concrete floor.

While herding sheep for the Mentaberry family, Tomás made a discovery that would bring financial security to the Alcorta family for years to come. Tomás was gathering rocks to build a *harrimutil* (stone boy), the distinctive rock cairn often built by sheepherders as markers to pass the time, when he noticed a stone of dark red hue that was heavier than the others. He had the ore assayed and discovered that it was a very high grade of cinnabar, the mineral from which mercury is

Tomás Alcorta's sheep camp during lambing time at Battle Creek, Oregon, April 1919. Tomás is in the center behind the man smelling the bread, a staple in the desert. The bread was baked in Dutch ovens buried in the hot ashes of a sagebrush fire. María Dominga is washing dishes while a hired girl holds her youngest daughter, Tomása.

Seldom recorded with a camera, this image captures the characters and trademarks of life on the desert in the early days. At lambing, family and hired hands pitched in to ensure a profitable start for the year and worked for the survival of the newborn lambs in the unpredictable springtime weather in the desert. The herders in the background are saluting the photographer with their *makilak,* rifles, and tin cups of wine. (Alcorta Family Collection, courtesy of The High Desert Museum, Bend, Oregon.)

refined. Tomás and his partner, Eusebio Aznarez, leased the rights to develop the claim to several mining companies over the years. The Cordero Mine established on the site was in production until 1990. At the time it closed, it was the most productive mercury mine in the world.

The family continued to live an unpretentious life in McDermitt. Tomás was generous with his good fortune, lending money to those in need in the community and seldom worrying about collecting. At home he enjoyed playing the *txistu* (the traditional Basque flute). Tomás's only concession to prosperity was wearing clean white shirts and enjoying good cigars as he made his rounds about town, greeting friends made over the course of a lifetime in the community.

Tomás Alcorta (right) and an unidentified friend, ca. 1910. At this time, Tomás was herding sheep out of McDermitt, Nevada, and ranging as far north as the Steens Mountain. (Alcorta Family Collection, courtesy of The High Desert Museum, Bend, Oregon.)

The Alcorta family at the Cordero Mine in McDermitt, Nevada, 1931. (Alcorta Family Collection, courtesy of The High Desert Museum, Bend, Oregon.)

Maria Dominga died in 1945, but Tomás lived until 1972. Each birthday was an occasion for a family get-together of his children and ten grandchildren.

Urbano and Marie Pedroarena of Alturas, California

Urbano Pedroarena grew up in the village of Aria, Bizkaia, Spain. He had begun to learn the trade of a blacksmith when he immigrated to America in 1914. He went first to California, then worked for the Union Land and Cattle Company in Deeth, Nevada. Urbano herded sheep on the deserts in northeastern Nevada in winter and moved to the high country of the Ruby Mountains in the summer. As was the case with many young herders, he found the life to be difficult and lonely, but Urbano had other options. In 1918 he went to work for a Gardnerville, Nevada, blacksmith shop, taking up the trade he began as a boy.

Gardnerville was home to a number of Basque boardinghouses, which also served as meeting places for young people. Working in the Overland boardinghouse as a maid was Marie Barnetche, a young immigrant girl from a village in the French Basque Country. Marie had worked for a brief time in a local candy factory before traveling to Nevada in 1921. During this era, boardinghouses served as important

The Barnetche family in Suhescun (Suhuskne), Nafarroa Beherea, France, in 1921—the year Marie Pedroarena immigrated to Nevada. *Back left to right:* brother Bernard and Marie. *Front left to right:* sister Felice, mother sitting, and brother Pierre. (Arena Family Collection, courtesy of The High Desert Museum, Bend, Oregon.)

meeting places for young, and unmarried, Basque men and women. Urbano, the blacksmith, and Marie, boardinghouse maid, met, courted, and were married in Gardnerville on April 28, 1923.

The young couple continued to live in Gardnerville, saving for the future and beginning their family. Daughter Elvira was born in 1924 and son Albert in 1926. In 1929 they moved to the farming and ranching community of Alturas, in northeastern California. Urbano bought a blacksmith shop, and the family built the Buena Vista Hotel.

With their two enterprises the family prospered. The Buena Vista boarded herders who worked for the sheep outfits that ranged the Warner Mountains and deserts of northwestern Nevada. Urbano's skill at the forge and as a machinist brought in a steady business from the community and outlying ranches, as well as from the Forest Service

A sheepman leading pack mules, with herder Urbano Pedroarena in the background, in northern Nevada, ca. 1914–18. (Arena Family Collection, courtesy of The High Desert Museum, Bend, Oregon.)

Mary (Marie) Pedroarena at work in the kitchen. The large iron cooking stove occupied most of the space. (Arena Family Collection, courtesy of The High Desert Museum, Bend, Oregon.)

Urbano Pedroarena at work in the blacksmith shop, Gardnerville, Nevada, ca. 1923. (Arena Family Collection, courtesy of The High Desert Museum, Bend, Oregon.)

and logging outfits. The Buena Vista closed in 1962, but the blacksmith shop continues operation today. Albert Arena, who grew up working in the shop and learned the trade from his father, continues to operate the local landmark that has been in the family for more than sixty-five years.

Pascual and Catalina Eiguren of Jordan Valley, Oregon

Jordan Valley began as a way station on the freight and stage route from California to the Owyhee mining camps. Today's large Basque community in the region traces its beginnings to 1889 when Jose Navarro and Antone Azcuenaga set out from McDermitt, Nevada, to explore the possibilities for sheepmen in the Owyhee country. On foot, with a packhorse loaded with supplies, the two young Basques became lost in the desert and nearly died of thirst on the five-day crossing.

Business success in Jordan Valley enabled Jose to take a trip back to the Basque Country to marry and to make arrangements to bring over his twelve-year-old nephew, Pascual Eiguren. As was the case with many young Basques, the hardship of life on the family farm compelled him to leave home. In later years, he often told his son Fred, "I would have never left the Basque Country if I had enough bread to eat."

Pascual Eiguren (seated), with fellow herders, ca. 1910. (Eiguren Family Collection, courtesy of The High Desert Museum, Bend, Oregon.)

Pascual Eiguren, with a band of Joe Navarro's sheep, at the Baxter Creek shearing corral, ca. 1918. (Eiguren Family Collection, courtesy of The High Desert Museum, Bend, Oregon.)

Pascual arrived in Jordan Valley in the spring of 1901, worked at his uncle's stable, and began school. The following year, Jose bought property on the Owyhee, had a Basque stonemason construct a stone home, and went into the sheep business. In the years that followed, Pascual herded for his uncle, became a partner, and acquired his own place, the historic Sheep Ranch at Arock, Oregon. Today, members of

Sitting in front: Catalina Eiguren, Jose Navarro, Pia Navarro. *Standing left to right:* Marie Arritola, wife of Rufino; Pascual Eiguren, husband of Catalina; Inez Telleria, sister of Pascual; and Rufino Arritola. Jose Navarro was uncle to Pascual Eiguren and Inez Telleria and was one of the first Basque settlers of Jordan Valley, Oregon. (Eiguren Family Collection, courtesy of The High Desert Museum, Bend, Oregon.)

Catalina Eiguren, wife of Pascual, with son, Fred, at their family ranch, Arock, Oregon, 1918. (Eiguren Family Collection, courtesy of The High Desert Museum, Bend, Oregon.)

the fourth generation of young Eigurens are growing up along Jordan Creek in a landscape first viewed by their great-grandfather almost a century before.

Cipriano and Juanita Barrutia of Mountain Home, Idaho

For many Basque sheepherders who had saved enough to buy their own band of sheep, this was also the point in their lives when they could look forward to marriage and family. Cipriano Barrutia worked as a partner with the Whitson Brothers when he first came to the United States in 1918. He had to return to Spain to serve in the Spanish army, however, because he was not yet a citizen of the United States. While in Spain, Cipriano began his courtship of Juanita Mandeola, and the couple were married in Semein in 1921, shortly before they emigrated to America.

Cipriano and Juanita journeyed to America with little more than their passage money, since he had turned over most of his savings to his parents in order to avert a financial crisis that would have taken the family *baserri* and left them with nowhere to live. They returned to Mountain Home, looking forward to resuming the sheep business Cipriano had started with the Whitson Brothers three years before. However, when they arrived in Mountain Home, they were confronted with the bad news that the business Cipriano had started was bankrupt and all assets were gone. Cipriano and Juanita had to start all over. Cipriano went to work for the Gandiaga Sheep Company, and the couple slept under the stars, on the ground with only a bedroll, in the desert along the foothills outside of Mountain Home. His first month's pay enabled the couple to buy a $6.50 tepee tent. This was their first home in Mountain Home.

For Cipriano, as for many of the herders who came to this country, the avenue to prosperity was to work hard, save, and buy in as a partner in a sheep company. Cipriano, after a few years, became a partner with the M. S. Swain Sheep Company. Although many Basque women helped out at lambing and shearing time, they lived in town while the men tended the bands in the deserts and mountains. Juanita, however, insisted on following her husband. She worked side by side with him the year round. Even with the birth of their children, Juanita continued to make their home the sheep camps in the Boise and Sawtooth National Forests. Camp wagons sheltered the family while crossing the deserts, and tents housed the family while they were in the high

The Barrutias pose in front of their winter home—a sheep wagon in the Grandview, Idaho, desert, 1921. The couple are dressed up for this photograph that was taken for their families in the Basque Country. Juanita is proudly showing off her ten-dollar "American dress." (Barrutia Family Collection, courtesy of The High Desert Museum, Bend, Oregon.)

The Barrutias and their pack animals loaded with supplies for their sheepherders' camps in the mountains above the old mining towns of Featherville, Atlanta, and Rocky Bar, Idaho, 1924 on Atlanta Summit. (Barrutia Family Collection, courtesy of The High Desert Museum, Bend, Oregon.)

Juanita Barrutia at the stove and Cipriano Barrutia holding their firstborn son, Ralph, camped at Lincoln Creek. They were herding sheep on the summer range above Cayuse Creek and Rocky Bar, Idaho. (Barrutia Family Collection, courtesy of The High Desert Museum, Bend, Oregon.)

mountain ranges. There was a strong sense of family even under these spartan conditions as they tended the bands of sheep of the Yuba Sheep Company. Children were born, five in all, but two were lost in childbirth, and the sadness of burying them in mountain mining towns was deeply felt. It was only when their three remaining sons were of school age and needed the stability of a permanent home that the family rented a house in Mountain Home. This is where all three sons received their schooling and worked on the family farm that was purchased as the permanent home.

Cipriano passed away in 1966, but Juanita lives in Mountain Home, where she can still view the desert land near the foothills where she spent her first nights on the ground in 1921. Her active nature has

Juanita Barrutia at the county fair, Glenns Ferry, Idaho, 1991. Juanita was among a group of women, all over ninety years of age, who were brought together to select a pioneer queen for the county. (Barrutia Family Collection, courtesy of The High Desert Museum, Bend, Oregon.)

not diminished with the years. In her home are medals and certificates she won while competing in the Senior Games in Boise, Idaho. On the urging of her son and grandchildren, she competed in the hundred-meter dash and won handily in her age group: age ninety-two at the time. She is now ninety-six years old and insists that she must feed and water every day the few livestock left on the farm on which she still lives alone—but under the watchful eye of her family.

Jean and Shirley Lekumberry of Gardnerville, Nevada

Throughout the era of Basque immigration to the high-desert country of eastern California, Nevada, southeastern Oregon, and southern Idaho, opportunity was the magnet that attracted young Basques to the region. This held true from the 1870s until the 1970s, when the economy and standard of living in the Basque Country improved and the high-desert sheep industry declined.

Among the young Basques who came to America in the last wave of immigration following World War II were the Lekumberry brothers: Jean, Pierre, and Leon. In 1947 they left their village of Ortzaize, France, for Nevada. From a boardinghouse in Gardnerville, Nevada, they signed on to herd sheep where the desert meets the Sierra Nevada, along the California-Nevada border.

For more than ten years the brothers worked as sheepherders or camptenders. They spent the cold winter months on the desert with the sheep or in one of the Gardnerville Basque boardinghouses and moved the sheep to the high mountain meadows of the Sierra in the summer.

One summer, Jean met Shirley Mallinckrodt at Twin Lakes Resort in the Sierra. The young Los Angeles girl and the sheepherder were married in 1957. In 1960 the couple purchased the JT Hotel, Bar, and Dining Room from John Jaunsaras and Jimmy Trounday. Jean and Shirley lived above the hotel with their children. Marie, Robert, and Jean Baptiste experienced a life common to the families of boarding-house owners. From an early age, they did whatever work needed to

Leon Lekumberry in the Sierra above Markleeville, California, with a *makila*. Leon still wears his beret, which is unusual. Most sheepherders favored felt hats with a brim for protection from the sun and weather. (Lekumberry Family Collection, courtesy of The High Desert Museum, Bend, Oregon.)

Jean Lekumberry, *left*, with sheepherder Aurelio Casaus in the Sierra above Bridgeport, California. At this time, Jean was working as a camptender, packing supplies on a weekly basis to sheepherders in the high mountain canyons. (Lekumberry Family Collection, courtesy of The High Desert Museum, Bend, Oregon.)

The Lekumberry family of Osses (Orzaize), Nafarroa Beherea, France, gathered together for the 1963 visit by Jean Lekumberry (back row near door), in front of the family home, Motxondonia. This was his first trip to the Basque Country since his departure in 1947. (Lekumberry Family Collection, courtesy of The High Desert Museum, Bend, Oregon.)

be done, from scrubbing floors and making beds to working in the kitchen and dining room. Beyond the immediate family was an extended family of herders who regularly stayed at the Lekumberry's JT Hotel each year and viewed the boardinghouse as their home.

Today, almost forty years after their parents purchased the JT, the younger generation continues the family tradition of providing Basque hospitality to travelers and local patrons.

7

Confessions of a Basque Sheepherder

RENE TIHISTA

Northeastern Montana is known for its cold winters, and the winter of 1956 was the coldest I remember. Our home place was on twenty acres on the outskirts of Nashua, an Indian name that means "meeting of the waters" and refers to the confluence of the Milk and Missouri Rivers only five miles away. We lived in the shallow valley of the Milk River alongside Big Porcupine Creek. Cottonwood, ash, alder, birch, and box elder trees lined the rivers and creeks. On the western end of the Great Plains, this is prairie country, and the rolling hills and coulees of this corner of Montana are dotted with wheat farms and ranches. It's harsh country with extreme weather but beautiful in a way all its own.

February was especially cold that year. The mornings dawned crystal clear. The snow glistened, like it had been scattered with diamonds, and squeaked when you walked on it. The air was still. I poked my head out from under layers of blankets and scraped the thick frost from the window so I could make a clear spot. The thermometer outside my window read 52 below. "Jesus," I shivered, and ducked back under the blankets. I would soon have to get up and do the morning chores: milk the cow, feed some alfalfa to her and her calf, and scatter grain to the chickens before going to school.

I could hear my mother downstairs in the kitchen clanking around the stove. She was always up at dawn, even in polar conditions. Soon I could smell bacon frying. But it was so damn cold not even that heavenly aroma, which usually lured me from the warmth of my bed in a hurry, could entice me to get up.

"All rrright meestre, you get up outta dat bed, rrright now." My mother's voice rang like a chime through the cold house, her rolling *r*s somehow making the command more melodic. She still had a heavy Basque accent to her English, even after more than thirty years in Montana.

I groaned, eyeing my Levi's and V-neck sweater laid out on the other bed. It was customary for me to leap out of bed, grab my clothes, and run downstairs to dress in front of the kitchen's warm wood stove. Today it seemed foolhardy: I would surely freeze to death before I got there. "It's 52 below, for chrissakes," I whined to myself. But I did it. Flinging off the covers, I plunged into the frigid room, swooped up my clothes, shoes, and socks, and ran downstairs. My breath hovered in the air before me as if to say, "You gotta be kidding. Let me back into those warm lungs, man. It's freezing out here."

Another winter morning in northeastern Montana. Looking back I sometimes wonder how I survived life in that country. Good thing I was young. The year 1956 was a particularly memorable one. I was a junior in high school and turned seventeen in April. My school life centered on basketball. I was starting guard, point guard they call it now. I played ball every spare minute, even in the cold outside where I had a half-gallon tin syrup can with the bottom removed hanging on the side of the coal shed. Not too high, so I could dunk. The rubber ball was a little larger than a grapefruit. In the dense, cold air of winter the ball would not bounce. It would hit the ground with a thud and lie there as though it had been shot dead. So only "pretend" dribbling would work. When, on rare occasions, some friend or one of my older brothers would play ball with me, we got into continual arguments over whether or not one of us had "pretend" double dribbled.

Although this early February morning was too cold for outdoor basketball, it was not too cold to perform my most-hated winter morning chore, milking the old black cow. My wife, Mary, once asked me the cow's name. I looked at her incredulously. "Name?" "Yeah, like Clo, or Daisy, or something. Cows usually have names don't they?" I laughed. It somehow struck me as hilarious to give a cow a name. "She was Old Black Cow," I replied.

Fortunately she was gentle. But in the winter her teats were often cracked and hard, sometimes streaked with dried frozen blood. I had to massage them with warm tallow before I could get any milk out of them. As I sat there on the stool milking her, the steam from our breaths made the interior of the barn foggy. I leaned into her flank as close as I could to absorb the warmth of her body. I remembered the puppy I had a few years back. He would follow me into the barn and I'd squirt the milk into his mouth and sometimes all over his furry little face. He loved it.

I finished milking as fast as I could to get out of that cold barn and into the warm house for breakfast. My oldest brother, Ed, was at the table when I came in. He'd been out feeding the sheep at our farm on the Milk River three miles west of Nashua. After I dumped the milk into the cream separator, I sat down to eat.

"So you guys think you can beat Poplar tonight?"

"Ah, we'll clobber those guys," I grunted disdainfully.

I loved playing Poplar. The year before, when I was a sophomore, I'd had a career game against them, scored 24 points, and they were the conference champions. But that was 1955. This was 1956, and we were a better team. We'd already beaten them once and would do it again. I heaped pancakes, bacon, and eggs onto my plate. The cold gives you an appetite.

"When you goin' to let me wash those Levi's?" my mother asked.

"Jeez, Ma, they're perfect right now."

"They're dirty," she proclaimed with a disgusted look. She just didn't get it. The Levi's had to be stiff and look lived-in. Besides, they weren't really dirty. They were more . . . greasy like. That's how they were supposed to be.

"Your brother alaways went to school with clean, neatly pressed corduroys or kahkis, and a clean shirt," she lectured, nodding at Ed.

"God, Mom, that was 1941. Guys don't dress that way any more."

She gave me a withering look. "Buh, tierrriet," she muttered one of her unfathomable Basque expletives. I think it meant something like "Yeah . . . right." Or maybe not. I thought I knew all the Basque cuss words there were. My father had been a very inventive swearer. But Mom had expressions that even he didn't use. They weren't really cuss words, though she definitely knew how to swear. She always said that she had no choice, what with rearing six boys and being around menfolk all her life. "You boys wouldn't pay no attention otherwise," she once explained.

The weather stayed around minus 50 degrees for nearly two weeks.

We had to use the head-bolt heaters to get our vehicles started. That wasn't unusual in winter, but this year even the head-bolt heaters didn't always work. We sometimes had to wait until noon when it warmed up a little, to 40 degrees below, before the engines would turn over. And as soon as the sheep were fed in late afternoon, the heaters were plugged in again.

There wasn't a lot of snow that winter, so the horse team my brothers had bought from Joe Laumeyer two years back wasn't used much. It did come in handy for feeding sheep. If everything went right, one man could do the job. The hay was loaded onto the wagon that had sled runners. The team was "sort of" trained to walk in a circle while the hay was thrown off to the sheep. I say "sort of" because the team's mare was spooky and unpredictable. Every now and then she would bolt, spooked by something, and the team would take off. I saw it happen once to my brother Jerry. He fell over as the team bolted, and before he could get up to grab the reins, the horses had run into a cottonwood tree, one on each side. The singletary smashed and Jerry was bounced, crashing up against the hay rack. He came off that hay rack cussing in English, then, as if he'd run out of American cuss words, started cussing in Basque. Nobody was quite able to figure out why the mare was so jumpy. Both horses were large, one a Belgian the other a Percheron. The gelding was mellow, but that damn mare was so unpredictable.

Once when my brother Mike was putting the mare's harness on she jerked her head up, catching him under the chin with such force that she almost broke his jaw. He had to eat liquids through a straw for more than a week. This was torture for him because he was one prodigious eater.

March Is a Lion during Lambing

March was an important month because it was the month of lambing. March also saw the beginning of an incredible series of disasters that befell us that year. I was usually taken out of school for the first two weeks of lambing, when most of the births occurred. We ran our sheep up on the Fort Peck Indian Reservation, about twenty miles north of our home place on the outskirts of Nashua. Our lease was prime grazing land, about eighteen thousand acres on Tomato Can Creek, and it included adjacent Mud Lake.

It was fine range land, tall blue-joint grass with plenty of water in the Tomato Can and several good springs. It was, after all, the type of country that once supported millions of buffalo. Livestock thrived there. We owned a section of land where the creek was deepest. There, on a bench above the creek, we had a two-room line shack. In the rear was space for a bed. The front had cupboards, counter space, a table, and my mother's cast iron Majestic wood stove that she said was as old as Methuselah. Old maybe, but the bread she could bake in that stove was famed throughout the area. Grade-school superintendent Homer Loucks used to make excuses to stop by our house for a couple of hot buns with cheese. He seemed to have an unerring nose for when Mom baked buns.

Shortly after World War II, my three older brothers, who were working in Alaska, bought Mom a new stove. This one, a modern technological marvel, was half electric and half wood and coal. We got the best features of both: quick electric heat for cooking, and wood and coal for heating up a cold Montana kitchen in winter. When she got the new stove, her old domestic was moved to the line shack.

We also had the mother of all sheep sheds on that bench above Tomato Can Creek. It was about two hundred feet long and had been acquired from the Scott Brothers ranch several miles to the east on Little Porcupine Creek. It was one of three built before the First World War by the Murray-Jamieson sheep company. For years, this large sheep outfit ran thousands of head on the hills and coulees of the Little Porcupine and Tomato Can.

My brothers bought one of the survivors and moved it to Tomato Can. It was quite a project. The shed was so long it had to be sawed in half and moved in parts by Pop Davis, the area's best mover of houses. It had to be transported slowly across ten miles of bumpy prairie tracks, two creeks, and finally up the rise to the bench above the Tomato Can.

It was a wonderful shed. At one end were gears and wooden pulleys, no longer operable, that were part of the original shearing mechanism run by a gas generator. The shed was large enough to hold several hundred ewes and lambs. Inside, we set up "jugs," little stalls for one ewe and lamb.

During lambing, my brothers Mike and Jerry herded the sheep as they grazed. One was on horseback, the other at the wheel of our Farmall tractor pulling the "gut" wagon, which could more appropriately be called a maternity wagon. It had twelve stalls, and as lambs were born, ewe and lamb were caught and placed in the wagon. When it was full, it was driven back to the shed, where Ed put them in jugs. The idea was to help the ewe and lamb bond until the lamb was strong enough to be let out to graze with its mother. Usually this meant a few days in the jug. March weather in northeast Montana can be treacherous, and young lambs die easily in a blizzard or sleet storm.

At night the "drop bunch," the ewes who hadn't yet lambed out, were brought into the corrals at the shed. Lambs born at night were the responsibility of Leo DeBray. Leo ran three hundred head of sheep with us. As part of his grazing fee, he worked the corrals at night, sleeping during the day in his sheep wagon. My job was herding lamb bunches. As the ewes lambed out during the month, they were put in bunches according to age. There's quite a difference in size and stamina between lambs born just two weeks apart. So we divided them into small bands that were scattered around the range. I spent my days riding between them, seeing that they were OK and chasing off coyotes. Usually it meant riding all day, since the bunches could be scattered five or six miles apart in various locations.

Lambing was an exciting time. Of course it was critical to our success as sheep ranchers. Without lambs to sell in the fall, we'd be out of business. But it was also exciting and fun in other ways. My mom had the one good bed in the rear of the line shack. Jerry, Mike, and I slept on rollaway beds. I had to sleep with Mike, a harrowing experience since he tended to flail his arms and talk—sometimes even yell—in his sleep. Ed, because he was the oldest, got the sheep wagon all to himself.

We were up at dawn, and Mom would fry bacon, ham, a couple dozen eggs, and hotcakes on the old Majestic. It was a good thing we produced most of our own vittles, because we were all big eaters. During lambing there was a lot of good-natured banter, and my older brothers actually refrained from bickering. That in itself was unusual. Normally they argued, yelled, cussed, and on occasion took a swing or two at each other. Jerry and Mike were in their early twenties, and Ed was in his mid-thirties. He'd returned home after my dad died to take over the business. As the oldest, he was head honcho and didn't take kindly to lip from his younger brothers.

Jerry and especially Mike were equally headstrong and often resisted Ed's authority. Ed himself was normally jovial, quick to laugh and very funny, but he took his responsibility as head of the family seriously. Jerry was kind of excitable, and everybody tried to talk at once. Amid all this energy was a lot of laughter too.

Etxe Monoua

We were *Amerikanuak,* a pretty typical Basque sheep-ranching family of the American West. My father was from the village of Banca in the Pyrenees of France. His family ran sheep in the steep mountains and valleys near that tiny village. The sheep operations were very small compared to those in Montana. Farms were not more than a few acres. Dad was the youngest of six, and his three older brothers emigrated to the United States early in the century. His two sisters stayed in France. Dad came to America in 1912 with his good friend and partner Pierre Uharriet, who was also my mother's uncle. They went into the sheep business near Rock Springs, Wyoming. During the eight years he spent in Wyoming, he courted my mother by letter. She fondly remembered the letters years later.

"Yourr father was a poet," she would say. "He wrote the most beeaauutiful letters." Her eyes would glaze over with the memory, and her accent made *beautiful* sound delicious.

My dad was a *bertsolari* (also referred to as a *gopledea* by Mom), a troubadour who performed at weddings and festivals in the old country. While traveling in the Basque Country in 1970, I stopped at the farm of Dad's neighbor. They were astonished to meet the son of Michel Monoua. (*Monoua* was the name of my Dad's "house." In old-country Basque culture, the identity of one's house or domicile was more important than the surname.) My wife noted the old ladies would smile when they recalled my dad and his performances.

He was known all over the valley. When I told my mother this story, she exclaimed, "O' courrse. He was a wonderful singer and veddy handsome." In fact she always insisted that none of us boys were as handsome as he.

My father returned to the Basque Country in 1920. He had sold his sheep in Wyoming and left the sale of his last wool crop in the hands of his partner. Prices were depressed, since the end of the First World War had reduced the demand for wool. Apparently Dad didn't make much money from the wool that year. After a one-year, in-person courtship, my parents were married in 1921 in Urepel, the village where my mother was born. After the marriage, Dad was supposed to go into business with my mother's father, Grandfather Ippeagurre. It wasn't meant to be. They didn't get along well and couldn't be in business together.

"Your father didn't like partners," my mother said. "He was very independent."

Ed was born in Urepel and was the focus of a great deal of love and attention from his grandparents. My dad's father, Bernard Tihista, was still working sheep in the Pyrenees above the valley where Banca lies.

"The old man would come down outa the mountains to see Edward," my mother exclaimed. "He was sooo proud of that baby. My father too. He had to hold that baby on his lap when he had his coffee in the morning."

When Mom and Dad finally decided to return to America, Ed was a year old.

"Everyone cried, o' course," Mom remembered. "And you know, your father didn't tell his dad we were leaving."

I was astonished. "Why not?" I asked.

"I guess he knew it would break the old man's heart. All four of his sons left for Amerrica, and he was afraid he'd never see them again. Your dad didn't want to face his father, knowing how it would hurt him."

It seemed insensitive to me, hearing the story many years later. But I imagine there were millions of examples of similar pain and sorrow during emigration, not just among the Basques. As it turned out, Bernard was never to see my dad again. Of all his sons, only Pete returned. A few years after my folks left, he came back and married Aunt May, also from Banca, then returned to Montana. Ed was the only one of Bernard's eleven American grandsons and three American granddaughters he ever saw.

Basque culture was carried to Montana, however. When I was a kid all the holiday gatherings with my uncles and cousins were held at our place. Mom raised a huge turkey for Thanksgiving and one for Christmas. Dad played the accordion and violin and sang Basque songs. Of course wine flowed freely during our get-togethers. I would sit on Dad's knee and sing "Uso Zuria," a song he taught me about a white dove that travels to Spain. It was the only Basque song I knew, but it must have been a hit because the grown-ups made me sing it over and over. We knew all the Basques in eastern Montana. Unlike the large Basque populations of Idaho and Nevada, there weren't that many in Montana.

There were a few bachelor Basque sheepmen like John Burrocua and Pete Musho in business nearby, and they were always invited. Pete Musho was a great singer, and he and my dad would harmonize beautifully.

During World War II, my dad, Pete, John, and my uncles Pete and Pierre would gather at Vick's Bar in Nashua. After a few beers, they would start singing the Marseilles. Dad had been in the French army before he came to America and was very patriotic. He also had three sons overseas, and though he never said much, my mother told me that he worried a lot about them. Fortunately they all returned, and only John ever got in harm's way. He was wounded while fighting in New Guinea, where he also contracted malaria, an affliction he suffered from for years afterward.

My mother was scandalized at what she felt was a demeaning treatment of the French national anthem.

"They shouldn't have sung that song in a bar," she muttered disgustedly.

She too was patriotic, and her favorite singer was Kate Smith, or "Kata Smeet," as she pronounced the name. When Kate Smith sang "God Bless America," a popular song during the war, Mom would get tears in her eyes. Years later, her great-granddaughter Tona Meldrum, a member of the University of Montana chorus, taped a version of it for her. It would make Mom cry to hear it. "Listen to that girl sing," she would exclaim rapturously. Tona sang the song at Mom's funeral in 1994. There wasn't a dry eye in the house.

Many times on Sundays a carload of Basques from Sidney or Miles City, two hundred or so miles away, would arrive in the yard. Mom would immediately set about feeding them. She would kill three or four pullets, expertly chopping off their heads with a one-handed blow from the ax. My job was to grab the flopping chickens and stick them in a bucket of boiling water.

She would clean them quickly and within a short time have a big roasting pan of Basque chicken and rice in the oven. It contained garlic, onions, and canned tomatoes from our garden and a couple of scalding-hot red peppers Mom picked from a little plant she grew. An impromptu party would begin. After dinner, my dad and the other Basque men would drink wine and play *mus,* a card game I could never fathom.

Etxe Iriania

My mother was from Urepel, a beautiful, picture-postcard village nestled in a valley a few miles from the Spanish border. It was only a few miles from Dad's village. Mom's parents ran a store, a drayage business, and a coach service. Pulled by a mule team, their coach ran down through the little villages to Saint-Jean-Pied-de-Port, the largest market town in the region. One of Mom's duties involved an old practice among the Basques of the border region. They all smuggled Spanish wine into France. A cousin of my grandmother's had a team of smugglers who would bring the wine over the border at night, sometimes with mules, sometimes on their backs. Then my grandmother and my mom would take the wine into Saint-Jean-Pied-de-Port in the landau coach. The wine was hidden under a trunk of clothes. In case they were stopped and searched, the story was that my mother was going to school in Biarritz. The trunk of clothes was to lend plausibility to the deception. Mom always talked about those trips with excitement.

"Were you ever searched?" I asked her.

"No, the gendarmes always believed us. But just in case, my mother always brought a big cheese and plenty of bread to give them."

On my first visit to Urepel in 1970, I discovered that relatives of mine were still smuggling wine. A distant cousin, Fernando Zabaleta, invited me to dinner. He was the nephew of my godmother, Domenica Granada. Fernando had spent eighteen years in Montana working for Domenica and Fred Granada at their ranch on the Little Porcupine. He returned to Urepel in 1967 and married. His farm was small and his home was a typical old-country farm home, with pigs in a barn under the house. At dinner, Fernando pulled out a jug of red wine and poured. After I'd had a couple of glasses he lowered his voice conspiratorially and asked, "You like this wine, Rene?"

"Yeah, it's pretty good," I replied.

"It's Espanish wine," he said, grinning. "I smuggled it over the border myself."

"Why?" I wondered. "Can't you get French wine?"

"Oh sure, but the Espanish wine is better and it's cheaper," he confided. "All the farmers around here smuggle dere wine from Espain."

I suspect that history and tradition also had something to do with it. Fernando clearly enjoyed the smuggling process itself.

Grandfather Iriania

My mother and her sister, Germaine, often described their father, my grandfather Michel Ippeagurre, as a "hard" man. Mom would occasionally describe him as a "son of a beech."

"He was loving in his own way," she would say. "I did his books for him, and he was tight as a tick. He was strict and not very affectionate or demonstrative like your dad. After we were married, your father would sometimes put his arms around me and kiss me. He was very affectionate. I was embarrassed and would pull him behind a door or into another room so my folks couldn't see us. Your dad would laugh and remark, 'We're married, you know. We're allowed to kiss.'" She would laugh as she recalled these episodes. "You boys get your affectionate nature from your father."

Her mother, Louisa, was jolly and loved by everyone. My mother didn't think she loved my grandfather.

"He was so estubborn," she said. "And kinda cold too. But my mother was happy-go-lucky and a wonderful woman."

Mom frowned and lowered her voice and said, "But my grandmother, Oy Yoy Ama Mitia, I hated her. She wasa so estrict. She ruled the roost you know."

My great-grandmother Domenica had been a seamstress of some renown in the area. When my mother's parents got married she lived with them, as was the custom in those days.

My mother went on, "She kept a little set of chime bells next to her bed, and when she wanted me, would ring those bells. Of course I had to immediately go to her. I rebelled against her even though I was punished for it. Once I wanted to go to a beeg dance. Oy yoy, I loved to dance. But because I sassed her she wouldn't let me go. Oh, I was so mad. I snuck out of the house and went anyway. She was furious, but my mother intervened and I wasn't punished."

She continued, "You know Germaine has that chime. Once when I was visiting her in San Francisco, I was taking a nap on her couch and I'll be damned if she didn't ring that chime. I jumped right up out of asleep. I thought it was my grandmother. Can you beat dat?"

Apparently my grandmother was in love with a handsome young border guard. He would come to dine at my grandparents' store, which was also a restaurant. But my great-grandmother had arranged a marriage for Grandmother Louisa. Michel Ippeagurre was a businessman from Zuberoa, another Basque province. He was obviously considered a more suitable match. The fate of the jilted guard is unknown.

My grandfather was always referred to as "Zuberoa," because he came from a different region of the Basque country. I didn't realize how deep labels go in Basque culture. In the 1970s when I worked in San Francisco, I dined often at the Hotel Obrero, which was owned by Catherine Goyenetche, also from Urepel. Catherine was younger than my mother and a distant cousin. The Obrero was a well-known Basque family-style restaurant and hotel. A few old retired Basque men, some former sheepherders, also lived there.

One day I stopped by to say hello. As I was climbing the stairs up to the restaurant, Catherine's sister Anna was standing at the top peering down. When she recognized me she exclaimed, "Oh it's you, Zuberoa." In her mind I was identified with my grandfather. My aunt Germaine added more anecdotal information about him. She had stayed behind in Urepel and took care of her folks until they died. She, too, had a hard time with him. Although her language was more refined than my mother's, her description of Grandfather Ippeagurre was essentially the same.

In 1973 I was working in San Francisco, director of a mental health clinic in North Beach. In the mornings when I walked to work through Washington Square, I'd weave my way through groups of elderly Chinese doing Tai Chi. On the benches were clusters of old Italian men visiting, talking in loud voices and gesticulating flamboyantly. One day I noticed a group of old guys on a bench across the park. I immediately recognized them as Basques. There were several small hotels in North Beach and Chinatown run by Basques that in the old days harbored retired Basque sheepherders. By 1973 there weren't many left. On this morning I walked over to the five old guys. They stopped talking when I approached them.

"Nola zira," I said, greeting them with the Basque version of "Hello, how are you?" They looked surprised.

At that time I had a full beard and my hair was shoulder length. I must have looked like a hippy to them. One of them jumped up and started speaking rapidly in Basque.

"Whoa," I said. "My Basque isn't good enough to follow you."

The man, who identified himself as Pierre, switched to English.

"Where are your parents from?" he asked.

"My dad was from Banca, my mother from Urepel," I replied.

"Urepel?" His eyes widened. He was about seventy years old. "I'm from Urepel!" he exclaimed. "What's your mother's name?"

I told him, "Marie Ippeagurre."

He frowned. "What's the name of her house?"

"Oh, that's right," I said, remembering that the house name was more important than the surname. "Marie Iriania," I said.

"Marie Iriania? My God, I know your mother. I know your father, too. I was at their wedding. I went to school with your aunt Germaine."

He was excited. He turned to the other old guys and, in rapid Basque, described our conversation, even though all them could speak English. I heard "Marie Iriania," "Michel Monoua," and some reference to my grandparents.

Pierre turned to me. "Well I'll be damned, Rene. You're a son of

Marie Iriania," he said in wonderment. "I knew your whole family. I knew your grandparents too. I'll be . . ."

Then he paused a moment, looked at me warily, and lowered his voice. "You know, Rene, your grandfather was a son-of-a-bitch." I burst out laughing. He looked relieved that he hadn't offended me.

"Well, that does it," I said. "My mother and Aunt Germaine were right after all. They told me the same thing."

Pierre laughed. "He was a good businessman though," he said, seeming satisfied that he found some redeeming feature in my grandfather.

"Well, at least," I replied, "he was an *impressive* son-of-a-bitch."

The irony of the situation amazed me. Here I was standing in a park in San Francisco talking to a stranger I'd just met who not only knew a grandfather I'd never known but corroborated the descriptions of him by my mother and aunt. I guess I shouldn't have been surprised, because Mom always insisted that all Basques were related or knew each other.

Standing there in Washington Square talking to these old Basques, two of whom were former sheepherders, stirred up memories about my sheepherding days in Montana and our life in that unpredictable country. My thoughts returned to the spring that followed that frigid winter of 1956. Mother Nature was not kind to us that spring.

Back at the Ranch and the Big Bad Wolf

The first disaster came about two weeks into lambing. One morning I rode up to a lamb bunch and found dead ewes and lambs scattered all over a coulee. I counted twenty-six dead. I assumed it was coyotes at first, but this carnage was unlike the work of coyotes. They usually took one lamb at a time. I couldn't believe this.

The sheep were spooked, but I herded them together and took off on a gallop back to the shed to tell Ed. He grabbed the .30-.30, and he and Leo jumped into the Jeep pickup and went looking for coyotes. As I rode to the other lamb bunches I could see the pickup in the distance.

It would appear on a hill a few miles away, disappear, then reappear on another rise, moving rapidly. Ed and Leo were chasing something, but I couldn't see what it was. This went on for a while until they disappeared from sight into a coulee near the Little Porcupine. Later that day I rode back to the line shack and found everyone standing around the carcass of what I thought was a coyote. In fact it was an eighty-six-pound timber wolf.

We'd always had coyote trouble. In those days a government hunter named Happy Jaycox, who worked for the Bureau of Land Management, went around hunting them. Usually, he would place the carcass of a sheep or old horse near a coyote run and put poison in it. This usually worked. It certainly kept the coyote population in check.

On rare occasions if coyotes were particularly numerous, we'd get the Etchart boys to hunt them from their Cessna. Swooping down over the coyotes, they would blast them with shotguns. This method was expensive and not very efficient, though I'm sure it was fun for the hunters. Poison worked better. Coyotes were tough to bag. In the four summers I herded sheep I shot at several but never got close enough to hit one. They had an uncanny ability to know when I had the rifle with me and when I didn't.

On one occasion, riding from Mud Lake back to the line shack, I stopped in a coulee to take a leak. Glancing up, I saw a coyote standing on the side of the hill about fifty yards away, just staring at me. I jumped on the horse and chased him. He ran just ahead of me, looking back once in a while as if he were laughing. I ran him to the edge of a cutbank, and he slowed to a lope at the bottom, turned, stopped, and stared some more, as if issuing a challenge.

Later that summer, I walked out of the sheep wagon early one morning and a coyote was again standing about fifty yards away watching me. This time I had the .30-.30 in the wagon. I casually strolled back, acting as if I hadn't noticed him. When I came out with the rifle, he was three hundred yards away running at top speed. I fired a couple of times, but he was gone. He somehow knew I had that gun.

But a wolf—this was unprecedented. Jerry threw the wolf into the back of the pickup and took it to Glasgow for the game warden to inspect. The Montana Fish and Game people came, weighed and examined it, took pictures, and proclaimed it the first timber wolf killed in Montana since 1919. Just our luck that she chose our sheep. But that was the kind of year 1956 was.

About a week after the wolf incident, we got a sleet storm. These storms were especially bad because the youngest lambs didn't have enough wool to withstand the freezing wet. It also meant the sheep would move during the night with the wind and driving sleet, trying to find shelter. I had to follow. Fortunately there was only one bunch of ewes and lambs, about one hundred or so, camped on an exposed hillside. The rest were hunkered down in the creek or near the shed, where there was sufficient shelter. This bunch was five or six miles from camp, so I herded them into a coulee filled with chokecherry and buckbrush. Sometime late they finally settled. I could have ridden back to camp, but we were having a lot of coyote trouble, and the memory of the wolf attack was still fresh. It seemed like I should stay with them, so I threw the saddle down, tied the horse to my foot, and scrunched under some buckbrush. The heavy wool saddle blanket and my canvas slicker and rain pants kept me reasonably dry.

I was really hungry when I came into camp in the morning, and my mother was worried. She had urged my brothers to go out and bring me in, but they figured I was OK. They had all gone through something similar over the years. That was part of sheepherding. We lost several lambs in that storm. Then, with the typical capriciousness of Montana weather, the sky cleared, the temperature rose twenty degrees, and it was spring again.

Toward the end of March, most of the ewes had lambed out, and I went back to school. I had to make up a few tests, but it was not that unusual. Lots of farm kids, boys mostly, had to be let out of school in the spring to plow and seed crops. It was built into the system, and the school adjusted.

After Lambing — Late Spring

In the sheep business there are cycles of major events. Lambing is the first, then docking, when the male lambs are castrated and their ears are marked and all the ewes and lambs are branded. Unlike cattle, sheep get branded with paint. Years ago, my dad and uncles docked lambs the old way, with sharp knives. The lambs were laid out on a bench, and with a swift swipe of the knife the bottoms of their scrotums were cut and the testicles were pulled out, usually with the teeth, because they were too slippery to grasp with fingers. The tails were cut off with a quick slash.

My dad was fast at this practice. By 1956, however, we were employing modern methods. We used a rubber "emasculator," a device that resembled a pair of pliers with short columns on one end. A small, thick rubber band was placed over the columns and expanded so it would fit over the testicles. Another rubber band was stretched over the tail. These rubber bands, once secured, would gradually cut off the blood circulation. After a few weeks the testes and the tails would fall off. It was painful for the lambs, at first anyway, but they got over it fast. I guess any animal-rights people reading this would be horrified, but that's the way things were done and probably still are.

Docking was usually done on a weekend and was a festive occasion. Sometimes neighbors would come, and Leo Debray would bring his family to help catch lambs in the corral. One year Ed Boner, the high school biology teacher, came to observe. My brother Ed was a showman of sorts and liked to shock visitors with an exhibition of dad's method of castrating lambs. The time Ed Boner came, brother Ed gave him a demonstration, slashing the end of scrotum and biting down and ripping the testes out with his teeth. He grinned, the bloody testes dangling from his mouth. The science teacher got sick. My brother Ed thought this was hilarious. The other Ed, the science teacher, thought it was barbaric.

There was always plenty of food during docking. My mom would make a huge dutch oven of Basque beans, a big potato salad, and a roast mutton hindquarter. Of course there were lots of fresh baked buns and homemade butter, too. I don't think Ed Boner stayed for dinner on that occasion, though.

Docking usually took place in late April or early May. The next major event was shearing. Because of the fickle Montana weather, shearing was done in June. Normally, there was a reasonable expectation that June weather would be mild, but it was certainly not a sure thing. Not even July could be counted on for nice weather. In early July 1951, the day after my dad died, we got a heavy snowstorm. June can be beautiful or hellish. The old saying about March coming in like a lion and going out like a lamb could easily apply to June in Montana. The opposite could also be true. June 1956 proved to be the month of the lion. And the lion roared, causing another disaster.

Shearing

The shearing was done by a crew of Mexicans from Texas. A man named Martínez—I never knew his first name—came every year with a crew of ten or twelve and a mobile shearing outfit run by gas generator. Martínez had been coming to Montana for years. My folks usually sent him money to gather up his crew, and he would show up like clockwork around the first of June. He worked a few other small sheep ranches around the area at the same time, but he always started with us. The year after my dad died, Mom bought a money order to send to Martínez, as usual. Ed was aghast.

"You mean you're going to send that guy $150 just like that? What if he never shows up?"

Mom was indignant.

"Martínez is an *Honest* man." She pronounced the *h* in *honest,* as had my dad. "O' course he'll come."

Ed was dubious, but sure enough, Martínez showed up a few weeks later.

The shearers pulled into Tomato Can and set up camp. They had a cook and ten shearers besides Martínez, who was the fastest. One year they brought a woman with them. My brothers and Leo Debray snickered and made innuendoes about the woman's role in that operation. Martínez said she was the cook, but we never saw her do any cooking, during the day at least. In previous years I used to go down in the evening and listen to the shearing crew sing Mexican songs. They always had a guitar and one of those miniature accordions. I think it's called a concertina. But the year they brought the woman, Mom wouldn't let me go down to their camp. I was baffled as to why, but I knew better than to argue with her. She could be hell on wheels when she was mad.

We always gave the crew a yearling wether, which is the sheep equivalent of a steer. They would butcher it and throw the carcass into a big pot filled with water, onions, beans, and mysterious Mexican spices. They ate out of that pot for the whole week they were there. Mom would give them loaves of bread, which they took gratefully, but they mostly preferred the tortillas they brought with them. Although tortillas are commonly known today, in the 1950s they were a novelty in northeast Montana. I'd never seen one before and didn't much care for them when I first tasted one.

Shearing took about four or five days. The shearing truck had a gas generator attached to the shearing machine, which sat atop the truck bed. There were five shearers on each side. The sheep were herded into the corrals, and the shearers would grab one, lay it on its haunches, and go to work. They were very skilled and fast, though at times they would nick a sheep and cause some bleeding. The cuts were never very serious, and Ed or Leo would daub the nicks with sheep dip. When the ewes were let out of the corral, it was pandemonium. They milled around and created a cacophony of bleating as they desperately looked for their lambs. My job was to herd them away from the corrals. It wasn't easy. The ones who couldn't find their lambs would try to head back to the corrals, and I had to constantly round them up and get them away. The sheared ewes were kept separate from the others until shearing was over. But some would be separated from their lambs for a couple of days. They were the most difficult to handle. Three thousand agitated ewes and lambs are a handful. Eventually, though, when shearing was over, they all mothered up. Usually that meant the start of my summer of sheepherding. In 1956, however, Mother Nature had another harsh lesson in store. It came the day shearing ended.

Ama Nature Strikes

The sacks of wool were loaded onto our Chevy flatbed truck. They were ten feet long and stacked high on the truckbed. Then they were tied down securely for the trip to Glasgow and the consignment barn near the railroad tracks. From there they were shipped off to the buyer's destination, usually St. Paul, Minnesota. About midday, Ed left for Glasgow with the wool. My mom had gone back to Nashua. Jerry was getting ready to head home, too, and Leo Debray had hitched up his sheep wagon to the back of his pickup and was getting ready to leave.

I was with the sheep down on the creek a quarter mile or so below the sheep shed. Off to the north I could see a band of dark clouds. A storm was coming. The sheep were still agitated from shearing, and now the wind was starting to kick up and the temperature was dropping.

I rode back to the shed at a gallop to catch Jerry before he left for town.

"I think we better put these sheep in the corral," I urged. He seemed annoyed and disagreed.

"Just bed them down out of the wind below Two Buttes," he said, nodding toward the twin buttes about a mile away.

"That's not enough shelter there." I was pleading now.

"They'll be all right," he said, dismissing my concern.

"Dammit, they won't," I said angrily. "They're already starting to run."

The sheep were basically naked, and it was getting colder. This is eastern Montana, and temperatures have been known to plunge quickly. In his book *Eastern Montana,* John Alwin describes temperature drops and rises of a hundred degrees or more in a few minutes. I had seen rapid drops in temperature many times and so had Jerry. That's why I was urging him to help me put the sheep into the corral. But he was more interested in going home to his wife and new baby, so he left. I then rode over to Leo, who was hitching up his sheep wagon.

Surely Leo would be smart enough to see I was right and would help me. Leo was a middle-aged man, supposedly descended from French-

Indian trappers and wise to the ways of nature, or so I thought. It was he who had immediately recognized the wolf he and Ed had assumed was a coyote.

To further complicate matters, our old sheep dog Ring was useless. He had one bad leg and was too old to keep up with me even when I walked the horse. Leo had a big yellow dog that wasn't bad as a sheep dog, but we didn't let him around the sheep much because he was vicious. Instead of nipping them around the legs like a good sheep dog, Leo's dog would tear into them, ripping flesh. I once got so mad at that dog I got the rifle and was about to shoot him when Leo intervened. He had been indignant. "You don't know how to handle that dog," he said. That was true. But he was a killer and I didn't like him.

Leo also reassured me that the storm wasn't serious. I pleaded with him to help me but he dismissed me disdainfully. I was only seventeen years old. What did I know?

So Leo left, and I was alone with three thousand milling ewes and lambs and a storm now beginning to hit. Even the dog abandoned me and went back to the line shack, where he could slink under the porch. The cold rain hit and soon turned to sleet. The sheep began to move fast. I managed to get back to the sheep wagon and grab my heavy canvas overalls and rain slicker.

By the time I got back to the sheep, they were running with the wind and sleet across the flat, heading southeast toward the Little Porcupine about six miles away. I tried everything I could to stop them. I screamed, yelled, tried to call them with a pppppPRPRRRRRRRRrrrrrr, an ancient Basque sheep trill they would ordinarily respond to. Nothing worked. I jumped off the horse and grabbed them and tried to turn them around, but it was futile. At one point I took off my belt and tied it around a ewe in an attempt to make her into an instant lead sheep. I thought maybe I could get the others to follow, but they ignored me and kept running. I was so mad I was crying. The driving sleet against the lenses of my glasses nearly blinded me. I cursed Jerry, Ed, and Leo.

"What's the matter with those damn fools?" I thought. "These are their sheep."

The sheep stampeded past me, trying to get out of the frigid weather. Many just laid down on the prairie and died. I tried to urge them to get up, even lifted some to their feet, but they just took a couple of steps and dropped. They were dying of hypothermia. All I could do was urge them to run faster toward the Little Porcupine where there was heavy growth of buckbrush, chokecherry, willow, and cottonwood trees. The sheep knew what to do. I just followed them.

Most of the herd finally arrived at the Little Porcupine and plunged into the wooded shelter. The wind had let up some, but the rain was still coming down hard, shifting from sleet to rain to hail. It was getting dark, and I was still trying to locate small bunches of ewes and lambs and herd them into the brush. Although it can stay light until 10 P.M. in the Montana summer, the storm brought on early darkness. After what seemed like hours of riding through wet brush, I had located all the ewes and lambs I could and hunkered down under a cutbank sheltered by some chokecherry. I was hungry and cold. There wasn't much I could do but stay with the sheep. So I took off the horse's saddle and used the heavy wool blanket to sleep under. It was soaking wet, of course, but wool is the warmest fiber there is. The blanket was also still warm from the horse's body, and the heat from my body eventually permeated it. I used the reins to make hobbles for the horse so she could graze, and I went to sleep exhausted. I had stopped crying but felt angry, guilty, and disgusted, all at the same time. I dreamed of the day I could leave Montana forever. I never wanted to see another sheep, ever, for the rest of my life.

By morning the storm had stopped. The sun was shining, and there were dark clouds racing across the sky. The sheep began to mill about and started grazing. I was famished. We were on the Scott Brothers range, and I had to move the sheep back up out of the Little Porcupine and head them toward Tomato Can. Then I remembered that the Scott Brothers had a line shack up on this creek not too far away. I moved the sheep out onto the flat and rode over to the shack. It was just an old clapboard and tar-paper shack with a sheep camp stove, a bed springs, and a cupboard. Much to the joy of my growling stomach, there were two cans of Van Camps Pork & Beans. I used my jackknife to pry open one can and gobbled down the contents.

Food had never tasted so good. I thought about eating the second, but decided that someone else might be in my position someday and left it. Later that summer I replaced the can I ate. It was obvious nobody had been to the line shack since my visit.

Driving the sheep back across the flat was depressing. There were dead ewes and lambs strewn across the five- or six-mile stretch they had run. A few lambs hovered around their dead mothers, bleating as if they were imploring the ewes to get up. I had a hard time getting them into the herd. Most were old enough to graze on their own, so they would survive. About midday Jerry arrived. I could see his pickup rattling across the prairie. He pulled up and looked at me with what I thought later (pun intended) was a sheepish, guilty look. I lit into him.

"Look at this, goddamnit," I yelled. "I told you we should put them in the corral. But no, you wouldn't listen. You and that son-of-a-bitch Leo think you know everything. I'll tell you something. Someday I'm going to get out of this godforsaken country and never look at another goddamn sheep again."

Jerry said, "OK, OK, you were right. Take it easy. Let's get these sheep back to Tomato Can."

But I wouldn't stop. "What the hell do you think I'm trying to do?"

He changed the subject. "You want something to eat?" He produced a couple of ham and egg sandwiches, and after eating, I calmed down a bit.

We counted the black sheep. Three of the seventeen were missing. Black sheep were important because they were markers. If a black sheep was missing it meant that other sheep were gone, too. Jerry drove off in the pickup looking for strays. He came back with a few later that day, but there were no blacks among them. I spent the rest of the summer during the hot middays riding into the coulees and brush of the Little Porcupine looking for strays. It took until the first of September to find them all.

For years afterward I would feel myself get hot when I thought about this event. I could never understand how those older guys could have let this happen when I tried to warn them. Maybe I was angry that they wouldn't listen to me because I was just a kid. I guess this episode was more traumatic for me than I realized. It was branded into my memory. At family gatherings, long after we were all out of the sheep business, my mother would use this example to praise me as "the best sheepherder in the family. Joost like his father," she would say. My older brothers would tease her that she only said that because I was the baby of the family.

Mom would shoot back indignantly, "Buh teirrriet! He was the best sheepherder in the family." End of discussion. Although we would all laugh and it made me a bit self-conscious, I had to admit she was right.

I often tried to figure out why my older brothers could make such a stupid mistake. In Jerry's case, it might have been the fact that he had a new baby daughter and was anxious to get home and be with her. He wasn't that old, only twenty-four, and though he could have been a good sheepman, he was not really happy in the business. As for Ed, I have concluded that there might have been a cultural element involved, which I'd never before considered.

The area around Nashua is really wheat country. There were some cattle outfits and a couple of sheepmen, but the economic elite were wheat farmers. They were our neighbors, many were friends, and some of them made a lot of money wheat farming between the end of World War II and the 1960s. I believe Ed felt somewhat self-conscious about being a sheepman. He never was very good at it, though he worked hard. But he was sensitive to any hint that he wasn't much of a sheepman. He'd left home soon after graduation from high school, and after the war and a short stint at the University of Montana, he got a job in Adak, Alaska. A huge airbase was being built on Adak, and Ed worked as an expediter and ran the PX. My mother used to say that Dad referred to Ed as a *botechia,* which apparently meant "storekeeper." In fact, Ed was a good salesman of appliances and of cars, which is what he did after leaving the sheep business. Mom was convinced it was his Ippeagurre blood.

Ed always took the wool to town after shearing. He made it clear that this was his job. I think that when he drove through town with the huge load of wool sacks he was making his statement—it was his harvest—just as the wheat farmers announced theirs when they pulled into the town grain elevators with truckload after truckload of wheat. He ignored the oncoming storm because he'd been eager to make his harvest parade through town, perhaps as a boost to his self-esteem.

The Fire

Except for a couple of nasty thunderstorms, things were uneventful until late August, when still another disaster struck. Our leases, Tomato Can and Mud Lake, were adjacent open ranges and considered one lease. There was no dividing line as such, although a pass coulee ran between the Tomato Can west to Mud Lake. The distinguishing feature of the two leases was that the Mud Lake lease, about eight thousand acres, had water only in the spring after the snow melt. There were no springs like Tomato Can, which had not only a creek with water holes but four springs.

Because it had no water, Mud Lake was not as desirable a lease as Tomato Can. Mud Lake was an alkaline lake of about 250 acres. If we had had a heavy winter, the water from the snow melt might last until July before drying up. It was never more than a few inches deep and was muddy and foul-tasting to boot. Livestock would drink from it only in an emergency.

I had a herding routine to take advantage of the plentiful grass on Mud Lake. I'd graze the sheep there one day and on Tomato Can the next so they got water every other day. The day the prairie fire started

I happened to have the sheep down on the creek. In hot weather, sheep don't graze from about ten in the morning until around four in the afternoon, when it begins to cool. They bunch up close together with their heads down to catch the shade of each others' bodies. The creek bottom had no grass. What little there was amid the alkali and gravel had been grazed down. This proved to be fortunate. I was sitting on a hillside above the sheep late in the afternoon. They had just started to move, grazing slowly up the hill toward Mud Lake. I would gradually graze them over the dividing ridge, thick with blue-joint. At dark I would bed them down below the sheep wagon, perched on the highest point overlooking both Mud Lake and Tomato Can.

Off to the southeast, above Mud Lake, lightning began flickering down from blue-black clouds. A storm was coming. My first thought was, "Damn, I hope it isn't hail." The previous summer I'd been caught in a nasty hailstorm with hailstones the size of large marbles. I'd hunkered down below a cutbank of the creek under an overhang of sagebrush. It wasn't much shelter. When those hailstones started hitting the horse, I couldn't hold her. She roared, squealed, whinnied, and finally broke away from me and took off. Fortunately the storm didn't last long. Aside from a few bruises I was OK, but it had taken me hours to catch the mare.

As I sat on the hillside dreading the thought of hail, I noticed smoke billowing up about a mile away. "Fire," I said to myself. "What the hell else could happen this year?" Soon the smoke was rising in thick bluish columns over Mud Lake. I quickly moved the sheep back across the creek to the other side and rode to the top of the ridge. There on the big flat above Mud Lake was a line of fire moving quickly across the dry blue-joint.

The wind was from the southeast and blowing hard enough to kick up dust swirls around the creek. The fire continued to move rapidly. I rode back down to the creek and made sure I kept the sheep down there. There was no grass to burn, so they were probably safe. I shuddered at the thought of their being on Mud Lake that day. An image of three thousand roasted mutton passed through my mind. The smoke got so thick it began to get dark. The fire became visible and was burning up toward the sheep wagon. I thought, "Oh, oh, that wagon is a goner." My can of high-test gas used for the lantern was sitting away from the wagon. The fire was burning right toward it. But I was in luck. The sheep had bedded down near the wagon and had trampled and eaten the grass down to stub. The fire burned to about twenty yards from the gas can and died out. It then began to burn down the ridge toward the creek but again ran out of grass to burn and went out.

Within a couple of hours after the fire started, there was no visibility to the west. I stayed on the creek with the sheep and wondered if the fire would reach the farms nearby. The Furhmans, Zvonars, and Joe Hollis were within its path. Jerry and Ed had been haying down on the Milk River Valley. Jerry spotted the smoke and knew instantly that it was Tomato Can. He jumped into his Plymouth and drove as fast as he could toward the smoke, rattling across the prairie, on and off roads. In the thick smoke I heard a vehicle. Soon, bursting through the smoke on the ridge above the creek, came Jerry's '53 Plymouth. He skidded to a stop. I rode up to him. He was pale.

"You all right?" he asked.

"Yeah. So are the sheep." I nodded to them down on the creek. "A case of pure dumb luck," I exclaimed. "If this fire started yesterday we'd have had three thousand roasted mutton." He swore to himself softly, and after we talked a while and he was satisfied I was OK, he left. Later that afternoon Mom came up to the line shack to see if I was all right. She brought some fried chicken and potato salad. A side benefit of the fire, I thought. I was getting pretty tired of my own cooking.

A week or so after the fire, a weather front came in, and it rained for three or four days. It was slow, steady rain and fortunately came just after wheat harvest. By early September the burned acreage was sprouting green grass. The next year Mud Lake again had a thick, deep layer of blue-joint. You'd never know there'd been a fire.

I came in from the hills in early September for my senior year and didn't go back to Tomato Can again until early October. I was quarterback of the Nashua High football team, and that occupied my interest until it was time to ship the lambs to market. Ed and I trailed the lambs from Tomato Can down the Little Porcupine and through the Buggy Creek drainage to the stockyards at Oswego. We moved them slowly, taking three days so the sheep could graze. We didn't want them losing weight. Weight translated into dollars. We had nice eighty-pound lambs that year.

As we trailed the sheep to the stockyards, Ed loved to tell stories about when he and John were in college at the University of Montana after the war. Like millions of other veterans, they had gone to school on the GI Bill. The money wasn't much and they were always broke. When they had hocked their radio and everything else of value, Ed would take John to the bar of the Florence Hotel in Missoula and ply him with dime beers. After enough beer, he would persuade John to send a telegram to my uncle John and ask for some money. They didn't want my folks knowing they did this. I'm not sure why. Uncle John was my brother John's godfather and namesake and would do anything for him.

After Ed had gotten John sufficiently stoked with dime beers, John would send off the telegram asking for $100. Uncle John never failed to deliver. It was not easy for him to get to town. Someone had to take him from the sheep camp into Wolf Point so he could wire the money. But John was his godson so of course he would do it. Later, when he retired, he lived with John and his wife in Missoula when John was in college. They used to take him dancing. He loved it. All the young women would dance with him, and he probably had the best time of his life. It's hard to imagine how he danced at all, since he could barely walk, but somehow he did.

Uncle John was my dad's oldest brother, born in 1878. I always knew him as an old man who had one leg shorter than the other. Although he wasn't crippled, he had a severe limp and walked with a cane. He was a quiet, kindly old guy whom we all treated with deference because he was the oldest member of the family. I remember one Christmas when Mike and I had a puzzle on the floor of the living room. It was almost completed. Uncle John, who had come for dinner, entered the room and walked right over the puzzle, messing it up completely. We started to groan, but my dad shot us both a look that meant "Not a peep out of you guys, understand?"

Uncle John stopped right in the middle of the puzzle, oblivious of our discomfort. "Well, Renald," he said, "you sure are growing now." He slipped his hand into his pocket and pulled out a half-dollar. "Here's something for Christmas." I have no idea why he called me Renald. I hated the name, but of course I never said anything. He might have confused me with my cousin Ronnie, whose name was Ronald. I don't know. But the half-dollar sure was welcome. That was a fortune to me in those days.

A lifelong bachelor, Uncle John, as Mom used to say, spent fifty years in the sheep wagon. He came to the United States in 1902 to work for a Basque sheepman in Jordan Valley, southeastern Oregon. He didn't stay there long. No one is quite sure where he herded, but we know he ran sheep around Mount Charleston, not far from Las Vegas, Nevada, and near Reno. Years later my mother explained his limp. In 1906 Uncle John was herding sheep in the mountains outside Reno and was thrown from a horse and broke his leg in several places. He was brought to San Francisco to the French Hospital, the oldest in California. He was in French Hospital when the 1906 earthquake hit. Mom didn't know if the limp was caused by his horse injury or if it happened in the earthquake.

Uncle John, Uncle Pete, and Fred and Domenica Granada were in the sheep business together for years. They ran sheep on the Little Porcupine, Buggy Creek, and other areas near Frazer and Oswego. Domenica was my godmother, a cousin of Mom's. Once in a while during the summer when I got tired of my cooking, I would ride down to their ranch for a real meal after the sheep had bedded down. It was only about three or four miles from Mud Lake, and I could get down there before dark. Domenica was a great cook and fed me until I couldn't stuff anything more down. I remember riding back to the sheep camp in the moonlight, so full I'd almost fall asleep on the horse.

Rene Had a Little Lamb

When we got to the stockyards, we had to separate the ewes from the lambs. That year we sold the wether lambs and only half the ewe lambs, since we needed some to restock the herd. It took nearly all day to get them separated, and then we had to load them onto the boxcars for shipping. That meant I had to go to work with my partner Mamie, the lead sheep. I had raised Mamie from a bum lamb. She was now about four years old. As a lamb she used to follow me all over like a dog. I had to lock her into the corrals when I went to school or she'd follow me. My brothers used to tease me by chanting, "Rene had a little lamb." She was named after Mamie Eisenhower. It was my mother's idea. She thought Mrs. Eisenhower was wonderful and was sure she'd be proud to know our most prized bum lamb was named after her.

Mamie was a good lead sheep. I would get a rope on her, we'd walk into the lamb herd, and then I'd lead her onto the boxcars, the lambs following behind. I guess we must have filled up seven or eight boxcars, and Mamie never quit on me.

A couple of years later when I came home on leave from the army, Ed and Jerry bet me that Mamie would still remember me. It was winter, and the sheep were in the pasture of our farm on the Milk River west of Nashua. When we went down to feed them I got out of the truck and called her name. Sure enough, she came out from the middle of the herd and ran up to me. Ed laughed, "She's still your pet." I've always considered sheep stupid and was surprised that she remembered me. She didn't stay around long when we started throwing the hay off the truck. But when we left she looked back at me and gave me a good-bye bahhhh!

I spent one more summer herding sheep after graduating from high school. I promised Ed and Mom I would stay until we shipped the lambs in October. This was 1957. After the lambs were shipped and the sheep trailed back to Tomato Can, my sheepherding days were over. A high-school buddy, home on leave from the navy station in China Lake, California, was returning to his base. I decided to leave Montana with him. I said good-bye to Mom and Ed, and we piled into my friend's '55 Olds 88 and took off for Las Vegas. My brother John lived there, so my buddy dropped me off for a visit before I enlisted in the army. My dreams were finally coming true. I was off to see the world.

Jerry left the partnership a couple of years later and went to broadcasting school in Minneapolis. His sheepman days were over, too. Ed and Mom finally sold out in 1962 and moved to Las Vegas. The combination of low wool and lamb prices and some bad years finally convinced them to sell.

The Tihistas were finally out of the sheep business. My cousin Jed, Uncle Pierre's youngest son, and his sons are still in the livestock business. So is his brother Bud's son. But they are cattlemen. The Tihista sheepmen are no more. It was a pretty good life. We never had much money, but as my mother always said, "We had plenty to eat."

All of us are scattered now. Ed died of a heart attack in 1989 the day before his sixty-seventh birthday. Jerry was killed in a car accident in Seattle in 1992. Mom passed away in the summer of 1994 and is buried alongside my father, uncles, and cousins at the cemetery in Glasgow, Montana. My brother Mike lives in Seattle, Paul in Glasgow, John in Las Vegas. My only sister, Irene, married soon after graduating from high school, about the same age as my mother did, and started her own family. She is the only one of us who stayed on the land. Her son and one of her daughters farm winter wheat in the High Line community of Gildford, in north-central Montana, an area known as the richest winter-wheat belt in the world. She raises a big garden every year and cans vegetables, just like my mother used to do.

We're all fully assimilated Americans now. The only Basque most of us remember are the cuss words, which flowed freely around our place. There are now grandchildren and great-grandchildren, second and third generations, typical Americans. None are sheepherders, though.

8

Santi's Story

WILLIAM A. DOUGLASS

Santiago Basterrechea Irazabal, son of Gregorio Basterrechea and Donata Irazabal, was born in 1940 on the *baserri*[1] Goikola in Gerrikaitz-Munitibar, Bizkaia. Times were tough. The Spanish Civil War had ended only a few months earlier, and Europe was embroiled in the Second World War. Throughout Santiago's formative years, Spain, under the dictatorship of Francisco Franco, remained an international pariah and was left out of Europe's dramatic postwar economic recovery. For the young Santiago, Goikola provided plenty to eat and solid shelter, but there was regular rationing of many of life's necessities and luxuries—bread, cooking oil, sugar, and tobacco. "We grew our own wheat, and there was a mill in the village. So we always had good bread. After school they gave us rationed bread to carry home. It was almost black, and we would feed it to our pigs. We got by, but I always thought of us as being poor."

Above all there was also the political oppression:

Our schoolteacher was not Basque and we were not allowed to speak the language. We had a kind of *cartera,* or wallet, that passed from one student to another. If you had the cartera and heard someone speaking Basque you gave it to him. At the end of the month whoever had it had to pay a fine of two or three pesetas.

At that time there were a lot of Spaniards coming to work in the Basque Country. We kids called them *belarri motzak* ("short ears"). They knew what it meant and you could get punished for saying that.

I hated the Spanish *guardias civiles;* just seeing them in their uniforms made me angry. They could be pretty rough with you. When there was a festival in the village they would come, and sometimes they might slap you on your legs with their guns.

Lots of young men came back to our village sick after military service. They were paid so little and the food was so bad that their families had to send them bread from home. I heard lots of bad stories about the Spanish army.

So in 1957, at age seventeen, or just before he became eligible for military service, Santi emigrated to the American West. Although Goikola was a traditional baserri in a backwater village, Santi's world was anything but circumscribed, for this was an area of Bizkaia with a strong tradition of emigration. Gregorio Basterrechea was the youngest in his family. He was also adventuresome. In 1920, at age sixteen, he had emigrated to Idaho. Unlike many a young Basque immigrant he had neither relatives nor friends in the New World, although all three of his elder brothers had herded sheep in Idaho and then returned to the Basque Country to live. Through a Basque hotelkeeper in Boise, Gregorio managed to secure a job as a sheepherder near Twin Falls on the Bell Newman ranch. After twelve years with the same outfit he returned to his home in Gerrikaitz-Munitibar.

At age thirty Gregorio married Donata Irazabal. They were the same age and cut from the same cloth. Donata was the eldest of six children. Her mother, Florentina Mendiolea, was widowed early, when Donata was only sixteen, and had raised her young family on Goikola. When Donata was about thirty, Florentina decided to turn her baserri over to one of her sons, as was the custom, but she also wanted ten thousand pesetas for it—a large sum of money at the time. The only son in a position to consider the offer was her second-born, Benito, aged twenty-eight, who had herded sheep in the American West and then returned to Gerrikaitz with his savings. But Benito thought the price for Goikola too dear, and he also wanted to return to the United States. Donata offered to buy the baserri out of the twenty thousand pesetas she had accumulated working for years as a maid in the coastal town of Lekeitio. So Gregorio married the "heiress" of Goikola, and they set up housekeeping there with Florentina, as was the custom.

Gregorio did not fight in the Spanish Civil War (1936–1939). During the conflict and afterward he farmed Goikola. Gregorio was a mountain of a man, famed throughout the region as a weight lifter. He competed frequently in the contests held during village festivals. He also harbored the dream of returning to the American West and, in 1950, managed to do so. No longer young, Gregorio wanted to blaze a trail for his four sons.

In 1953 he brought his eldest son, Luis, aged seventeen, to Idaho to work for Bell Newman. Gregorio had a knack for study and whiled away his time in the sheep camps learning English, a language in which he became quite fluent. But it was more than a pastime for him. In the early 1950s the contracted-herder program was emerging.[2] While it permitted sheep ranchers to recruit Basques in Europe, it also limited the length of their stay in the United States to three years. So in 1955 Gregorio passed his examination and became an American citizen, a status that allowed him to facilitate the unrestricted entry of his sons into the country.

In 1957 Gregorio sent for his second-eldest son, Juan. In that year the Bell Newman ranch was sold, and Gregorio, Luis, and Juan all went to work in sheep for Manny Patterson in Gooding, Idaho. Despite being the most experienced, Gregorio remained a herder so that his sons could camptend and engage in general ranch work. He believed that it would give them more knowledge, exposure to American life, and opportunity. "I always wanted to come to America. My father was there, my uncle was there. Luis and Juan were there. My father always told me that whenever he got off the plane in New York he was so happy he would kneel down and touch the ground. He was an American citizen, so I didn't need a sheepherder contract—I could go as a student. But I wanted to herd sheep and make lots of money. That was my idea."

Thus in 1958 an excited seventeen-year-old Santiago Basterrechea took the long taxi ride from Gernika to the Madrid airport and boarded an airplane to the United States. Unlike the often weeks-long ship-and-rail journey of earlier generations of intending Basque sheepherders, Santiago's trip would be measured in hours. Yet, curiously, it recounts many of the same anxieties and sense of wonderment.

When I was in Madrid I was afraid of the authorities. I didn't feel like I was in my own country. I thought that for some reason they might stop me from getting on the plane, but they didn't. During the trip they offered me some food, but I wasn't used to American cooking and I couldn't eat it. The man next to me kept talking in English and I couldn't understand a thing. I could tell that he wanted me to eat something.

In New York they took me to a small room and told me (in Spanish) to stay right there. I waited for three or four hours and I was getting very hungry. Then someone came for me, but he only spoke English. With gestures I made him understand that I needed something to eat. He took me to a restaurant and ordered me a big plate of spaghetti. I really enjoyed it, but then I started to worry. I had a ten-dollar bill and I wasn't sure if it was going to be enough.

I handed them my money and pretty soon they came back with nine one-dollar bills. They looked just like the ten-dollar bill—the same size and color. I wasn't used to that. I thought this is a pretty good country!

Then they had me wait with some other passengers and a black man sat next to me and started talking. He touched my shoulder, which made me jump, and the other passengers started laughing. That was the first black man I had ever seen, and it scared me when he touched me. At that time I had no idea about the problems between blacks and whites in this country, but it still scared me.

I changed planes again in Salt Lake. My father met me in Boise and I sure was glad to see him!

Gregorio took Santiago to Gooding to work for Manny Patterson. At first Santi worked as a herder, summering his sheep near Ketchum.

I had good days and bad days. When you're young you're always thinking about going to town. But I enjoyed herding. I loved those Idaho mountains and big rivers. I liked to hunt and fish. But there was no future in herding. There was more opportunity in construction. For the first couple of years I thought of saving money to go back to the Basque Country. I told my father[,] "I'm gonna save $10,000 and then go back." He told me that was a good idea, but that I would change my mind. He was right about that, because after two years I decided to stay here. And then they made me camptender for my father, so I was with him all the time.

In 1961 Gregorio sent for his youngest son, Antonio. So, briefly the father and all four sons were in the United States together. That same year Gregorio returned to Gerrikaitz, after an eleven-year separation from Donata.[3]

Luis was the first of the Basterrechea brothers to leave herding. First he went to Gooding, where he worked in construction, but then he secured a position tending bar in the Stockman's Hotel in Elko, Nevada (owned by Dan Bilbao—another Bizkaian immigrant). Luis worked there for several years and then married an American woman. Eventually he moved back to Idaho and founded Basterrechea Distributors, which has become one of the major trucking firms in the Gooding and Boise areas. With a fleet of thirty-five trucks, the business now specializes in long-distance hauling, primarily for Idaho's Simplot Corporation (the supplier of potatoes to the McDonald's restaurant chain).[4]

For a while Santiago, Juan, and Antonio continued working together for Manny Patterson. But Antonio hated sheepherding, so his older brothers sent him to their uncle, Nicasio Irazabal, who was living in Eureka, Nevada.

Nicasio had come to the United States during the 1930s as a merchant marine. By then his brother Benito had returned to the United States (after refusing to purchase Goikola) and was again herding sheep in Idaho. Nicasio jumped ship in New York and made his way to his brother's side. Later they both left herding and went together to Ely, Nevada, where they found jobs at the Kennecott copper mine. Subsequently, Benito went back to the Basque Country, married the heiress of a farm in Munitibar, and lived there for the remainder of his life. Nicasio, however, married an American woman and eventually acquired a roadside restaurant, motel, and service station on Highway 95 fourteen miles east of Eureka. Nicasio (Nick) had no children, so he was pleased that his nephew wanted to come to work for him.

Juan was the next to leave Manny Patterson. He went to California for a job herding sheep near Sacramento. Juan and Santiago corresponded, and Santiago joined his brother in 1962. They decided to move to Reno to look for jobs in construction. "I loved Nevada. The first time I saw Elko I liked the gambling and the twenty-four-hour life. I was young and single."

In Reno the two brothers first stayed at the Santa Fe Hotel. During their initial few days there, Joe Moulian, a Gipuzkoan Basque foreman for Arlington Nursery, called the hotelkeeper looking for some workers. Juan and Santiago were hired and worked for the next six months in landscape gardening. Meanwhile, Santiago had become friendly with José "Joe" Bengoechea, who was from Gizaburuaga, Bizkaia. Joe was driving a truck for Helms Construction Company, Reno's largest. By then it had a reputation of preferring Basque employees; at one time it had more than thirty. Joe put in a word for Santiago, and he went to work for Helms in 1963.[5]

Antonio had been living in Eureka for a year and had tired of life at the remote roadside business, so he joined his brothers in Reno, working first as a dishwasher at the Holiday Inn and then as a construction laborer for Helms. The three Basterrechea brothers shared a house with Joe Bengoechea and another Bizkaian Basque that they knew from the old country, Ramón Jayo (from Munitibar). All five bachelors worked for Helms Construction.

Santiago began attending night school in order to pass his citizenship examination. In 1963 he became a U.S. citizen—"that was my proudest day." It also allowed him to return to the Basque Country for a visit, with impunity from obligatory military service in the Spanish army.

In 1964 I went back to the Basque Country on my first trip. I wanted to see my mother. I bought a car in France and was just traveling around from place to place enjoying myself. I thought I might stay for a few months. Well, one day I came across an accident on the road between Bermeo and Gernika. Two women were going to Bermeo in a taxi—Carmen Maruri and her boss. The boss owned a coffee shop in Eibar. The taxi was hit by a truck. Carmen was injured only a little bit, but the other lady was more serious. So I drove them to a doctor in Gernika.

The next week I was in Gernika and I saw Carmen. She was waiting to catch the train to Eibar. We started talking about the accident and I offered her a ride. After that we started going out together. When it was time for me to come back to America I changed my plans. I stayed there for almost a year before Carmen and I got married. She was from the baserri Kosmena in Murelaga. We came to Reno together, and I went to Helms Construction. They gave me my old job back.

Carmen immediately began studying English both privately and in classes at Reno High School.

Meanwhile Juan had decided to join his uncle Nicasio in Eureka. He worked there for a year, returned briefly to Reno, and then went to work for his brother Luis, driving a truck in Idaho. When Nicasio died a widower, the four Basterrechea brothers inherited equal shares in the

Eureka roadside business. It was decided that Juan would operate it. He stayed there for three or four years until the business was sold. He then returned to Reno to work for Helms and, in 1981, succumbed to cancer at forty-three years of age. Juan had never married.

In 1972 Antonio returned to the Basque Country and while there he married a woman from the town of Mendata. They returned to Reno, where he worked as a construction laborer until his untimely death in a traffic accident in 1998.

After bringing his bride back to Reno, Santiago Basterrechea drove a truck for construction companies — primarily Helms — for the next thirty years. He and Carmen have two daughters — Gloria (Maria Gloria) and Rosie (Rosa Maria). In 1995, at fifty-four years of age, he went into semiretirement to care for his rental properties and to enjoy more free time. During his working years Santi had managed to construct for his family a beautiful home in one of Reno's better neighborhoods. He also built four rental houses in the burgeoning Galena Creek area, doing much of the work himself with the help of Carmen's brother Tony. The two brothers-in-law both own rental homes that they assisted each other in constructing on weekends and after their regular work hours. Santiago and Carmen also own a five-plex apartment building and have managed to provide each of their two daughters with their own house. Santiago states with great pride, "It's all paid for. I owe nothing."

Santiago and Carmen are clearly an example of the American immigrant success story. They have also faced throughout their adult lives the immigrant's dilemma: how to reconcile two worlds. Both had their parents and other family in the old country. Culturally and linguistically, life in the United States meant conscious, daily adaptation to what a "native" takes for granted.

Carmen was very homesick here in Reno. So in 1971 she went back to the Basque Country with our two girls for a visit. She started looking around and found a condominium to buy in Gernika. I sent her the money, and then I went there to see my family. I thought maybe we would have to live in the Basque Country if my wife was unhappy in America. I considered putting in a bar or café like some other emigrants have. I was a truck driver, so I also thought about buying a truck and going into transportation for myself, like Luis had done in Idaho.

We furnished that condominium and I really thought we were going to live there. But then Carmen changed her mind. She decided that life in the United States was better and she wanted to come back! So we sold the Gernika property, and I left the money there in a bank account. When it looked like the peseta was going to be devalued, in 1975 I called my brother-in-law Juan in Aulestia and told him to find me some real estate. They were building some new condos in Markina Etxebarria, which is just a few miles from Gerrikaitz-Munitibar. Juan bought me one, and it sat vacant for a year, until our next trip. That's when we furnished it. So now whenever we go back for a visit we have a place to stay. The rest of the time it just sits there empty.

Once back in the United States and committed to an American future, Carmen became a licensed baby-sitter. For the past twenty-three years she has provided professional child care in her home and thereby contributed to the family's economic security.

Another challenge was the "Americanization" of the family inherent in the birth and upbringing of the next generation in this country. "At home we always spoke Basque to both of the girls. When they went to school they didn't know English, but after a few months they didn't want to speak Basque. We always talked to them in Basque, but they answered back in English. One time they wanted bicycles. I agreed to buy them if they would promise to talk to me in Basque. I brought the bicycles home and the girls were so excited. They said, 'Oh Dad, thank you very much.' So that was that!"

There were, however, many ways both small and large to create a "Little Bizkaia" within the confines of one's own private space and leisure time. Like that of many Basque-American homes, the Basterrecheas' family room is adorned with family photographs, reminiscent of the formal living room in the Basque baserri. Their den is decorated with two Basque-dancer dolls, the Zazpiak Bat Basque nationalist escutcheon, a *bota* bag from Pamplona, a pair of traditional Basque footgear (*abarketak*), and several carved wooden plaques, including an escutcheon of Bizkaia that also commemorates Iparraguirre's "Gernikako Arbola" (the Basque national anthem). Santi is proud of his collection of Spanish wines.

The Basterrecheas' Reno world also encompasses extended kin. Santiago's brother Antonio and sister-in-law Severina have five children. And then there is Carmen's brother, Antonio Maruri. He came to Los Banos, California, in 1969 to herd sheep on a three-year contract. But within two years his sister had taken out her U.S. citizenship and was able to formalize his permanent residency. He was, therefore, able to leave herding before his contract was up. He moved to Reno to work in construction and as a plumber. He married an American woman, and they have two daughters. So nine cousins in the next generation of Basterrecheas/Maruris have grown up in Reno, Nevada. To this day the three families socialize frequently, celebrating holidays and family events, or just getting together for a backyard barbecue.

Nor were Gloria and Rosie Basterrechea cut off from their Old World relatives. In 1974 their grandparents, Gregorio and Donata, visited Reno—as did Gregorio by himself in 1978 and 1981. Both their old-country maternal uncle and paternal aunt and uncle have visited Reno, as have some of their European cousins.

Then there were the family visits to Bizkaia. Since their return to the United States in 1971 Santiago and Carmen have gone back to the Basque Country for visits in 1975, 1980, 1982, 1986, 1990, 1992, and 1994. "From now on Carmen and I plan to go to the Basque Country every year. We have that condo to stay in. We both like to go for a month or so, but I can't see us retiring there. America is our home now. Our family is going to be here."

Gloria and Rosie are thoroughly American. They attended Reno schools and both have impressive professional careers. After graduating from the University of Nevada, Reno (UNR), Gloria got her law degree from the University of Arizona. She lives in Las Vegas with her non-Basque architect husband. Rosie graduated from UNR with a dual degree in criminal justice and social work, did graduate work, and is a social worker for Washoe County. Yet both daughters did receive special exposure to their Basque heritage as a part of their formal education.

I spoke to Gloria about going to school in San Sebastián on the University of Nevada's program. I used to read the newsletter from the Basque Studies Program, and I thought the San Sebastián opportunity was ideal for my daughter. Gloria liked the idea. I had taken her to the Basque Country several times, but my girls were kind of afraid and shy when speaking with their European cousins. Gloria and Rosie could understand Basque—and Spanish, too. They studied Spanish here in high school. But they didn't have much confidence speaking either one. So Gloria went to San Sebastián, and a few years later so did Rosie. Now Rosie asks me, "When are we going to the Basque Country?" She really wants to go back. Gloria wants to take her husband there as well. But when they do they plan to see more of Spain, and France and Italy, too.

Santiago has also sustained Basque associational and friendship ties in Reno throughout his adult life. While he was still single, or in the early 1960s, there was a move to found Reno's Zazpiak Bat Basque Club. Santi became one of the founding members and movers of the effort. Over the years he has served several terms on the club's board of directors and has frequently chaired the games committee that organizes the athletic competitions during the annual Reno Basque festival. He still specializes in cooking *chorizos* for the club to sell to the public during the festivities.

Santiago and Carmen attend four or five Basque festivals each summer. They usually manage to visit Bakersfield, Los Banos, Elko, Boise, and sometimes Winnemucca in this fashion. They have also attended two of the three *jaialdis* (large cultural happenings) held every few years in Boise. So whether serving as sponsors to visitors of the Reno festival or attending the Basque festival in other communities, about half of the Basterecheas' summer weekends are configured by their Basque heritage and contacts.

And then there is Santi's friendship circle, particularly in retirement. He and Ramón Jayo and Tony Silonis (from Ea, Bizkaia) hunt chukars together each year in northern Nevada. They use the cabin at Buffalo Meadows owned by the Basque sheep rancher John Espil. Santi describes their time there as "going to the sheep camp," an experience that carries its own special nostalgia. They also traveled together recently to fish for trout in Idaho's Snake River.

Santi also has a regular group of friends that includes Joe Bengoechea, Ramón Jayo, and Juan Acordagoitia (from Ereño, Bizkaia). All four men are now retired, and every Wednesday they go together to Gardnerville, Nevada, to eat lunch at the Country Club restaurant or the Overland Hotel (both are Basque establishments). They then spend the afternoon playing the card game *mus* together.

When asked to sum up his view of the future of Basque-American culture, Santi replies,

> When I first came to this country there were a lot of Basques and more arriving all the time. But then the herding was over and hardly anyone comes now. The Basques here are getting older and are dying off one by one. There are still quite a few Basques left in Reno—

both French Basques and Spanish Basques. I think the Reno club will last for a few more years, but after that I'm not sure.

When they were teenagers my girls didn't want to go to the Basque picnics; they liked American activities more. But now they are a little bit more interested. So I don't really know what will happen in time with Basque culture in this country. I'm not too optimistic.

Santi's story epitomizes the rapid evolution of the Basque-American experience during the second half of the twentieth century. By the time that he came to the United States in the late 1950s he was following a well-worn course charted by his father, both his paternal and maternal uncles, and two of his siblings. Indeed, by 1957 the Basterrechea nuclear family was as much established in Gooding, Idaho, as in Gerrikaitz. Gregorio was an American citizen, although Donata was not. Gregorio headed up the "Gooding household," which included three of his five children; Donata managed Goikola, where her daughter and youngest son continued to reside. It would be the sister, Maria Gloria, fourth-born within her generation, who would marry and inherit Goikola—all four of her brothers having opted for a New World future. This was decidedly *not* the custom—and is a prime example of the changing dynamics in late-twentieth-century rural Basque society as well.[6]

Although he didn't know it at the time, Santiago was entering the world of the Basque sheepherder during its waning years. While exempted from the contract-herder program, most Basques herded sheep under it and were required to leave the United States after three years. This, of course, meant that herding, for the most part,[7] had ceased to be an effective avenue whereby some Old World Basques entered the United States, passed through a period of purgatory in the sheep camps, and then eventually settled on ranches or in small towns— thereby renewing the Basque-American community. Santiago was able to follow such a career path, thanks to his father's foresight. Most of his fellow herders did not have their Gregorio.

Santiago's arrival coincided with another development within the Basque-American community. Cut off from adequate recruitment of Old World–born members, Basque-American culture faced the prospect of reproducing itself or simply dying out. Given that many Basque-Americans had but scant knowledge of Old World–Basque culture there was also the challenge of forging or inventing some sort of viable Basque-American cultural reality.[8] A kind of syncretic Basque-American cultural symbolism emerged, fragments of both Basque and U.S. rural traditions (peasant farmsteads and western ranch life). By the early 1960s there was a burst of associational energy among Basque-Americans that resulted in the creation of two dozen Basque clubs, many of which formed their folk-dance group and sponsored an annual Basque festival. Indeed, attending part of the "festival circuit" each summer became one of the prime ways to both express and reinforce one's "Basqueness."

As we have seen, Santiago was instrumental in the founding and maintenance of Reno's Zazpiak Bat club and in the staging of its annual festival. However, as Basque-American culture moves further away from its Old World–peasant and American West–sheep-ranching roots and closer to the new millennium, it is becoming apparent that the club and festival syndrome is itself evolving.

The emergence and activities of NABO, the overarching North American Basque Organizations, Inc., have regionalized or even nationalized Basque-American culture in the United States. The creation of the Autonomous Basque regions of Euskadi and Navarre, as well as the devolution of some powers from Paris to the regions in France, have empowered Old World–Basque politics and created a climate in which the "Mother Country" is now able to reach out to her diasporic offspring. All of this is, of course, greatly facilitated by the technological and transportational advances that have transformed the contemporary world into a global village.

The ease with which the Basterrecheas move between Reno and Gerrikaitz, the many visits from their Old World relatives, and the course work of both Gloria and Rosie in San Sebastián as part of their American university education are all manifestations of the evolving new reality of the Basque immigrant in the United States, as well as that of his/her descendants. In short, Santi's story is that of the transition of a thoroughly traditional Bizkaian farm lad into a thoroughly modern Basque American. It is also an individualized version of the collective Basque-American experience in late-twentieth-century America.

Part III

Modern Basques

9

Lyda Esain
A Hotelera's Story

JERONIMA ECHEVERRIA

One could easily argue that Lyda Martinto Esain was destined to become a *hotelera*.[1] Several members of the Esain and Martinto families had been Basque hotelkeepers before her. Lyda's mother, Marie Amestoy, left her natal village of Banca, France, in spring of 1900 after securing a job at Jean Pierre Martinto's Basse Pyrenees Hotel in Tehachapi, California.[2] From the neighboring village of Ortzaize, Martinto left his hometown thirteen years before Marie, intending to herd sheep in Kern and Fresno Counties for one of his older brothers.[3] After eight years of herding, Martinto began investing in property in the town of Tehachapi, eventually purchasing six unimproved lots on Main Street, building the town's largest hotel, and putting up an adjoining livery barn. Not long after opening the hotel and livery, Martinto also constructed a handball court of stone and cement on the premises. The handball court received a great deal of attention from local players as well as from Basques throughout the state.[4] Between 1895 and 1908, when the Basse Pyrenees enjoyed its peak years of business, hoteleros Jean Pierre and his wife, Veronica, sent for young Basque women from the Banca-Orzaize region. Like Lyda's mother, they came to work as cook's helpers, as housekeepers, and as serving girls.

During the two years she worked at the *ostatu,*[5] Marie met many local Basques, as well as those traveling to and from Los Angeles and Bakersfield. A regular at the Basse Pyrenees was Jean Pierre's younger brother Dominique, who worked at the Tehachapi lime kiln at that time with a few other Basque woodchoppers.[6] In 1902 Marie and Dominique married and, shortly thereafter, decided to move to San Pedro, where Dominique's older sister Marie Martinto Laffargue helped them find work among a small colony of Basques employed in the local shipyards and docks.[7]

After about five years in San Pedro, Dominique and Marie were once again considering other opportunities. This time, another of Dominique's brothers, Jean Fermin, urged them to move to the San Joaquin Valley and try their hand at farming. By this time, the couple had a son, Victor, born in 1904, a daughter Grace, born in 1906, and a third child on the way. Dominique began traveling between San Pedro and central California to work with Jean Fermin on valley ranches. In the fall of 1910 the Martinto brothers bought an eighty-acre farm off Highway 99 near Malaga, and Dominique returned to San Pedro to move his wife and children north. Although the brothers knew little of raising, caring for, and selling Alicante and Zinfandel grapes, alfalfa, or fruit produce when they began, they learned quickly. A few months after moving to Malaga, on February 5, 1911, the third Martinto child was born. Within weeks, Lyda Martinto was baptized at the Roman Catholic Church in Tehachapi so that her parents' friends and family could celebrate the occasion at Uncle Jean Pierre's Basse Pyrenees Hotel.

Lyda's childhood was much like that of non-Basque children growing up during the same years. Like others, all the Martinto children were born at home with the help of a midwife in modest circumstances with relatively little fanfare. Lyda recalls the birth of her younger sister Jeanette: "In 1916, when I was five, my mom was making lots of noise one day and the French neighbor who was a midwife came over. She told us kids to go sit by the highway and watch the traffic for awhile. When we came back, we had a baby sister."

In the same year, Lyda began attending Malaga's four-room schoolhouse. She, Grace, and Victor walked the mile to and from school every day throughout their grammar school years. With the help of her older brother and sister, and the urging of her teachers, Lyda learned to read and write in English; at home only Basque was spoken. After graduating from Malaga Grammar School, Lyda attended Fowler

High School. From first through twelfth grades, she and her siblings were the only Basque children in Malaga and Fowler schools. As Lyda quips when talking about their situation, "They didn't even know what a Basque was. . . . Sometimes I think the kids thought we were saying we were *fish*!" Although no Basque families lived in Malaga, the Martintos always spoke *Euskara* (the Basque language) at home and frequently received acquaintances, friends, and family driving nearby Highway 99. In addition, they often traveled south to Tehachapi to visit Uncle Jean Pierre and Aunt Veronica. Or, when there was a wedding, baptism, anniversary, or birthday celebration among Fresno County Basques, they would join in at John Bidegaray's Hotel Bascongado on the west side of the Southern Pacific railway tracks in downtown Fresno.[8]

After graduating from Fowler High in 1929, Lyda considered a career in nursing. For a time, though, she had agreed to help her parents at the Malaga ranch. Lyda joined her mother in the daily cooking for the family, ranchhands, and guests, seasonal canning of fruit and jam, and occasional curing of meats such as *lomo* and *chorizo*.[9] In addition, she helped with household chores and cleaning, picking grapes during peak seasons, driving family members to and from town, and irrigating the fields when needed. As Lyda put it, "There was lots of work to do. Everyone knew about the ranch. People would stop by and Mother would cook for them. Sometimes we'd laugh among ourselves. We'd call the Ranch the 'Free Hotel.'"

One day in 1930 Felix Esain came out to the Martinto ranch to talk with Marie about helping him and his partner at the Santa Fe Hotel on Tulare Street. Esain and Javier Eleano had leased their ostatu and enjoyed a steady clientele but were having trouble finding a suitable cook. Knowing Marie's culinary skills, and that she had worked at Tehachapi's Basse Pyrenees years earlier, Esain pleaded with Marie to work for them until they could hire a permanent cook. Marie reluctantly agreed, knowing that Lyda could drive her to and from town as well as pitch in a bit more at the ranch.

When they arrived at the Santa Fe on Marie's first day of work there, Marie invited Lyda to go inside with her. Lyda declined, replying, "What am I going to do in there with all those men?" On the second day, Lyda's curiosity prevailed, and she went in—and met Felix Esain. As Lyda described it, "He was so nice I didn't mind going back every day. In fact, after a while, I'd go in to see if I could hire extra grape pickers from the hotel boarders." Lyda and Felix began dating and, in

1932, were married. During their first few months together, the new-lyweds vacationed in California and Nevada, often staying in Basque boardinghouses or camping with other couples in the Sierra Nevada.

After trying a brief stint of chicken ranching on the outskirts of Fresno and working a second job at a bar in town with Paul Yturri, Felix began looking for something else. In 1934 the Esains learned that the owners of Fresno's Basque Hotel were looking for new renters. The original Basque Hotel had been constructed by the Laxague family near the turn of the century and was operated in subsequent years by Juan Villanueva and then by John Bidegaray. The Esains knew that the establishment had long been a popular mainstay for Fresno's Basques and had the potential to be a successful business venture. After driving between two jobs for a few years, and after the birth of their son Victor in 1933, the Esains saw the Basque Hotel as an opportunity to live and work in one place as a family. So in 1934 they decided to lease the hotel from Julie Bidegaray.

At the time, the two-story boardinghouse contained twenty-eight dormitory-style rooms upstairs, with bathrooms and showers at the ends of an L-shaped hallway.[10] Downstairs contained a small two-bed-room apartment for the Esains, a long bar, an ample kitchen, a small office, and a very large dining room lined with long, family-style tables. In 1934, when the Esains took over at the Basque, boarders paid a dollar a day in exchange for three meals, a room, and one straight shot of whiskey, which they called an "eye opener." Boarders ate in the large dining room, but the Esains sometimes preferred family meals in the kitchen.

Until they could afford to hire additional staff, Lyda and Felix were the Basque Hotel—they cooked, cleaned, tended bar, washed laundry, helped the boarders find jobs, and performed numerous unexpected tasks. When needed, Marie came in to town to help prepare for large parties or sometimes to play with her grandson Victor. After four years at the Basque Hotel, in 1937, the Esains decided to stay and contracted for a 6 percent loan to buy the hotel outright. Within three years, they were able to pay the loan in full. As their business grew, they added wash basins to each of the upstairs rooms, expanded the kitchen and dining rooms, and added a dance area. In 1941 they built a large, partially covered *cancha* alongside the north side of the building, where Felix, Victor, and dozens of local and visiting Basques enjoyed daily games of *pelota*.

In many ways, Lyda and Felix were the ideal hotelkeeping couple. Born in Euskal Herria (the Basque Country), Felix's command of

Basque and Spanish exceeded his English by far. Lyda, on the other hand, had a strong command of English but could communicate readily in Basque and Spanish. An Old World Basque like Felix and New World Basque like Lyda were able to offer their clients an ideal combination of services and skills. If a boarder needed assistance with some aspect of surviving in the greater Fresno community, for instance, he asked Lyda to advise him. Oftentimes, Lyda accompanied her boarders during doctor's appointments or to consult a lawyer, for example. If a visiting herder wanted to open a savings account at the local bank, Lyda was the likely candidate to serve as translator. Felix could not have served in this capacity as well; but he did help boarders find work, and he tended to represent and maintain the Old World social and cultural aspects of the Basque community that were vital to Basque boarders. Felix, for example, organized all the *mus* (Basque card game) or handball competitions at the hotel. He also made a point of stopping to visit other hoteleros in Fresno, buying drinks for their customers and encouraging neighborliness on a regular basis.[11] In the Basque Hotel itself, Felix discussed local ranching and the concerns of his customers and shared relevant information with his boarders and clients in Euskara.

In 1951, after seventeen years of hotelkeeping, Lyda and Felix decided to sell their hotel. When asked why they came to that decision, Lyda responded, "Well, after nearly twenty years of working every day, a person gets tired. No matter how much you love it, you get tired." If one assesses their decision to purchase the Basque from only a financial perspective, one would have to claim the venture a success, for the $15,000 the Esains invested in the Basque multiplied in value over seven times by the time they sold it in 1951.

The Fresno Basque Hotel was not simply a financial or economic venture, however. Instead, as Lyda has stated, "We worked together for nearly twenty years, under one roof, at the Basque. It wasn't just going to work, to our jobs. It was our daily life. It was where we lived. Everyone gathered there." The spirit of Lyda's remark has been echoed by many other hoteleros, suggesting that those running the boardinghouses knew they were doing more than earning their daily bread. In fact, the boardinghouses offered a number of conveniences that helped newcomers cope with the unfamiliar.

Hoteleros located in transit centers were often called upon to assist with the details of traveling across the American landscape. From 1890 to 1940, the peak decades of Basque hotelkeeping, a Basque arriving by train in Fresno, Bakersfield, Los Angeles, Winnemucca, Reno, Elko, or Ogden had only to gaze across the street in front of the depot to find a Basque boardinghouse he had heard about at his last stop. Of the nearly five hundred hotel sites found in one study, only a handful were beyond the train conductor's whistle.[12]

Once inside the hotels, the Basque immigrant discovered that a number of additional conveniences were provided. In some instances, if a Basque did not have a job upon arrival, the hotelkeeper was likely to set about in search of work for him or her in the community, on a neighboring ranch, with a sheep outfit in the area, or in another customer's home. In the meantime, the hotelkeeper might extend liberal credit, room, and board in exchange for the newcomer's future business and eventual repayment.

Among Basques and those who write about them, the *ostatuak* are often referred to as "home away from home." When asked what made the boardinghouses their second homes, boarders have been most likely to include the following characteristics in their answers. A brief review of the list makes evident that while the newcomers may have depended on the boardinghouses in diverse ways and in varying degrees, each was undoubtedly dependent upon them for their assistance:

1. Basque language
2. Basque cooking
3. Basque games
4. Basque music and dancing
5. Help finding work
6. Short-term loans and/or credit
7. Advisers/*etxe amak, etxe aitak*
8. Place to find a mate
9. Place to find other Basques
10. Help with translating in town
11. Help with travel to other towns
12. Storage place for gear and/or Sunday suits
13. Place to receive mail
14. Place in town where wives might deliver children
15. Place in town to recuperate from injury and/or illness
16. Place in town to board children while in school
17. Place to celebrate family's special occasions

Further, each ostatu and its hoteleros played a part in establishing the larger network of Basque ethnic boardinghouses that fanned out throughout the eleven western United States. By the twentieth century, hotelkeepers were aware of the reputations of other boardinghouses throughout the American West and referred clients regularly. The emergent network contributed to solidifying the settlement of Basques in the western states as well as helping second- and third-generation Basques remember and revisit their ethnic roots.

There are many ways in which a hotelera—like Lyda Esain—played a key role in the greater scheme of Basque hotelkeeping. Although Basques have often referred to a specific boardinghouse by the name or surname of the *etxe aita,* the personality, hospitality, and graciousness afforded by the *etxe ama* often influenced the quality of their stay much more.[13] Thus, a boardinghouse might have been referred to as Arrieta's, Barbero's, or Fermin's, but its popularity may have been more dependent upon the hotelera. In fact, by considering a few women who operated ostatuak, one begins to sense that the hoteleras were often more critical to the success of their enterprises than first imagined.

Reports of Maria Echanis, for example, lead one to believe that she was the heart of her boardinghouse in Ontario, Oregon. After herding sheep in eastern Oregon for five years, Jack Echanis returned to Mutriku, Gipuzkoa, to seek the hand of his childhood sweetheart in marriage. Maria accepted, and when the two went back to Oregon, they joined Jack's partners in a sheep outfit in Stinking Water. There Maria cooked for two of her brothers-in-law, the two Urquidi brothers, and a few hired hands. She also worked a bit at the Urquidi boardinghouse in nearby Crane.[14] Because Maria was popular as camp cook and had gained experience working at Urquidi's, her friends and customers talked her into opening her own *ostatua*. When she and Jack moved into Ontario, they opened their home on Oregon Street as a boardinghouse. That wood-frame structure burned down in 1929, and a new, twelve-bedroom structure replaced it in 1930.

In addition to raising her own five children in the ostatua, Maria also addressed other young customers as if they were her offspring. Many of them called her Etxe Ama or simply ama. In Maria's words, "These boys and girls were so far away from home. They not only needed good food and a room they could call their own, they needed companionship."[15] Thus, "Mom Echanis's place" became a second home for many of Oregon's young Basques and provided a maternal figure for comfort, advice, and encouragement.

Maria Echanis was known for her generosity throughout the four decades she served the Ontario Basque community. As her daughter once stated, "In looking back, I don't see how Mother managed it all. Sometimes, during fair time, she would be cooking breakfast, dinner, and supper for as many as forty people. Then, in the middle of the morning would come a younger brother who was hungry and would ask her to fix him some chorizo or something. She always did everything for them, and so cheerfully." [16]

Depictions of other well-loved hoteleras are also available. One Boise Basque, remembering mother and daughter Letemendi, stated that "almost everything I became in America I owe to Letemendi's. . . . I don't think I could have made it here without them." In fact, Boise author Patrick Bieter suggested that the term "tough love" best described Leandra Letemendi.[17] Showing up late for one of Leandra's meals, for example, usually resulted in a serious tongue-lashing. Yet a young Basque who learned the importance of punctuality in Leandra's house also benefited from her compassion. When she discovered one young man alone, crying on his first birthday away from home, for example, Leandra put her chores aside, sat down, and talked the young man through his homesickness.

In Elko's Overland Hotel, Gregoria Sabala was known for taking young herders and serving girls under her wing, acting as their mother, counselor, and nurse. Expectant mothers in their final months of pregnancy left their Nevada ranches and traveled to Elko's Overland to be closer to a midwife or physician in case problems arose. By necessity, most were delivered by Gregoria instead. As Gregoria was known to quip, by bringing so many lives into the world, she specialized in "rural free delivery." [18] In addition, when the dread influenza epidemic of 1918 struck Elko, the Overland's rooms and hallways were strewn with fifty to sixty afflicted patients. Once again, Gregoria called upon her nursing skills, and as she later boasted, she did not lose a one.

In Bakersfield, "Mama Elizalde" was one of the San Joaquin Valley's most well-known and well-loved hoteleras. Like many of her boarders at the Noriega Hotel, Graciana Elizalde loved to gamble and wagered on an array of events ranging from pelota matches in the adjacent cancha to the vagaries of human nature. As one might suspect, betting has not been unusual among Basques of either gender. Graciana's generosity upon winning, however, was. On one occasion, Graciana began wagering on the gender of a serving girl's expected child. When Grace was proven correct—against the wagers of most of her customers—she collected their money and opened an account in the child's name. "Mama Elizalde" is a legend in part because of her forty-two-year tenure at Noriega's, but also because she shared her resources and time whenever she thought the cause warranted.

In Carson City, Nevada, Theresa and Dominique Laxalt opened their small French Hotel a few streets from the state capitol. In *Sweet Promised Land, The Basque Hotel, Child of the Holy Ghost*, and *Deep Blue Memory*, their son Robert and granddaughter Monique describe how Theresa stepped in to run family business matters, discipline children, manage and cook for the small hotel, and generally keep things going while Papa was away in the sheepcamps.[19] These depictions remind us of the many hoteleras who have served as the primary operator of the family ostatua and done so with grace and generosity.

Laxalt's account of his mother's role at the French Hotel is reminiscent of another accounting of women's work in an Old World fishing village. In that study, Charlotte Crawford describes the multiple responsibilities that wives assumed as their fishermen husbands left for the five-month cod season.[20] In each of these chronicles, women of the village took on full accountability for their families in the absence of their husbands. In many instances, they did not fully relinquish their responsibilities upon their return.

Lyda Esain, Maria Echanis, Leandra Letemendi, Gregoria Sabala, Graciana Elizalde, and Theresa Laxalt are representative of the hundreds of Basque *etxeko andreak* who managed and tended their boardinghouses. Out of necessity, these transplanted countrywomen learned and mastered their lots in life. Learning to live in a new land, attending to the birthing, nursing, nurturing, and caring for others, all the while combining these traits with a successful business enterprise, was complicated, challenging, and unfamiliar. As Lyda reflected, "That idea I had at eighteen of being a nurse at Saint Agnes Hospital went out the window. I never got there, but I probably did more nursing in the hotel than I would have in the hospital anyway! Sometimes our boarders needed insulin shots, special feeding, or special care. Whatever it was, we did it."

Perhaps the most basic characteristic shared by hoteleras was that they were in the hotels at all times, with only a few, rare exceptions. Although their husbands or business partners may also have worked seasonally in sheepcamps or on ranches, or locally as blacksmiths, lumberjacks, miners, or construction workers, the women dedicated their entire effort to the concerns of the ostatuak, even raising their own children in and around the steady demands of hotelkeeping. Thus, a Basque seeking any sort of assistance from the hoteleros knew he or she would be able to locate the etxe ama on the premises at all times. Examples abound of hoteleras dropping their work to respond to a customer's emergency.

The significance of the etxe amak is reflected in the powerful association between maternal figures and our homes. Perhaps the young men and women of Euskal Herria, having established an ostatua as their second home, found it comparatively easy to associate with their own mothers the familiar language, foods, and caretaking provided by hoteleras. Eventually this seems to have led to the symbolic acceptance of a surrogate maternal figure. Whether Basques consciously considered the strong association between their a "new homeplace" and accepting a "second mother" as adviser and parental figure is doubtful. Nonetheless, that it happened frequently is unquestioned.

Three recent studies have touched upon the role of the hoteleras.[21] One suggested that compared with their male counterparts, hoteleras did more than their share of the work and had more rigorous schedules than the men. Although the majority of informants for these studies have been female and could be accused of bias, the distribution of work between men and women in the hotels is certainly worthy of consideration. Moreover, one former male resident of Los Angeles's "Basque town" reported that the women he remembered working in the hotels were virtually slaves, performing every variety of task needed to keep the enterprise going.[22] Daily work began around six in the morning and lasted until the last customers were served, with breaks and/or free afternoons granted during lulls in the hotel's busy routine.

Undoubtedly, work for the etxe ama, the serving girls, cooks, and *criadas* in the hotels was difficult and challenging. A number of variables affected how burdensome the hotelera's tasks became: the hotel's popularity, the relationship between the hotelkeeping couple, the years the ostatua was in business, the hotel's location, and the intensity of local competition. In fact, in reporting the difficulty of her work, a hotelera for whom "times were good" and who remembered in later years "making a good living then" was less likely to emphasize the irksome workload because she had often been able to hire enough people to staff her boardinghouse. In smaller and less profitable enterprises, however, hoteleras have proven more likely to focus on their daily toil.

As one would suspect from examining life in the *ostatu euskalduna*, hoteleras never reported that work in the boardinghouses was easy or light. In cases where the hotelero worked outside the boardinghouse— perhaps in nearby sheepcamps on a seasonal basis or in a local enterprise that took him away from the premises on a regular basis—hoteleras were more likely to state that they were often tired, sometimes embittered, and occasionally depressed. Because they carried the primary responsibility for the ostatua on their shoulders, these women no doubt had a heavier workload in their boardinghouses than did their husbands. Further, hoteleras have preferred to remain anonymous if discussing the amount of work they performed in comparison with their deceased husbands, as they resist seeming disloyal.

Even though the hotelera's daily routine was subject to unpredictable events and sudden demands, it was also surprisingly consistent. The list below contains a composite or prototype of a hotelera's daily schedule based upon hundreds of interviews and discussions with hoteleras.

HOTELERA'S DAILY SCHEDULE

Time	Activity
5–6 A.M.	Wake up; organize kitchen, make sack lunches for boarders and children; begin preparation for midday meal
6–8 A.M.	Cook and serve breakfast to family and boarders
8–10 A.M.	Organize and oversee cleaning girls; set up noon meal; clean rooms, common areas; washing, gardening; errands in town—groceries
10 A.M.–noon	Set tables; cooking in earnest for noon meal; continue with housecleaning details
noon–2 P.M.	Noon meal
2–4 P.M.	Errands in town; clean up after lunch; continue unfinished work from morning; gardening, sewing, canning
4–6 P.M.	Oversee children returning from school; set up evening meal; cooking
6–8 P.M.	Dinner
8–10 P.M.	Clean up; visiting with friends; children to bed
8 P.M.–midnight	"Special occasions" (dances, family parties)
Midnight–2 A.M.	Weekend entertaining; often early breakfast or card crowd

Although the extensive list of daily chores often meant an eighteen- to twenty-hour workday, women like Lyda Esain who toiled two, three, and four decades alongside their husbands offer another perspective. In such cases, one is more likely to hear terms such as "our work" and "our business" rather than differentiations between "his" and "her" work. Much more commonly, hoteleras reflect that although the work was hard, these were the best years of their lives.

Thus, although most Basques who lived and worked in the ostatuak freely acknowledge the women's rigorous workload, one would be hard pressed to claim that their lot was always more difficult than the men's. John Beterbide's sons in Alturas, California, for example, remember that their father worked a daily twelve-hour shift in the local lumber mill before returning to their family boardinghouse, eating dinner, tending bar until closing time, and cleaning the premises thereafter.[23] In sum, it seems misleading to generalize that all hoteleras outworked their husbands when hotelkeeping families vary in their assessments.

Distinctions are easier to make, however, when discussing the nature of the division of labor on a gender basis in the boardinghouses. As mentioned earlier, Felix Esain's responsibilities tended to be the barroom, cardroom, cancha, and outside employment contacts, whereas Lyda's were in the kitchen, dining hall, laundry, and rented rooms. Remembering that the combination of an Old World male and an American-born Basque female often yielded the most successful hotelkeeping couple, the list below contains an overview of the hotelkeepers' characteristics, responsibilities, and duties, as they have most commonly been reported. Some functions—such as visiting with other hoteleros at neighboring ostatuak, running in-town errands, or accompanying customers to dental or physician's appointments—do not appear below because they may have been shared.

HOTELKEEPERS AND THEIR DUTIES

Felix Esain	Lyda Martinto Esain
Old World–born Basque	New World–born Basque
More Basque, less English	Less Basque, more English
10–14 years older	10–14 years younger
Tending bar	Keeping house
Maintaining stockroom	Buying groceries
Organizing mus games	Canning and preserving foods
Organizing pelota tournaments	Organizing cooks and staff
Keeping family accounts	Overseeing children
Overseeing livery, stables	Gardening
Repairing building	Mending and sewing
Cleaning after hours	Doing laundry

Not all women working in the hotels were hoteleras, however. Like Lyda's mother, Marie, in fact, a majority of young Basque women joining former neighbors or family members in the boardinghouses had prearranged work in the ostatuak. In general, the domestic chores of cleaning, cooking, and serving were their lot. In addition, a clear majority of them met their husbands while working in or while attending dances and social functions in the ostatuak. In fact, of 150 Basque subjects interviewed, 85 percent met their spouses in the boardinghouses.[24] Such high endogamous rates among first- and second-generation Basques can be explained in part by a common culture and language, for many spoke Euskara upon arrival.

In 1918, for example, Margarita Osa arrived in Boise holding a contract to work as a maid in Boise's Barbero boardinghouse.[25] As was the practice of the day, part of her monthly wage of eighteen dollars was withheld to repay her transportation from Euskal Herria to Boise. Her daily duties at Barbero's included typical chores such as house cleaning and laundry. Similarly, the fifteen-year-old Lucy Alboitiz Garatea contracted to work with her aunt and uncle at Boise's Aguirre Hotel, also known as Zapatero's. Both women described bleeding knuckles from hand cleaning with scrub boards, sore backs from long work hours, and "housemaid's knees" from crawling on their knees while polishing floors.[26]

Margarita and Lucy eventually became hoteleras in their own right. Margarita and her husband, Marcelino, bought the Plaza Hotel in Burns, Oregon, in 1928 and managed it until 1945, when they sold the establishment to Joe and Paulina Lizundia. Four years later, the then-widowed Lucy Garatea bought the Plaza and managed it for sixteen years. Margarita and Lucy Garatea are examples of young Basque women who came to the United States, gradually saved enough to collect a grubstake, and bought their own ostatuak.

In 1955, Catherine and Pierre Goyenetche came to the United States for the second time. They selected San Francisco as their new home, and she worked at Loustou's French Laundry and he as a gardener. After six years of intense saving, the couple leased the Obrero Hotel, reserving three of the Obrero's rooms for their family and renting the remaining seven to boarders. Only on special occasions did Catherine hire help, for she usually served as cook, Pierre as bartender and host, their son as busboy and dishwasher, and their daughter as waitress and hostess. At the Obrero in the 1960s, for as little as $2.50 per serving, the family successfully produced legendary meals for sixty to seventy people at one evening seating.[27]

From 1961 through 1975 Catherine and Pierre leased the Obrero. To their consternation, they were never able to buy the building because its owners refused to sell. During the 1960s the Obrero and Goyenetches were a central part of San Francisco's busy Basque neighborhood. Catherine regularly passed Basques on Broadway and Powell Streets as she ran errands or shopped in the afternoons. As in other locations, the young men called out to her using the familiar ama in their greeting. Older San Francisco Basques fondly remember Catherine's delicious meals and the raucous after-dinner singing that she often directed.

As in the ostatuak of San Francisco, California, or Burns, Oregon, Basque women in other settings worked extended hours. In fact, work schedules similar to those in the ostatuak could be found among Basque women working alongside their husbands on the ranches of the high desert, where they prepared and served meals to family and ranch hands, cleaned dishes, darned clothing, raised gardens, tended to children, canned vegetables and foodstuffs in the summer, and made chorizo and blood sausage in the springtime. On more than a few occasions, Basque women conducted these activities from sheepcamp tents, which meant cooking over open fires, baking underground with campfire coals, roasting on spits, and laundering clothes on washboards along rivers.[28] Later, when the herds expanded and their husbands prospered, these women enjoyed the comparative luxury of two- and three-bedroom ranch houses, but they generally continued with strenuous daily tasks nonetheless. In addition, Basque women have worked extended hours in the laundries and bakeries of San Francisco, Bakersfield, and Stockton.

Further, one account of Basque hotelkeeping in Nevada suggests that Basque men and women differ in the way they viewed life in the ostatuak. As Gretchen Holbert stated, some sheepherders clung to the independence afforded them by life on the open range: "The hotels, however, were a mixed blessing to the independent herder. This woman-tended haven was both solace and confinement to him, fellowship blended with the loss of absolute freedom. Like the sailor come home to a landlocked village, the herder entered the hotel conditionally, determined to leave. The hotels would be there, red-bricked sentinels of a new order, awaiting his return."[29]

Holbert's commentary underscores the centrality of gender in the daily operation of the ostatuak and the particular role that the *etxeko andrea* played. As ethnic historian Donna Gabaccia has recently reminded us: "Immigrant women carried with them not merely Italian or Japanese or German ways, but also the distinctive female traditions found within their native cultures. To become 'American,' these women invented 'ethnic' female identities. Most immigrant women—like most men—creatively blended old and new in doing so." [30]

Like many other immigrant women who came to the United States during the late nineteenth and early twentieth centuries, the Basque hotelera was blending the familiar into the new while creating a new, hyphenated identity to help her fellow Basques embrace the United States and its culture.

Other authors have suggested an elevated interpretation for Basque women in Old World Basque society. The anthropological and sociological studies of Teresa del Valle, Jacqueline Urla, and Roslyn Frank claim that Basque women play a much more important role in family development, financial matters, and societal development than they are often credited. In other words, the New and Old World *andreak* are much more influential than they seem. [31]

In a U.S. counterpart to such studies of Basque women, Deborah Fink's *Open Country, Iowa* outlined three modes of women's work on the Great Plains. [32] In the first case, women labored on the farm to help sustain the family, perhaps raising crops, milking cows, and preserving food items. In the second, women worked within the house or farm to produce goods—such as weavings, butter, preserves, or eggs—in exchange for products outside the home. In the third, women toiled outside the household in order to earn money to help support the household. Basque hoteleras participated in a combination of all three strategies. They raised crops, hogs, chickens, and cattle for their kitchens, they sewed for their customers and families, and they traded for goods not found in the ostatuak. Finally, they lived with their families in their workplace.

Certainly, the *Euskaldun andreak* played a greater role in the survival of early communities than Basque-American literature suggests. All too often, such literature has featured the "lonely Basque shepherd" who roamed the American West with his band of sheep. True, a majority of Basques arriving at the turn of the century intended to herd for a few years and then return to Euskadi (the Autonomous Basque Community in Spain), but sheepherding is not synonymous with Basque identity. In fact, many Basque men married girls from villages in their home provinces, found other forms of work, and planted roots in the western United States. [33]

Further, the Basque shepherd needed an elaborate support system in order to succeed. The Basque ostatuak and the hotel network helped fulfill this need and thus were critical factors in the newcomer's transition to America.[34] This was especially true in the earliest decades of Basque immigration in the United States, from 1880 through 1930. Beyond those years, however, we have witnessed the settling of Basque immigrants. Those young Basque bachelors began to find sweethearts, marry, and raise children, just as Lyda and Felix had done in the early 1930s.

After sixteen years of providing a support system for Fresno-area Basques, the Esains decided to sell the Basque Hotel to Jean and Marie Nouqueret in 1951. Then Felix, Lyda, and Victor vacationed in the Basque region for four months. Working at the ostatu without a family vacation probably encouraged them to take the long trip to Euskal Herria, as did Felix's fondness for the village and family members he had left behind in 1916.

Just as thousands of Basques before them, the Esains stopped to visit with Valentin Aguirre in New York City when they departed from and returned to the United States. Lyda remembers that Valentin greeted them at the docks upon their return and asked, "What did you miss most about America?" To her surprise, many months later, a Christmas card from Valentin arrived, restating her answer: "Good ol' American whiskey!" Not accidentally, Valentin and Lyda shared a characteristic common among successful hoteleros—they remembered their customers' preferences.

After returning to Fresno, during their first year of retirement, the Esains began considering the restaurant business. "After all," Lyda stated, "it's not the right thing to be just sitting around. One has to do something." Felix and Lyda opened the Villa Basque Restaurant on North Blackstone, and "business just zoomed" from 1955 to 1971. On good days, for example, they and their staff served two hundred or three hundred meals, and on days like their last Mother's Day at the Villa Basque, they served a thousand people. In 1971 Felix began having health problems, and the two decided to retire. As Lyda says, "That time we went from semi-retired to real retirement."

For more than two decades after, Lyda remained a vital part of Fresno's Basque community until her death in March 1999. One had only to sit beside her at the old Basque Hotel for a few minutes before realizing that one was accompanying a local dignitary. Whether at the bar, the tables, or the front door, her old customers were likely to walk over and ask, "Do you know this lady? I tell you, I think she did more for me than my parents," or "Lyda, she sure helped me in some rough years. She was another mother to me."

When one asked Lyda about her years at the Fresno Basque, she enthusiastically replied: "Those were the best years of my life. I worked side by side with Felix, and Victor grew up there—our whole life was in that hotel. We worked hard, we played hard, and we had such fun." Whether it was because uncle Jean Pierre was a well-known hotelero or because her mother and aunt were also successful hoteleras, Lyda clearly provided ample evidence of her unique role as etxe ama to Fresno Basques. Her hospitality, warmth, and good cheer earned her well-deserved acclaim in Fresno and throughout the San Joaquin Valley. Her life and words illustrated those of countless other hoteleras throughout the American West.

10

Pete Cenarrusa
Idaho's Champion of Basque Culture

J. PATRICK BIETER

On the afternoon of August 2, 1968, in the Spanish Basque city of Irun, Meliton Manzanas, a Spanish police commissioner, was shot several times at close range by a single assailant. Although no clear description of the gunman was given by Manzanas's wife, the attack was presumed to be the work of the Basque separatist organization ETA (*Euskadi 'ta Askatasuna,* Basque Homeland and Freedom). Manzanas was well known among locals as a sadistically brutal official with a passionate vendetta against Basque nationalists. Scholar Robert Clark indicates that "he had been marked for assassination for some time, but it was not until ETA had its first casualty, in June 1968, that the struggle between ETA and the police spiraled upward in open bloodshed." [1]

In August 1968 Pete Cenarrusa was serving his second year as Idaho's secretary of state, a position to which he had been appointed by Republican Governor Don Samuelson. Cenarrusa had deep ties to his parents' homeland and believed passionately in both the American idea of liberty and the right of Basque self-determination.

These two apparently disconnected events—the killing of a Spanish police commissioner and the appointment of Cenarrusa to the highest office ever held by a Basque in Idaho—were to have an intimate relationship, one that continues to exist. This essay will attempt to tell the story of Pete Cenarrusa and his rise to be the champion of Basque causes in Idaho.

The Early Years

The history of Pete's parents parallels that of hundreds of Idaho Basques. His father, Joe, was born on a *baserri* (a small self-sufficient farmstead) near the Bizkaian village of Munitibar; his mother, Ramona Gardoqui, was from nearby Gernika. They both came from large, rural, Basque-speaking families, and as did thousands before and after him, Joe Cenarrusa began life in the United States as a sheepherder. His education was also typical: five or six years in a rural school and the informal education provided by life on a five- or ten-acre mountain farm, with milking, plowing with oxen, and taking trips to town to sell products from the farmstead, and the myriad of lessons taught by a close-knit religious family whose traditions were centuries old. Foremost among the values absorbed in this informal education were a fierce independence and a dogged work ethic. Basque men and women have undertaken some of the most arduous work the twentieth century has provided, from laboring in mines and steel mills in Europe, to cutting sugarcane in Australia, to working in the rubber plantations of Peru, to herding sheep in the American West. Basque immigration to Idaho has taken place virtually all within the twentieth century, affording scholars the opportunity to examine their rapid upward economic and social mobility. Of these trends Pete Cenarrusa is a model example.[2]

Pete's father, Joe, came to Boise in 1907 at age seventeen and, like many others, got his first job while staying at a boardinghouse. A Muldoon rancher named Rawson came to town and hired four young Basques for herding. Joe Cenarrusa was one of them. He later took a job with Tom Sanford, a pioneer Idaho sheep rancher and legislator from Carey. Sanford became something of a mentor for the young Basque immigrant, helping him with immigration problems and later making him ranch foreman. In a 1927 letter to Senator William Borah asking for help with Joe's immigration problems, Sanford gives us a glimpse of his regard for Joe and also of Basque beginnings in the sheep business. Sanford wrote,

> In 1907 a young boy seventeen years of age landed in New York from Spain, and I took him into my employ, for five years he worked

for me and his brother worked for me for four. . . . During the time that Joe Cenarrusa was in my employ I found him to be an exceptional foreigner, both in intelligence and character, so much so that he was received by my family as one of them. After he had severed his connection with me, he and his brother took their saved earnings and bought sheep, which they have operated successfully ever since, he also has invested in real estate and today he has a wife and several children all born in Idaho.[3]

Much of southern Idaho at that time was open range. Cattle, sheep, mining, and the beginnings of irrigated cropland formed the basis of the economy. Railroad centers like Shoshone became focal points of Basque settlement with the seemingly ubiquitous Basque boardinghouse as the center of that local culture. Basque herders lived by the seasonal rhythm of the sheep-ranging year, starting with lambing in the spring and then following the receding snow line into the foothills. Summer found them in the mountain meadows; lamb shipping at the rail centers came next, followed by ranch or boardinghouse life in the winter as they awaited the start of the cycle with lambing in the spring. The work demanded self-sufficiency more than strength, character and mental stability as much as skill. It was lonely, monotonous work, seen by most young Basque men as a starting place but certainly not as a lifetime career.

Joe Cenarrusa had met a young Basque woman named Ramona Gardoqui at Soloaga's boardinghouse, and in 1914 they were married. Although they had been born in the Basque Country in towns only a few miles apart and were about the same age, they first met in Shoshone, Idaho. As Sanford indicated in his letter to Borah, Joe, like many Basque men before and after him, bought his own spread and went into the sheep business. Joe teamed up with his brother Pete, buying a house in the old mining town of Bellevue. The Wood River Valley, now the site of world-famous Sun Valley, was one of the shipping points of a flourishing sheep culture in the first decades of this century. Although young Pete spoke only Basque, he started first grade in Bellevue.

When asked if he felt different or discriminated against at school Pete said, "[I think] the kids in Bellevue first wondered who these black-haired kids were who spoke [such a] strange language. We were ridiculed and pushed around for a while, but I was a determined kid, and I wasn't going to let anyone get the better of me. I whipped the biggest kid in my grade and didn't have any trouble after that. In fact we all later became like one close family." Classes were small in the Bellevue school. Pete graduated from high school with a class of eight. He remembers his childhood with great affection. He describes his father as strong and hardworking, his mother as loving and committed to the family. Five children were born to the Cenarrusas, two boys and three girls. His father came to speak excellent English; his mother, not quite as good but "certainly passable." [4]

Cenarrusa aspired to go to college and in 1936, in the midst of the Great Depression, matriculated at the University of Idaho with a degree in agriculture science. Taking what was called the "University Express," a Union Pacific train for college students, he headed for Moscow. Pete enrolled in an agricultural education program, was soon initiated into a fraternity, and went out for the university boxing team, which in those days competed nationally with the best boxing programs in the country. Pete started as a novice and finished his first year as a semifinalist among the Pacific Northwest lightweight class. He later competed while serving as a marine during World War II.

As Pete was entering the University of Idaho in 1936, a civil war was beginning in Spain. Insurgent Spanish army general Francisco Franco, together with his Italian and German allies, attacked the Republic of Spain from his base in North Africa. The Basques had been given their independence by Madrid in an effort to keep the industrialized Basque country as an ally in the war against Franco. One province, Navarre, joined the rebels, so the Spanish Civil War also became a Basque civil war. Pete's mother's hometown was Gernika, the site of the twentieth century's first saturation bombing of a civilian population. The civil war sent shock waves through Idaho's Basques, nearly all of whom came from the very hills and valleys that were the site of vicious fighting against the invading Franco troops. What was the American Basque response? For the most part it was one of official noninvolvement. By 1936–1937 most of the U.S. Basque population centers were mature and decidedly American. Relatively prosperous Basque homes lined the city center of Boise and other southern Idaho communities. The Basques were succeeding in the United States, and no matter how close the Spanish Civil War came to the old-country farms and villages, no concerted action was to be taken by American Basques to support their brothers and sisters fighting for their homeland. The organizations that existed among Basque Americans tended to be fraternal and social, aimed at mutual support in hard times like deaths or serious accidents. When a Basque Republic representative came to Idaho in 1937 to recruit men and money for the cause of Basque independence, he apparently received little of either.

Idaho's only representation in the war was a handful of leftist "Wobbly" miners from the Kellogg area who enlisted in the Abraham Lincoln or George Washington Brigades led by international Marxists in support of the Comintern's policy in Spain. Indeed, it was this Communist patina of the Spanish Republic that made the Roman Catholic Basques such uncomfortable allies of the Republicans and the choice of involvement such a complicated one for American Basques who felt caught in the psychological crossfire between their old-country roots and their adopted country's official anti-Red policy. It was the prudent thing to stay uninvolved, yet Pete Cenarrusa was uneasy about this decision.

He went to summer school in 1940 for additional course work in Fort Collins, Colorado, and began to study the reports on the Spanish Civil War and U.S. involvement. Hitler loomed ominously over all of Europe; Franco was the uncontested power in a ravished Spain and a divided, devastated Basque Country. Cenarrusa concluded from his studies that the United States had been wrong in its policy of isolation and neutrality and that if he ever had the chance, he would go to the aid of the Basque homeland.

Pete took a job teaching agriculture and coaching in the small west-central Idaho town of Cambridge. He was single and boarded with a local family. Those were uncertain times for a young Basque-American man, as they were for virtually all young American men. Pete had always wanted to fly, had taken an Army Air Corps test, and was reflecting upon the Nazi wildfire now threatening to destroy all of Europe. He wondered if the responsible thing to do was to enlist and be ready when the inevitable war broke out. He left Cambridge for the hamlet of Carey, Idaho, in his second year of teaching, to be near his family, who had moved there. Pearl Harbor ended his turmoil.

Pete went to the neighboring town of Twin Falls to enlist in the Army Air Corps on a Sunday shortly after the bombing of Pearl Harbor. The army office was closed and would reopen Monday—a teaching day for Pete; he would not be free. He was informed that the navy recruiter was in Twin Falls and that he was available on Sundays. Pete volunteered to be a naval aviator, and after finishing the 1941–1942 school year he left Carey for naval air training in Corpus Christi, Texas. He was on his way to combat in the Pacific as a Corsair fighter pilot when his orders were changed from Pacific theater sea duty to a marine dive-bomber squadron stationed at Cherry Point, North Carolina. After trying unsuccessfully to get his orders changed, Pete reported to Cherry Point. He later learned that these dive bombers were to be used in air support for the invasion of Japan, but the dropping of the atomic bombs ended the war abruptly. Separation from active duty brought him back to Carey, a new job, and soon a wife and family.

Returning rural GIs were in need of agricultural classes in southeastern Idaho; Pete was an agriculture teacher looking for work. The needs coincided, and Pete began work as a traveling vocational agriculture teacher in rural Blaine County. He was personable, knew the problems of veterans, and soon developed a reputation as both a teacher and an unofficial counselor of the returned GIs. Also he continued to fly in a war-surplus plane he bought and repaired. In his spare time he gave flying lessons. One of his pupils, Freda Coates, became his wife in October 1947. Freda's family was in the sheep business, as was Pete's dad, who was still living in Carey. As Freda puts it, "A sheepherder's daughter married a sheepherder's son and we've been in the sheep business ever since."[5] It was about this time that Pete got involved in politics.

One of the issues that caught Pete's attention was the highly contentious battle over local-option gambling. His county was divided along religious and economic lines, with tourist-driven Sun Valley and its neighbor Ketchum favoring gambling and the more conservative, Mormon-dominated rural areas opposing it. Pete, who was known throughout the county because he had taught in virtually every section of it, was urged to run against the Democratic incumbent, a former Mormon bishop. But the incumbent had alienated both sides by first supporting gambling and then opposing it, and Pete was elected—a Basque Catholic in a predominantly Mormon area. Thus began the political life of Pete Cenarrusa. For more than forty-five years, Cenarrusa has never lost an Idaho election, either in contests for the legislature or in seven quadrennial races for Idaho's secretary of state. No other Idaho politician can match that record.

Pete gained a reputation for unpredictability in the Idaho legislature. In the words of a colleague at the time, "Pete was considered something of a renegade in his early years in the House."[6] His reputation was as a supporter of sheep and cattle interests, a Blaine County booster, and a friend of education. An example of his local boosterism predates his election to the Idaho House of Representatives but illustrates two of his passions. The hamlet of Carey, which in the 1940s and 1950s had a population of about five hundred, had, under Cenarrusa's direction, built a small airport. A few days before its scheduled dedication Pete learned that President Harry Truman was going to spend the night in Sun Valley, resting from his whistle-stop campaign through the intermountain West. Pete thought of having the president stop in Carey and dedicate the new airport as he passed through the little town on the way to Butte, Montana, to resume the train tour. Pete contacted a Sun Valley–area journalist (who was also a close friend) to see if the two of them could be invited to the president's reception to make the pitch for his airport. They got invited, and Pete persuaded the presidential press secretary, whom he described as becoming "somewhat relaxed" at the time, that Truman's dedication of a small town's humble little airport would make good publicity for a "president of the people."

The next day the presidential caravan did stop in Carey, and Truman polished up his best prose for a place he had mistakenly assumed was being dedicated to the memory of a local service man killed in combat. In fact the airport was being named for a young woman from a prominent Carey family who had died with her boyfriend when they crashed while "buzzing" her home. The mother was in tears as the president went on about the son of Carey who gave his life for his country. A whispering informant set the president straight, and without missing a beat Truman went on about the "good American" young woman whose town thought so much of her that they would name an airport in her memory. Who knows but that simple airport dedication might have added to the Truman upset of Dewey in 1948.

Pete fought for his town and his district with the same feisty competitiveness he had displayed in the ring as a collegian. Perhaps the best illustration is an the incident famous among Idaho politicians of both parties: the Little Wood River bill.

The Wood and Little Wood Rivers provide water to the valleys of Pete's district in south central Idaho. Both are subject to occasional flooding, causing ranchers and homeowners along their banks considerable financial losses. Pete submitted a bill for the construction of a flood-control dam on the Little Wood. A similar bill was presented by eastern Idaho representatives for a flood-control project on a small stream near Rexburg. Both bills made it to the House floor, where Cenarrusa was attempting to shepherd his project. Voting was not particularly along partisan lines but apparently more along religious and philosophic differences, because some voted for Pete's proposal and against the "Mormon" project, some voted for both, some against both, and some only for the Rexburg dam. A legislator who voted for both bills, against both, or for Pete's was all right, in Cenarrusa's opinion. But legislators who had voted against Pete's and only for the eastern project got put on what came to be called "Cenarrusa's Little Wood List" and were made to pay a political price when Pete later took over the powerful position of speaker of the House. The paper napkin on which the list was recorded, which also shows the check marks that indicate retribution had been meted out, is framed and hangs in Cenarrusa's office. Perry Swisher, a former legislator, gubernatorial candidate, and Idaho public utilities commissioner, says that Pete was the friendliest of colleagues, but "no one crossed him with impunity." Swisher tells of another side of the Cenarrusa character, which he describes with considerable emotion. He had been a legislator from Pocatello, in the far eastern part of the state. Per diem allowances at the time were hardly enough to permit families to accompany legislators to Boise, and in the 1950s car or train travel was costly. Swisher tells of the number of times Pete flew him to Pocatello for weekends, going out of his way to help and refusing to take any payment. This kind of collegiality, certainly repeated for scores of others, largely accounts for Pete's selection by his party's caucus in 1963 as speaker of Idaho's House of Representatives.[7]

Pete was speaker for three sessions and presided fairly over the brutal debate on the sales tax. Idaho was deeply divided over the issue of the tax that proponents were urging as a source of funding for education. Opponents from "border" counties, particularly next to Oregon, which had no sales tax, predicted doom for business if 3 percent were added to, for example, the cost of a car. Farmers were won over with exemptions for machinery or other business-related purchases. Republican Governor Robert Smylie had made the sales tax a significant ingredient in his program for the state. Pete supported wholeheartedly the efforts of Rep. Chuck McDevitt, who led the floor fight for the tax. History proved Smylie, Cenarrusa, and McDevitt right: Idaho has been designated as having one of the fairest and most balanced tax programs in the nation. By the mid-1960s Pete was among the most powerful Republican leaders in Idaho, a delegate to national nominating conventions, and chairman of the Idaho delegation that nominated Ronald Reagan in 1980. He was still a part-time politician and full-time sheep rancher when, in 1967, he accepted the appointment by Governor Don Samuelson to replace the recently deceased Edison Deal as secretary of state for Idaho.

Idaho's secretary of state is an elected official who presides over several state functions, such as certifying candidates for elections, registering and supervising corporations, checking recall and initiative signature lists, and carrying out scores of other certifying and registering functions. Cenarrusa intended also to use his stature as a prominent state official "to assist his fellow Basques in any way he could legally help them both here and in the Basque country."[8] One of his most significant actions on behalf of Basque causes came at the time of the trial of the sixteen young Basques charged with the assassination of Meliton Manzanas.

Idaho's Basque Secretary of State

Immediately following the killing of Manzanas, Franco imposed a state of emergency in the three provinces of the Spanish Basque Country that had fought against him during the Civil War, namely, Gipuzkoa, in which the killing had taken place, Bizkaia, and Araba. Since the assassination was assumed to be the work of ETA, a wholesale roundup of suspected ETA members and sympathizers followed the killing. ETA had emerged in the 1950s first as a clandestine Basque language and culture study group among intellectual university students and gradually, in the 1960s, assumed a role as the rallying force for Basque nationalism and linguistic and cultural resurgence. Franco's regime had suppressed any overt expression of Basqueness at even the most local level. By a conscious program of controlling education and the press he seemed determined to eliminate the Basques as a challenge to his hegemony over all of Spain. By stationing huge numbers of heavily armed and brutally efficient state police in the Basque Country, he had an enforcement arm to his nationalistic policies that made any resistance perilous. After the killing of Manzanas, Franco was clearly determined to use the process of prosecution as a brutal and, he hoped, final episode in the continuing battle with the intractable and stubbornly anti-Fascist Basques. What, if any, would be the response to the situation among Idaho's Basque population? How would Idaho's secretary of state react? The answers to these questions form part of the history of the next decade in Idaho. Political scientist Robert Clark reports what happened after the killing of Manzanas. "Madrid declared a state of exception in the Basque provinces," he writes, "and began to round up suspects for questioning. In the course of these arrests, and the several that followed indirectly from the state of exception, 16 members of ETA were individually charged with the crime."[9]

I have interviewed individuals who were among those "suspects" rounded up, and each described, several years after the event, the grotesque interrogation methods used, involving torture of the most sadistic kind. In a society so closely interrelated as the Basque community, one can see how these tactics could politicize entire extended-family networks. Among those charged with the killing were two priests. Clark adds, "In all, five of the ETA members arrested in connection with the Manzanas killing were wounded during their arrest, and nearly every one of them claimed that he had been tortured during the first days of his imprisonment either to make him sign a confession, or simply to intimidate him. Each of the accused repudiated his confession when he had the opportunity to do so in open court." [10]

The trial was to be conducted in a military court. As Clark writes, "Access of the defense attorneys to their clients was sharply restricted. Cross examinations of adverse witnesses was not permitted. The accused were not allowed to testify regarding the brutal methods that were used to extract their confessions." [11] The trial lasted from December 3 to December 9, 1970. Shortly before the trial began, the German consul in Donostia, Eugene Biehl, was kidnapped by ETA. The group indicated that whatever happened to the accused in the Burgos trial would also happen to Biehl. The Basque community and concerned people throughout the world held their breath as the military court began deliberations.

Pete Cenarrusa, now Idaho's secretary of state, was being informed daily about the happenings in Burgos and the Basque Country. His young son, Joe, had studied in the northern Basque city of Uztaritz during the preceding summer and had been deeply impressed with the people involved in the fight for Basque autonomy. He had met ETA apologists and had talked with individuals who had been tortured by their Guardia Civil interrogators. Pete determined to marshal as much political support as he could in defense of those charged with the Manzanas killing. He induced Governor Don Samuelson to send the following:

November 27, 1970

His Excellency Generalismo Francisco Franco
Palacio de El Pardo
Madrid, Spain

On behalf of the citizens of Idaho and especially of its large Basque community, whose ancestors pioneered our state, I respectfully request, Your Excellency, that the forthcoming trial to be held at Burgos against sixteen Basque Nationalists, in which six death sentences and seven hundred and fifty years are demanded by the prosecution, be transferred from a military to a civil court.

I am not asking clemency for the prisoners but only that they have the right of due process of law in a free and open court so that their guilt can be removed or established. Reports of alleged confessions extracted by torture have produced strong reaction in our state among whose citizens are relatives of some of the prisoners and therefore I associate myself with the pleas addressed to you from many quarters including the Vatican and the Basque Bishops of Bilbao and San Sebastian in their joint pastoral letter of last Sunday in order that the due process be observed in this case before an open civil court.

Respectfully,
Don Samuelson
Governor of Idaho [12]

This most remarkable letter was drafted in the office of the secretary of state. Pete's "Basque was up," and he was determined that Idaho's Basques would not stand by once again while Basques experienced a gross injustice. The trial in Burgos was continuing.

A story in the *New York Times* revealed that "testimony from sixteen young Basques drew toward a close at their trial on charges of murder, rebellion, banditry, and terrorism. Most of the defendants admitted they are members of ETA, a Basque separatist organization, but denied the more serious charges." [13] The trial was being held under the tightest of security, and the most severe restrictions were placed against defense witnesses. What few impartial observers were allowed in the courtroom concluded that Franco was holding a show trial against the increasingly insurgent Basques. The trial set off protest demonstrations across the country, giving the regime its deepest crisis since Franco took power after the Civil War, in 1939.[14]

Some Idaho Basques read with increasing anger international press reports of the trial. One Idaho newspaper reported: "An explosion in the trial that began December 3 came when one of the six facing a possible death sentence, Mario Onaindia Nachiondo, a 22-year-old former bank employee, advanced toward the court shouting, 'I'm a prisoner of war.' The other prisoners, each guarded by two policemen in white helmets, struggled violently to knock their benches over." [15] Mario Onaindia had close relatives in the Boise Basque community.

Cenarrusa set about organizing Basques in Idaho to petition Franco and to enlist the aid of the Idaho congressional delegation, including influential Senator Frank Church, a member of the foreign relations committee. A Mountain Home Basque woman, Lois Richey, telephoned the White House in the cause of the prisoner Maria Arranzazu Arruti, a sister of her future son-in-law. Richey said, "I first called the Idaho Secretary of State Pete Cenarrusa, then I placed a call to the White House." [16]

A headline in a December 1970 edition of the *Idaho Statesman* read, "200 Basques in Boise Send Wire to Franco." [17] This message was the result of a protest meeting called by Cenarrusa to enlist Basque community support. Participants at the meeting called for state and nationwide appeals for clemency. In fact, that was already happening.

Two of the world's most totalitarian regimes—Marxist Russia and Fascist Spain—were targets of worldwide protests and demonstrations during December 1970. Associated Press stories reported that both nations were under pressure to commute death sentences imposed on six Basques and two Russian Jews. A report in the *New York Times,* for example, stated, "Italian longshoremen in the busy seaport of Genoa staged a 24-hour boycott of Spanish and Soviet ships and 10,000 commercial and industrial workers in the port struck for two hours in separate protests against the sentencing of the Basques." [18] Perennially neutral Switzerland, along with the Vatican, appealed for clemency. Meanwhile, Cenarrusa continued his efforts in Idaho. He sent a letter over Governor Samuelson's signature to U.S. Secretary of State William P. Rogers in an attempt to get state department support for clemency. The letter read in part, "Many Idaho Basques and those from other states have relatives and loved ones still living in Spain, and express anger and puzzlement why the United States should contribute so generously in financial aid to the Spanish government when these oppressive circumstances exist." [19] Governor Samuelson apparently trusted Cenarrusa as his source of information about Basque concerns. The worldwide protests, including those of Samuelson and the Idaho Basques, was about to pay off.

The outcome of the Burgos trial was complicated by the status of the West German consul kidnapped by ETA, which had indicated that Biehl would be released in exchange for lenient treatment for the Burgos prisoners.[20] Negotiations apparently took place between Madrid and ETA, and on Christmas Eve Biehl was released in good health. On December 30, one day before three prisoners were to be executed by firing squad, Franco commuted all the death sentences to thirty years in prison. Bottles of champagne were opened in the Basque Country.

A moment of silence was observed in thanksgiving at the Burgos prisoners' benefit dance in the Basque center in Boise.

Euskadira Goiaz (We are going to the Basque Country)

The Cenarrusas decided in 1971 to visit the Basque Country to see the hometowns of Pete's parents, to go to the village of Ziortza (Cenarrusa) in Bizkaia, and to make contact with the Basque government in exile in the north Basque Country. Pete was interviewed by a reporter from a Bilbao newspaper in August 1971, and the article included a comment on the unusual fact that Pete was "speaking the language of his birth, El Euskera, and the language of North America, English, both perfectly." They were also surprised that Cenarrusa spoke very little Spanish. When asked why he was visiting the Basque Country, Cenarrusa answered, "Because of love and a desire to preserve my heritage." Pete also "lectured" them a bit on one of his favorite topics: the influence of Basque thought and laws (*fueros*) on John Adams, second U.S. president and one of the founding fathers. When asked why Basques had done so well in the United States, he answered: "Their individualism, work ethic and sense of community."[21]

After an emotional visit to his parents' hometowns and meetings with "cousins I didn't know I had," the Cenarrusas traveled to Donibane Lohitzun in the north Basque Country. There he met officials of the Basque government in exile, including Telesforo Monzon, a cabinet member in the Basque republic and a passionate advocate of Basque nationalism. Monzon, a tall, articulate Basque speaker, was to have considerable influence on Cenarrusa. Indeed, it was this trip to Donibane Lohitzun and the conversations with ETA *gudariak* (soldiers) that convinced Pete that justice was on the side of the insurgents, and he resolved to aid them from America. "Euskadi Askatu!" (Free the Basque Country) became a driving force in his life.

The Memorial

When he returned to Idaho, Cenarrusa joined an organization to help the families of Basque insurgents who were then in Spanish jails or in exile. This organization, called Anaia Danok (Brothers All), was intended to be a political outlet for those Idaho Basques supportive of the insurgents. Pete also began association and correspondence with two individuals who were to have continuing influence on his perceptions of happenings in the Basque Country, Pedro Beitia and Inaki Zubizarreta. Beitia, then working for the World Bank, had been an official with the Basque Republic and became a civil war exile. Zubizarreta, also a Basque Nationalist in exile, was professor of architecture at North Carolina State University. Through these contacts Pete became aware of the worldwide network of Basque Nationalists organized and dedicated to restoring freedom to the Basque Country. Nearly all were members of the Basque Nationalist Party and were mostly professional men in their countries of exile. All dreamed of the day when they could return to their homeland. The Basque government in exile was located in Paris, where its president, J. M. Leizaola, directed strategy. From Paris, such projects as Radio Free Euskadi had been established. Since Franco's control of the media was nearly total, Radio Euskadi could help maintain the hope of freedom by informing Basques of the widespread support for Basque liberty. From Boise, Pete became part of this nationalist network. Among the results of this collaboration was the Human Rights for the Basques memorial. Pete began work on a document dedicated to improving Basque conditions after returning to Boise in the fall of 1971. He decided to make the appeal in the form of a memorial of the Idaho legislature. He thought that if a bipartisan document, passed by an essentially non-Basque political entity like the Idaho legislature, were publicized worldwide, international opinion might support the movement for independence for Europe's oldest ethnic group. After circulating a draft of the memorial to friends on both sides of the aisle, the document was ready for presentation. Cenarrusa's friend and fellow sheepman from Blaine County, John Peavey, sponsored the resolution, and Senator Frank Church entered the memorial into the *Congressional Record* in Washington with these words:

> Mr. President, during the second regular session of the legislature of the State of Idaho, a Senate joint memorial was unanimously passed urging the Government of Spain to extend the principles of the universal declaration of human rights of man as recognized by the United Nations, to all Basques and Spaniards and to allow general amnesty for all Basques and Spaniards now imprisoned or exiled for reasons of their political and social activities. I wholeheartedly support this statement and am pleased to share it with the Senate.[22]

The document was unique. Idaho had unanimously passed a declaration of solidarity with insurrectionists against a Cold War ally, whose support through leases of land for air and naval bases had been considered essential to the protection of Europe and the Mediterranean. How was this possible? Simply put, the answer lay in the deep respect with which Pete Cenarrusa and the Basques of Idaho were held within the state. Members of both parties indicate that they voted for the memorial because "Pete wanted it."[23] Former four-term Idaho governor Cecil Andrus, at the time of the memorial a Democratic state senator from north Idaho, said, "I voted for it for three reasons, respect and affection for Pete, belief in the Basques, and my personal antagonism to the Franco regime."[24]

It did not take long for copies of this remarkable document to spread through the Basque community worldwide. Inaki Zubizarreta wrote to Cenarrusa, "On my arrival from Caracas, the first thing my wife gave me was your cable. I had been confident that the memorial was going to be passed, but reading your cable filled me with emotion. It is a triumph of the Basque cause, the people of Idaho and the U.S.A., but most specially of Pete Cenarrusa. Thank you very much and my most sincere congratulations."[25] Zubizarreta indicated that he had widely circulated the memorial and that it was met everywhere with the same reaction: extreme happiness and great emotion. His letter continued: "In Caracas I showed it to my many friends of EGI [a Basque Nationalist youth organization], the Nationalist Party and many others. Some weeks ago I sent it to other friends in Boston and New York and yesterday in Washington. Happiness and encouragement arrives in the faces and the spirit of every Basque who reads it."[26]

Martin Ugalde, a distinguished Basque historian and Nationalist, wrote from the French-side Basque Country, "We are going to publish the memorial of Pete, which is very, very good. If you have a chance, give him my congratulations."[27] Zubizarreta added in a letter to Pete, "The Memorial will give hope to the Basque people and . . . confidence that there are still people in the world that not only speak of democracy but that also believe in the meaning of it. . . . What you are doing will enlighten many people, and certainly shake many more. It will enlighten the Basques, the political prisoners, the exiles. It will shake the ones in power. . . . [F]or all that, Pete, my thanks as a Basque, for the magnificent document."[28]

Copies circulated throughout the Basque Country, even though to be caught in possession of such an "inflammatory" document could result in swift and severe punishment from Franco police. The author was in the Basque Country in the summer of 1972 and can attest to the impact of the memorial. In a visit to a baserri one weekend, he found framed on the kitchen wall the translation of the memorial. It held a place of honor in the home. President Leizaola, who had earlier written Pete thanking him for his efforts in behalf of the Burgos prisoners, now lauded him for his work on furthering the cause of Basque independence through the memorial. Cenarrusa's document had indeed been read around the Basque world.

Idaho's Basque Elder Statesman

In 1972 Pete was invited to visit Basque communities in the main places of exile: Mexico City, Caracas, and Bogota. The invitation resulted in part because of Pete's increasing international reputation as a worker for Basque causes. An observer at the Basque center of Caracas wrote his observations of Pete's appearance there. Although the translator's prose is somewhat awkward, there is no mistaking his admiration. Pete was complimented for his "profound inclination toward the country of his progenitors" and for the fact that "he speaks fluently the beautiful (Euzkera) Basque that he learned to speak before his native tongue and that his parents transmitted like a precious heritage." He reports that Pete comes as an agent to help bring the Basque people of North and South America closer together in support of Euskadi. Pete assured his Caracas audience that "there is grand determination in the Basque Country for the right of self-determination." Cenarrusa described the Basque efforts to restore use of the Basque language through the *ikastola* (school) movement, outlining in some detail many of the obstacles that the Spanish government was placing in their path.[29] Many in his audience were former Basque Republican Gudaris or politicians—refugees, unable legally even to visit their homeland. They were working and waiting for the day when they could return to a free Euskadi. They saw Pete Cenarrusa's actions as an effort to help them realize their dream. He returned to Idaho and assumed the role as symbolic leader of Idaho's Basques. His office in the Boise capitol became a clearinghouse for Basque problems, and Pete became also a kind of ombudsman for local and old-country Basques. Miren Rementaria Artiach, an Euskera-speaking American-born young woman, became his office manager; Ben Ysursa, an American-Basque lawyer, fluent in Spanish, was his legal assistant and chief deputy secretary of state. In addition, Pete used his cordial relations with Senator Church and his friendship with Jim McClure, Republican junior senator from Idaho, to secure answers to immigration questions, particularly in helping political refugees from the Basque Country. The author knows of no Basque ever turned down when seeking Cenarrusa's help. Indeed, he showed a file replete with folders, each telling a story of the need for his help with passports, visas, extensions, herder tax problems, and citizenship issues. In fact, Pete became something of a thorn in the side of federal immigration officials because he seemed always to be badgering them for special considerations for one client or another. He was seen as an absolute friend of Basque causes, a true *abertzale* (Basque patriot).

Because Cenarrusa was the highest-ranking Basque in Idaho government, his office was the first stop of visiting Basque dignitaries. After the death of Franco in 1975 and the gradual restoration of some democracy to Spain, travel between the Basque Country and Idaho increased. A very emotional moment occurred when a group of Basque political party leaders came to Idaho as part of a tour studying American elections. In the group was Mario Onaindia of the Euskadiko Ezkerra party, then at liberty as a result of the post-Franco general amnesty proclaimed in a peace move by King Juan Carlos. Here in a Boise capitol conference room was Mario Onaindia, who had been one day from death by a Franco firing squad, conversing with Pete Cenarrusa, the man who had led the American Basque drive to have his death sentence commuted. This delegation was one of scores of delegations that he hosted. For Cenarrusa it was a labor of love.

The president of the Basque government, Jose Antonio Ardanza, and his wife visited Idaho as part of a tour of the United States in 1987. Pete and Governor Andrus were his hosts. Ardanza was received in Idaho in a manner befitting a chief of state. He was provided, for example, with the governor's official automobile, driven by two Basque-speaking former herders, then successful Boise businessmen. At a state banquet in his honor at the Basque Center in Boise, Ardanza declared Idaho the "Eighth Basque Province" in recognition of its efforts to maintain Basque language and culture in the state. Later Cenarrusa, as Idaho's official delegate, accompanied the Basque president to Washington, D.C., where Ardanza met President Reagan and hosted a reception for western congressional delegations with Basque constituencies.

The author can personally attest to Pete Cenarrusa's cultural commitment and generosity toward delegations. I had developed a small program through Boise State University to encourage college students to study Basque language, history, and culture in Euskadi. We had decided to locate the program in Oñati, Gipuzkoa, because of the prevalence of Basque spoken there and the availability of classrooms and dormitory space. As the program progressed and we made friends in the village, a plan emerged for a group of Oñati friends to travel to

Boise to meet the families of students they had come to know. By the time the plans were finalized, more than forty had decided to make the trip. We, in Boise, planned their tour here, starting the first day with a visit to the state house. We rented a tour train for a short trip around the city center and then pulled up in front of the impressive capitol steps. As we started up, a short, stocky, ruddy-faced man came bounding down the steps shouting, "Oñatiarrak, Ongi etorri, Idahora!!!" (Welcome to Idaho, Oñatians.) It was Pete. He guided the tour through the building, introducing them to dignitaries, including the governor, all the while keeping a running commentary in Basque. Later, Boise Basque friends were invited to join the Oñatiarrak for the final departure dinner in our backyard. In all, more than ninety attended. Pete, unsolicited, provided young lamb from his ranch for the entire group. That final night provided an unforgettable cultural experience of singing, dancing, and friendship.

After the Franco Years

Pete Cenarrusa returned to the Basque Country in 1977 to observe the first free elections there since 1936. He gloried in the commitment to democratic pluralism he saw as the parties prepared for the elections. The plurality of political parties assured that a parliamentary system of political coalitions was likely to characterize the legislature. Non-Basques from other parts of Spain now lived in virtually all provinces, with metropolitan areas like Bilbao having Basque speakers in the minority. Cenarrusa sent a press release back to Idaho in which he outlined the six-point program that would be incorporated into the newly formed Basque autonomous state. In essence the program called for removal of the Guardia Civil, the dreaded Spanish national police, in favor of a Basque police force; control of education with the creation of a Basque university; local power to tax with a flat amount sent to Madrid, as had occurred under the Fueros; Basque control over local radio, television, and other media; foreign relations under Basque governmental control, with a special department over relations with Basques living outside the homeland, estimated to number over two million; and Basques who were drafted into the Spanish military to be allowed to stay in Euskadi. Cenarrusa's intent with the news release was to inform Idahoans of the progress toward autonomy and to vindicate the efforts of the insurgents on whose behalf he had worked so long and hard. A new Euskadi was in the making. The task, however, was to prove arduous.

The Basque government that emerged from the autonomy negotiations contained most of these proposed elements of sovereignty and local control. Yet the liberty was too much for Spanish nationalists in Madrid and elsewhere, but enough *askatesuna* (freedom) for the most ardent ETA members and their supporters within the Herri Batasuna, a Basque patriotic political party. Indeed, the process of autonomy since Pete's visit in 1977 has not been smooth. Yet signs of progress are everywhere. Many of Pete's friends have returned from exile. Basque schools, the ikastolak, and even the public schools are now teaching Basque to the young. Local Basque-controlled city councils are progressively improving their communities. Pete looks back with pride at the restoration of democracy to his parents' homeland and looks forward to a new, freer Euskadi, which he can say he played a part in creating.

Pete Cenarrusa is now the longest-serving elected officer in the history of Idaho, passing Joe R. Williams, former state auditor, in 1997—not even counting his time in the legislature. In addition he has won more elections with a higher plurality than any other politician in Idaho history. Among the most significant requirements of the position of secretary of state is membership on the land board, which sets policy over state-owned forest and range lands. Idaho's rangelands have long been considered the special province of cattle and sheep ranchers who for the most part went about their business with little interference from politicians and the public. However, over the past three decades, recreational and environmental groups have begun to contest the sheep and cattle hegemony over the lands. Since the land board is required to return maximum profits to the public school districts as beneficiaries of the lands, bidding by environmental groups for state lands along steams and other ecologically sensitive spots has increased the cost to ranchers. Cenarrusa has, for the most part, sided with the sheep and cattle industry with his votes on the land board, arguing that a western way of life and culture is tied up in ranchers' access to these lands. Two of his passions have not changed throughout his public life: a total commitment to helping promote Basque-American culture and a passionate dedication to the ranching way of life.

Pete's term of office ended in 1998, when he was more than eighty years old. No other Idaho elected official has ever served his state as long as Pete Cenarrusa. Idaho's Basque culture is flourishing with a new Museum and Cultural Center, a vibrant Oinkari dance group, a choir dedicated to the preservation and performance of the music of the Basque homeland, language classes being taught every weekday, the prospect of a children's ikastola for preschool Basque language instruction brightening, and a North American Basque Organization dedicated to the promotion of the Basque heritage. Pete can look back with considerable pride for his part in these accomplishments. He can also look toward the Basque Country and know that he had helped inspire and promote the rebirth of Europe's oldest democratic tradition among its most ancient of cultures. He helped in a time of darkness by his unstinting commitment to Basque autonomy. And finally, he can look back on nearly a half century of public service and know that he had been a builder of dreams for the next generations. A former sheepherder whom Pete had helped had this to say about him: "Pete has the generous heart of a real Basque. He really believes in the Basque people and consequently they believe in him. No one who ever asked for his help was turned down."

11

Juanita "Jay" Uberuaga Hormaechea and the Boise Heritage School of Basque Dancing

ANGELINE KEARNS BLAIN

A swish of skirts and a dash of bright boleros . . . the Basque children of Boise Valley are dancing! And the vivacity which runs like a golden thread through the tapestry of their lives glimmers again in the lights of the city.[1]

This description of Basque children performing their heritage dances in Boise, Idaho, could not have been written without the efforts of Juanita Uberuaga Hormaechea, or "Jay," as she preferred to be called. In 1948 she started the Heritage School of Basque Dancing in Boise to teach Basque-American children traditional dances when they were in decline in Boise and other U.S. cities where Basques resided. The loss of Old World dancing to the ethnic group would have been felt throughout the Basque community. The classes became a living source of renewal for Basque culture. Jay Hormaechea's dancing project ensured that the sights and sounds of Basque music and dance would continue as part of Boise's cultural landscape, and by doing so, she made a major contribution to the renaissance of Basque culture in the American West that took place in the decades following World War II.

As early as 1937 Boise Basques were concerned that Basque dancing in their town was disappearing. In a newspaper article published that year, Jack Beardwood described the cultural changes taking place in the Boise Basque community. Arguing that "American" influences were undermining Basque character, he speculated that within a generation or two, as soon as the "Pioneer Basques" who populated southern Idaho and northern Nevada passed away, so, too, would the distinctive "individuality" of the Basque. He added, "The younger generation attended primarily American social functions. Basque dances, which used to be a regular treat for the Boise residents, are no longer held, except on special occasions."[2] Nearly a decade later, Domingo Yturri, a longtime resident of the Basque community in Jordan Valley, Oregon, voiced similar concerns about the fate of Basque dancing: "The young stuff don't pay attention much to the old Basko customs. . . . The young folks don't care and no more Basko dances because we old ones have got too old, and the young ones dance American."[3] These observations on the erosion of Basque culture were consistent with Jay's, that Basque-American children no longer knew how to dance the *jota* or the *porrusalda*. She also realized that the children knew little about their cultural heritage and what it meant to be a Basque.

Hormaechea had three goals in mind when she instituted Basque dancing classes in Boise in 1948: to preserve Old World traditions by passing on the traditional dances to the younger generation, to bring Basques closer together, and to maintain a Basque identity in the face of pressures to assimilate to the dominant culture. Judith Lynne Hanna, an expert on the role of dancing in society, asserts, "Dances are social acts that contribute to the continual emergence of culture."[4] Hormaechea's dance class project embodied this important insight. As a consequence of her activities, she would be asked to produce two major Basque pageants in Boise, *Song of the Basque* (1949) and *Basque Festival* (1950). Attracting thousands, these events represent a watershed in the history of Basque culture in the American West. Hormaechea's Heritage School of Basque Dancing would inspire her students to revitalize other aspects of Basque culture, particularly the use of the Basque language. It would stimulate original students in her classes to organize the Boise Oinkari, an internationally recognized Basque dancing troop that certainly helped to put Boise, Idaho, on the Basque-American cultural map. Finally, her history is a testament to the important role creative Basque women have played in the cultural life of Basque-American people.

A Child of the Holy Ghost

Ysidra Juanita "Jay" Arriola Uberuaga Hormaechea was born October 14, 1908, in Boise, Idaho, to immigrant working-class Basque parents. Her mother, Juana Arriola, was born in Mutriku, Gipuzkoa, Spain, in 1883. Juana later moved to Yspazter, Bizkaia, eventually emigrating to the United States on March 15, 1906. She arrived in New York City and later made the long, overland journey to Boise. Juana, as Jay pointed out, "thought she was going to California when she immigrated, but ended up going to Boise, like a lot of others [Basques] who also believed they were going to California but ended up in Boise." [5]

Juan and Juana Arriola Uberuaga opened the Saracondi Boardinghouse at 211 South Sixth Street in Boise in 1911, just after they were married. The Saracondi became a home away from home for Basque sheepherders. It offered lodging, food, drink, card playing, music, and dancing. Juana met Juan after her arrival in Boise. Nicknamed "Sarakondi," he was born on October 22, 1884, in Gerrikaitz, Bizkaia, Spain. Uberuaga arrived in New York from the Basque Country on February 2, 1905. Juana and Juan were married in Boise on July 4, 1911. They had eight children; Jay was the eldest. Hormaechea described her father as a hardworking person who took very good care of his family. "He always kept our home warm on the coldest of days. He did whatever he could for the family. He was a number-one person." Obviously proud of her father, she said he was the first man in Boise to own a motorcycle. Hormaechea's description of her mother was poignant. "She was precious, naturally, and wanted her children to go to school. She used to make homemade bread. My brothers' friends would come over and she always had a piece of bread for them. Bread, yes; butter on the bread, no! Butter cost too much. Times were hard then."

Survival for the Uberuaga family was difficult. Often called the "land of opportunity," the United States was a harsh place for newcomers until they gained a foothold. Jay's family, like others, fretted about the basic necessities of life. Meeting such demands left little time or money for frivolities. Christmas, as Hormaechea recalled, was a meager event: "It was never a big deal like it is now." Being the eldest of the children, Hormaechea helped to raise her brothers and sisters. "We never knew what Christmas was until I was grown up, went to work, and earned some money. I brought in a fresh Christmas tree to our home at 310 Grove, in Boise. It was the first tree that our family ever had. Christmas Day for us people was shared big suppers, dancing, and enjoying ourselves, in that way. . . . Maybe, a little package for the kids. That was it. . . . That's the way it was when I was a girl."

When Hormaechea spoke about her parents, she noted the gap between their marriage and the date of her birth. "Juan Uberuaga is not my real father, and I was made to suffer for that. My mother had me out of wedlock." Her illegitimate birth caused Jay to be stigmatized by some elders within the Boise Basque community. "I was told I had no right to be here." She described her existence as if some force ensured she be born, regardless of the social scorn she endured. "There were those who said I didn't belong to the family. . . . He's not your father," she recalled. Some people were cruel. Some of the kids, she claimed, were not allowed to play with her. When they were growing up, she wanted her younger brothers and sisters to know who she was. She was emphatic about this. "They knew because I told them! I held my head up high." She had to fight her way through life the hard way. She believes it made a better person out of her, because it made her understand what life is really like.[6]

This prejudice against illegitimacy among some of the elders in the Boise Basque community appears antiquated, more relevant to the Old World than the United States in the middle of the twentieth century. Yet Flavia Maria McCullough's 1945 study of Basque Americans in the Northwest records that the older generation adhered to a strict code of conduct and greatly feared their new homeland's liberalism in moral matters.[7] The distrust the older Basque generation exhibited toward their new environment may have reinforced negative Old World attitudes toward illegitimacy.

Growing up in Boise, Jay also experienced some racial discrimination. When she was a schoolgirl, she remembers, children would come up to her in the school yard and pinch her arm to make the point that her skin was not as white as theirs. She said, "I'd tell them that our skin was just as white as theirs. . . . Some called us dirty black Baskos. . . . It was hard." The belief that Basques in southwestern Idaho experienced little discrimination is unfounded. Hormaechea referred to a particularly vicious article published in the *Caldwell (Idaho) Tribune* in 1909, which contains examples of the name calling that Idaho Basques experienced at the time.[8] She said that immigrant groups who come to the United States still are forced to struggle before they are accepted, just as the Basques did. In spite of this prejudice, the Basques succeeded. "We had a hell of a good time just the same, and kept going. . . . We didn't let them stop us," she asserted triumphantly. "We shoved our shoulders back and kept dancing." This determination, she believed, is part of the Basque character.

In looking back, Hormaechea said she knew from an early age that life would be a struggle. But she was also determined that it would include good times. Her formal schooling ended prematurely because of economic stress in her family. She graduated from the eighth grade at Central Grade School and briefly attended Saint Teresa's Catholic School, both in Boise. Jay's family experienced the hard times, as she said, "heart-and-heart" together. She knew other Basque and non-Basque working-class families found themselves in similar circumstances. "Everybody, including children, worked to make pennies to take home, not to spend on ourselves, but to take home to our mothers. . . . [K]ids, even though they were born in the United States, had to struggle too."

The Little Maid

At age thirteen Hormaechea began to work as a domestic at the Anduiza Hotel, a Basque boardinghouse located in Boise at 607 Grove Street, which paid fifteen dollars a month, plus room and board. Her sadness about leaving school and moving out of her parents' home to live in the boardinghouse caused her deep unhappiness in her employment. "It was the coldest, the coldest of winters," she remembered. "My room was upstairs, a terrible location because the upstairs of the boardinghouse had no heat." She quit after three months. "I'll never forget," she stated, "but I couldn't take it." Jay did not blame her employer, Mrs. Anduiza, for the harsh working conditions. Like many women who operated boardinghouses as part of a husband-and-wife team, Mrs. Anduiza was expected to supervise the preparation of all the meals and the boardinghouse cook, as well as supervise the serving and cleaning girls. Besides taking care of the domestic side of operating a boardinghouse, owners' wives also had their own families to rear.[9] Jay's monthly pay of $15 plus room and board was comparable to the monthly wage of $15 to $20 that was paid to adult men who herded sheep in isolated areas of Idaho.[10] While she worked in the hotel, Jay gave her earnings to her parents.

Contrary to her first job experience, Hormaechea recalled, working in the Modern Hotel at 613 Idaho Street in Boise was very positive. The owner of the hotel, Estaquio "Boni" Ormaechea (no relation to Jay), hired Jay to work as a hostess in his boardinghouse to entertain the boarders by engaging the men in card games, billiards, and dancing. "It was fun to work there. I love people, and I was very outgoing," she said. The Ormaechea family, according to Jay, treated her like a member of their own family instead of a worker. It saddened her when they decided to sell the boardinghouse in 1927. The new owners, Benito and Thomas Ysursa, kept Jay on as an employee but under a new set of rules. The Ysursa brothers' wives, Asuncion and Antonia, Jay recalled, took her aside and told her that they did not employ her just to entertain the boys. Other duties were imposed. She was expected to clean the boarders' rooms, make beds, serve morning coffee, prepare the tables for meals, serve meals, wash dishes, and then entertain the sheepherders. "Luckily, the owners sent out all the heavy laundry to the Chinese laundry around the corner." With so many demands on her time, Hormaechea admitted, she had to cut a corner or two. The Ysursa women, she said, worked every bit as hard as their employees; they taught her the true meaning of hard work and self-discipline.

Hormaechea made no attempt to hide her affection for men, especially "good-looking men." She added, "I've loved men all my life; I've been around men all my life, and I hold them in high regard." During her stay at the Modern Hotel, as many as forty men lodged in the place, the majority of whom were single. Attempts at courting did take place. "I got several marriage proposals from various boys . . . some serious some not," she said. But she was not interested in getting married. The men would come into the kitchen where she worked, and say, "Why don't you get married, Juanita?" Some of Boise's non-Basque businessmen liked to eat in the Modern Hotel, too. Hormaechea recalled one of the bankers, who, impressed with her outgoing ways, suggested that she quit her job in the boardinghouse and take clerical classes at Links Secretarial College in Boise. After she completed the course, he said, he would offer her a job in his bank as a teller. "I never did go to secretarial school," she said. "I was too young, too frivolous, and having a lot of fun." In a bank or boardinghouse, outgoing, attractive women like Jay were viewed as economic assets.

Sunday afternoon dancing was one of the main attractions a boardinghouse offered to gain new customers. Asked how the boarders treated her, she recalled: "They'd tease. That's nothing! We did the same thing to them. There never was a smart remark, like 'Let's go to bed' or stuff like that. Never! Never! Sure, there were cocky little teasing remarks. We danced with the boys, I played cards with them. I played for money just like a man. I was a renegade gal."

Some owners would not allow their female employees to go dancing at a competitor's establishment. A rule like this did not sit well with

Hormaechea. She would sneak out and go anyway, dancing until dawn. As she put it, "That's the way it used to be." Asked if she was ever criticized by folks more "straitlaced" than she, she responded, "I never had a lot of girlfriends. . . . [N]one of the mothers would allow their girls to go with me. It wasn't allowed in the beginning because I was born out of wedlock, but they [the daughters] snuck around with me anyway." The same mothers who refused to let their daughters socialize with Jay would later become firm backers of her plan to teach traditional Basque dances to Basque-American children.

By the time Hormaechea quit working at the Modern Hotel during the Great Depression, she was making seventy to eighty dollars a month, most of which she continued to give to her parents. She also spent part of her earnings to buy clothing for her brothers and sisters and household articles for her parents. She was adamant about one point: She "loved" working as a maid in the boardinghouse and would not change any of it.

Hormaechea's bilingual abilities turned out to be an asset. Jay had no problem finding work as a sales clerk in Boise's most fashionable department stores, where she worked as an interpreter to wait on Basque customers who did not speak English. Later, she decided that she wanted a professional job. She enrolled in State Beauty College in Boise and graduated in 1937 with a license to practice cosmetology. Ruth Yurri, a Basque American who owned the Whitehead Beauty Salon in Boise, hired Hormaechea. Eventually, Jay bought the business from Yurri. Hormaechea continued to operate her business for forty-eight years, until, as she explained it, "her legs gave out."

When Hormaechea married her first husband, Eugene Aldrich, a non-Basque, she went against the wishes of the Boise Basque community. Basque parents encouraged their sons and daughters to marry only Basques. Jay realized there were good reasons for this practice. One of the most important was the language problem. A parent who did not speak English found it difficult to get along with a daughter-in-law or son-in-law who did not speak *Euskara* (the Basque language). The Basque Ladies Auxiliary denied her membership in their organization because she married a non-Basque. This action, which hurt her deeply, continued to puzzle Hormaechea. "I was never allowed to be a member. . . . I was voted out because I was married to an American, because my name was Aldrich." Excluded from the Ladies Auxiliary, she found a lifelong home in the Basque Girl's Club, which she helped found in 1936.

Jay Hormaechea, standing next to door on left, at work in the Whitehead Beauty Salon at Eighth and Main Streets, in the Eastman Building, in 1941. (Courtesy of Jay Hormaechea.)

Hormaechea's mother died in 1938, at the age of fifty-four, from complications related to high blood pressure. "Maybe if she had gone to a doctor for yearly check-ups," Jay surmised, "they might have saved her. People didn't go for medical checkups back then. It just wasn't done."

Jay's only child, Joanne, was born during her marriage to Eugene Aldrich. This marriage ended in divorce. In 1952 she married Jose Artolazabal of Nampa, Idaho, in Winnemucca, Nevada. This marriage also ended in divorce. In 1957 Jay married her third husband and life-long partner, Rufino Hormaechea, in Reno, Nevada. They remained a close couple until Rufino passed away in 1994.

The Basque is Born to Dance[11]

Jay learned to love the jotas and porrusaldas from the immigrant women and men who frequented the boardinghouses. Jay described the immigrants as "those wonderful men and women who came from across the sea. The old timers. I watched them dance. I picked them up just like that! Naturally, I was a dancer. I loved the dance. It did something to me." Because of her deep love of dancing, she wanted to see the dances performed in the traditional way. When she attended the Sheepherders' Ball in 1936 and noticed that a group of herders, newly arrived from the Basque Country, were dancing the Old World dances in the manner of a Western American "hoedown" rather than in the traditional, graceful style, she exploded and confronted the men about their performance. She recalled, "They did not dance like they should have. They were supposed to walk up to the girls and ask them to dance, not grab them! I told them, 'That's not the way to dance. Quit that. Dance like this! Separate! Don't grab her.'"

Despite the tongue lashing, the herders asked Hormaechea to teach them how to dance. She thought about giving the sheepherders dancing lessons but did not. Not until eleven years later, in 1948, when she realized Basque-American children were growing up without knowing how to dance the jotas and porrusaldas, did she finally act. Attending public schools scattered around the Boise Valley, a majority of the children had little opportunity to socialize with each other in order to share their ancestral background. Additionally, the annual Sheepherders' Ball and Basque Picnic, the two major social events for Boise Basques, were oriented to adults. Jay realized the children no longer knew much about their Basque heritage. A change would have to be made. If Basque-American youngsters were to be educated about their history, a structured learning experience would be necessary. Rodney Gallop, an authority on the Basques, has argued that Basque-American children needed to speak Euskara, to play *pelota,* and to dance properly if they were to be considered *Euskaldunak.*[12] Jay arrived at the same conclusion in 1948. She knew something drastic had to be done if the dances were to survive.

The inspiration to start dancing classes for the children came to Hormaechea while she was attending a Basque dance at the Spanish Hotel in Nampa, Idaho. "I'll never forget it . . . at Jimmy Jausoro's mother's boardinghouse in Nampa. Right there, I decided to teach the children the classes—not only to the children but to the older people as well. I could see things slipping away, and it broke my heart thinking about Basque children not knowing how to dance, because I loved to dance so much."

She first told the accordionist Jimmy Jausoro, a well-known Boise Basque musician who played at the dances, of her desire to start the dancing classes for the children. Jimmy strongly supported her dream. She also contacted Domingo Ansotegui, another Basque musician.

"When I asked Jimmy and Dom if they would play for me if I started the classes," Jay recalled, "they both said, 'Absolutely.'" When word got around in the Basque community about her plan to teach the children the traditional dances to preserve a vital part of Basque culture, the response was positive. She had tapped into a growing concern among members of Boise's influential Basque social club, Euskaldunak, which Jay asserts backed her efforts "one hundred percent!"

Hormaechea made the decision that only children of Basque descent would be admitted to the classes. It became a requirement that any child who took the classes had to have at least one parent in the Euskaldunak club. Two factors contributed to this decision: Hormaechea's belief in the urgent need to preserve traditional Basque dancing, and the necessity to reinforce a sense of a common Basque lineage among the class participants. Parents wanted to know what the classes could offer their children besides teaching them how to dance. Hormaechea pointed to the lasting friendships their children could make through the classes and how later in life the children might be able to assist one another in finding jobs or come to each other's assistance in hard times. As Jay saw it, "The dancing is important, but getting the children and their parents together was just as important. Dancing is the medium for doing all of that." Eventually, thirty to forty children, aged six to fourteen, enrolled in the weekly classes. Girls outnumbered the boys almost ten to one. "The boys," Hormaechea said, "thought it a sissy thing to do." [13]

There was some minor resistance to the dancing class project. A few people questioned her right to teach the children to dance. As she recalled it, some asked, "Who the hell do you think you are, teaching these children?" But they underestimated her resolve. She just put her head up and retorted, "The hell with you." The dissenters quickly changed their tune after attending one of the classes.

Hormaechea also had to locate a good place to hold the classes. A Basque center did not yet exist. Some in the Basque community had talked about the need for a meeting hall of their own, but the time for action had not yet arrived. Instead, Hormaechea frantically searched each week for a rehearsal hall for the children's classes. In the beginning, she paid the standard fifteen dollar rental fee out of her own pocket, a considerable amount at the time. Jay's daughter, Joanne Aldrich, recalled that her mother paid the fees because "she was so committed to what she wanted to do." [14] When she no longer could afford to pay the weekly fee, she began to charge twenty-five cents per lesson.

Jay Hormaechea and her daughter, Joanne Aldrich, ca. 1945? (Courtesy of Jay Hormaechea.)

The amount she collected covered the cost of renting a hall, with a bit left over. "We had a few dollars left over and I made the remark one time, 'This goes for our first brick for a Basque building,'" she said. "Nobody even thought anything like that could ever happen."

The dance classes, which were held on Sundays, were divided into two sessions. Children attended the early session, which started at noon, and youth, young married couples, and older adults participated in the later class, which lasted late into the evening. The gathering of children, youths, young married couples, and older folk offered a unique social experience. As word got out about the fun everyone was having at the weekly dances, enrollment escalated. Jay could not teach the classes by herself, so she trained Petra Cengotita and Marie Alegria to assist her as dance instructors. The women taught the students the jota and porrusalda, which were the most popular dances. The mothers, Hormaechea emphasized, were the ones who took on the responsibility to see that the children arrived on time.[15]

The Dance Mistress

The role of the dance mistress is not only to teach her students the dance forms but also to teach them the importance of self-discipline, self-confidence, and cooperation. Asked to describe her teaching style, Hormaechea replied that the kids hated her. She was very strict. When she told them to sit, they sat. When the kids saw her coming they would say, "Here comes Jay. You all quiet down." In fact, one little boy told her that he thought she was "the meanest thing that ever lived on this earth." A former student and lifelong protégé, Albert Erquiaga, recalled, "She was like a German drill sergeant. . . . Jay would stand with her hands on her hips, point her finger at us and say, 'Now you boys get out on the floor.' Jay reminded me of a person who has more than two eyeballs; even though she is seeing you over here, she knows what is going on over there. She would have made a wonderful teacher in a juvenile home because those kids would have never got away with a thing. . . . At the same time she had the ability to make you have fun and enjoy yourself. She had a way of dealing with kids." [16]

Erquiaga's parents enrolled him and his sister in Hormaechea's class to get them involved in Basque activities. His parents saw the class as a way to preserve the Basque culture. Their involvement illustrates Hormaechea's dream of getting the parents involved in the classes. As she correctly anticipated, "After you get the children, you automatically get the grandparents, mothers, fathers, and others involved. You get them together without them realizing what they are getting into."

Jay did not spend all her time organizing the dance classes. A woman of great energy, she had a family, a home, worked at her business six days a week, and set aside every Sunday afternoon to teach classes. Her whirlwind lifestyle makes today's "supermom" seem tame by comparison. Asked if her busy schedule, especially her taking time away from home to teach the classes every Sunday, affected her marriage, Jay frankly stated, "Nobody could stop me from teaching the children their dances. They didn't try to. If they did, they could get out in a damn hurry."

By the end of 1948, Hormaechea's dancing classes were becoming more publicly visible. Boise's major newspaper offered readers a vivid description of the activities taking place in Jay's classes in June.[17] An account of her activities also appeared in the *Spokesman-Review* (Spokane, Washington) in October.[18] After word spread about her classes, the director of the annual Boise Music Week program board asked Jay

Jay Hormaechea during *Song of the Basque,* May 1949. (Courtesy of Jay Hormaechea.)

if she would prepare a demonstration of Basque music and dance for their 1948 event.

Song of the Basque

The director's proposal to include an entire evening devoted to Basque culture represented a dramatic departure from previous music week programs. Historically, the programs focused on the celebration of "American" culture.[19] Hormaechea accepted the offer, assuming the mantle of director, choreographer, and producer of *Song of the Basque*. Her first priority was to achieve an authentic representation of traditional Basque customs, music, language, and dance movements and costumes. Approximately one thousand people showed up to see the dress rehearsal.[20] News quickly spread about the high quality of the production, and the people of Boise flocked to see the show.

The first performance of *Song of the Basque* took place in the Boise High School Auditorium on May 9, 1949. More than 150 Basques performed in the show, including performers from the southwest Idaho towns of Emmett, Nampa, and Mountain Home, as well as Boise. Two thousand people attended the show, and three thousand more were turned away because of lack of seating. With understandable pride, a local journalist hailed Jay's production as "the greatest night in the history of Basques in America."[21] *Song of the Basque* replicated the traditions of Basque people, their music, dancing, folktales, language, and songs, with performers dressed in colorful traditional costumes. As a favor to Jay, Boni Garmendi translated "God Bless America" into Euskara. Hormaechea ended the program with all of the cast singing Garmendi's "Gora Amerika."

The public demanded a repeat showing of the pageant. When they did, Boise's Euskaldunak organization made a decision to repeat the show and charge an admission to cover auditorium rental and production costs.[22] Additionally, it was decided to film the second performance and sell prints of the film. A thirty-minute record album of the music and songs was also made, which sold nationwide. After expenses, profits were earmarked to help fund the construction of a Basque center. Hormaechea's joke about setting aside "extra money" from her class to buy the first brick for a Basque building was becoming a serious possibility.

A group of Jay Hormaechea's dancers as they appeared in *Song of the Basque,* May 1949. (Courtesy of Jay Hormaechea.)

Sixteen hundred people paid to see the second showing of *Song of the Basque*. The pageant helped to enhance and project the Basque image throughout the American West. Basques and non-Basques alike received a more extensive view of New World Basque culture. Clearly, Hormaechea's production took Boise by storm, and Jay was asked at once by the directors of Boise Music Week to produce a second Basque pageant as part of the 1950 musical season.

Basque Festival

Jay's second production, *Basque Festival*, opened in Boise on May 18, 1950. This program featured eighty Basque participants, from four year olds to senior citizens. Five thousand people attended the festival, which included visitors from Nevada, California, Oregon, Washington, Montana, and Utah. Not surprisingly, Boise Music Week officials described *Basque Festival* as a significant milestone in the history of Basque Americans.[23] The pageant brought together the largest gathering of Basques in the history of Idaho. News of the event reached as far as New York City.[24] The *Christian Science Monitor* also recorded the success of the Boise event.[25] William Douglass has argued that "prior to 1959 . . . Basques of the American West were little noticed and they consciously maintained a low group profile."[26] The wide publicity and recognition accorded Hormaechea's productions appear to contradict this claim.

Song of the Basque and *Basque Festival* were colorful extravaganzas that brought together thousands of Basque and non-Basque people. As a gesture to non-Basque people, Jay ended both programs with the cast singing Boni Garmendi's "Gora Amerika." These two presentations introduced the audiences to the cultural traditions and history of the Basques. The shows also had the effect of bringing older and younger generations of Basque people together. Eventually, Jay's efforts would also play a role in the renewal of contacts between the old country and new homeland.

When asked what she believed contributed most to the success of the pageants, Hormaechea replied, "Those kids knew how to come on and off the stage. No two ever left together for the rest room; they went one by one. There was no monkey business. The children were wonderful." She received accolades from various important people concerning the pageants she produced. Patty Harris, a well-known dancing teacher in Boise during the 1920s, telephoned to compliment Jay on the discipline the children displayed in the pageants. Harris advised Jay to go to Hollywood to seek fame and fortune. "That was a real compliment coming from Patty Harris. Hollywood! Hell! I wouldn't go there for anything." In 1953, the Boise Chamber of Commerce received a letter from the U.S. vice-consul of Bilbao, Spain, Robert O'Neill, requesting information about the Boise Basques. In the letter of reply, Hormaechea was cited as the recognized authority on the cultural activities of the Boise Basque community.[27]

Jay's "Babies"

The dream of a "true" Basque community came to fruition with the opening of a new Basque Center at 601 Grove Street on March 28, 1949. Immediately, Jay moved her dance classes there, where they are still held today. At the same time, the classes came under the sponsorship of Euskaldunak, and the young dancers, whom Jay refers to as her "babies," were named the Boise'ko Gazteak. Only Basque children or the children of Basque descendants were allowed to participate. Jay continued to instruct the group until 1956.

A student in Hormaechea's classes, Adelia Garro Simplot, remembered going to the Basque Center as a young woman for the traditional dancing. "She was so vivacious and so energetic, just full of life. . . . [S]he had us all dancing. . . . [I]t was so much fun. . . . [I]t was wonderful." It was important to Mrs. Simplot that Jay be recognized as the one who saved the dances: "It's women who are the bearers of culture, and Jay has been a great inspiration for generations of young people."[28] Later, Simplot's love of Basque culture and history would motivate her to help establish North America's first Basque Museum and Cultural Center in 1984.

By 1959 the youngsters who had enrolled in Hormaechea's novice classes in the early years were young adults. Some of them had continued to meet regularly at the Boise Basque Center to dance and were interested in expanding Basque dancing in Boise. Albert Erquiaga and Delphine and Diana Urresti were the first of Hormaechea's babies to venture outside of the hometown to dance. The three participated in the First Western Basque Festival held in Sparks, Nevada, in 1959. After returning to Boise, they founded a new Boise Basque dance group called the Euzkaldun Gaztiek. Erquiaga was elected president, and Jay was appointed adviser to the group.[29]

In 1960 Jay and her husband, Rufino, traveled with members of the new dance group to the Basque Country. She was their chaperon. Hormaechea especially enjoyed seeing her former students dance with boys and girls in the small towns around the Basque Country. After returning to Boise, Albert Erquiaga was one of the principal organizers of the Boise Oinkari Basque Dancers, serving as the codirector of the troop from 1963 through 1968. In the opinion of John Bieter, a Boise Basque historian and a member of the Oinkari, Jay was the person who constructed the original foundation upon which the troop was built. It was brought into existence through Al Erquiaga and the Boise Basque Center.[30]

The Oinkari would ultimately go on to represent Basque American culture by performing at the New York World's Fair, in June 1964, and in Washington, D.C. Again, Hormaechea accompanied the group in her dual role as dance-adviser and chaperon. At the invitation of Idaho's Democratic senator, the late Frank Church, they were invited to dance in the rotunda of the U.S. Senate office building. This performance offered elected officials a rare opportunity to recognize the presence of Basque Americans in the United States—an honor, Jay stated, that almost took her breath away.

Members of the Oinkari soon became interested in learning how to speak Euskara. They contacted Joseph V. Eiguren, a Basque historian and native speaker, to see if he would teach them some phrases. This meeting led Eiguren to establish the first Basque-language classes in Boise, Idaho.[31] Eiguren said Jay's efforts at saving the Basque dances in Boise were comparable to what the Basque Nationalist leader, Sabino de Arana Goiri, did in preserving Euskara from extinction. Noted Eiguren, "I do believe that if she didn't save it from extinction there would be no Oinkari."[32]

Idaho historian Merle Wells finds it remarkable that a small ethnic group, like the Boise Basques, would give rise to a group of dancers who have achieved national and international recognition.[33] However, asserted Wells, until the time of Hormaechea's classes and the two Basque pageants, only a small portion of the non-Basque public had ever seen Basque culture publicly displayed. When Erquiaga was asked why he became so immersed in Basque culture and activities, he answered, "I was influenced by Jay's dance classes. . . . [S]ee, one step leads to another. . . . There has to be a beginning, and the beginning started, in my opinion, with Jay's classes. This is where this all evolved from . . . all from Jay's classes."[34] Erquiaga is not alone in his judgment. In her book *Basques from the Pyrenees to the Rockies,* Bernice

Brusen pinpoints Hormaechea as the one person who possessed the leadership and talent to have pushed the entire Boise Basque community into a greater awareness of the Basque folk heritage.[35]

After Hormaechea had formally retired from teaching dancing lessons in 1956, she took on the task of consultant for the Basque heritage classes. With additional free time, she and her husband made frequent trips to the Basque Country. She also focused on her beauty business while continuing to be involved with the Basque community. In the meantime, she began collecting Basque memorabilia from the previous fifty years. She filled 150 large photograph albums with newspaper clippings, magazine articles, journal features, letters, photographs, announcements of births, weddings, divorces, and graduations, obituaries, business cards, high school invitations, university invitations, and even a box of letters sent to her from ETA, the Basque Nationalist organization.

Honoring One of Their Own

Jay believed that one of the greatest experiences in her life occurred on October 13, 1985, when she became the first Basque-American woman to be inducted into the Basque Hall of Fame of the Society of Basque Studies in America. The Society of Basque Studies in America selected Jay as their recipient for the fifth annual Hall of Fame Award for extraordinary contributions to Basque culture. A member of the delegation traveled from New York to present her the award at the Boise Basque Center.[36] Hormaechea was profoundly affected by the recognition: "I nearly fainted. Can you imagine me getting a thing like that. I'm honored, I told them. I was proud to think that in the whole United States, I'd be the first woman, a humble person that came from little Boise, Idaho. It was quite an honor, coming from New York City, from the Basque Studies in America."

The year 1985 was also the twenty-fifth anniversary of the Oinkari dancers. To mark the occasion, the dancers put on a special performance in Jay's honor and presented her with a plaque inscribed with the following words: "We thank you for our beginning. The many hours of teaching. And, your support and guidance. Most especially, to thank you for your constant love and devotion." The family of the late Domingo Ansotegui, who had played for Jay more than forty years ago, also presented her with a bouquet of flowers in memory of Domingo. This occasion stood out in her memory as a very special time.

More awards have followed. On February 26, 1993, she received a Citation for Cultural Achievement from the Boise Basque Museum and Cultural Center. Bethine Church, the widow of Senator Frank Church, read Jay's tribute to the assembled crowd.[37] A year later the Basque community honored Jay by selecting her as their choice for the *Idaho Statesman* Distinguished Citizen Award.[38] Trisha Clausen Zubizarreta, a Basque poet who celebrates ordinary Basque life through her writings, composed a poem in Jay's honor, "Juanita's *Abarketak*," which praises her role in maintaining Basque culture through dancing.[39]

Clearly, Jay Hormaechea played a major role in the history of Basque culture in the American West. At the time this was written, Jay was in her mid-eighties and living with her daughter in Richmond, California, and was still an articulate and graceful woman. Her mind remained sharp and her spirit light, her body agile and graceful, testifying to a long life of vigorous Basque dancing. "I play one of the [Basque] tapes and dance around the living room every day," she stated.

It was Jay Hormaechea's deep love of Basque dancing and culture that made it possible for her and her dancers to realize the three goals she had set out to accomplish in 1948: to bring the Old World to the New by keeping the dances alive; to help unify Basque people in the American West; and to help invent and maintain a Basque-American identity. Her project to use Basque dancing to achieve these goals turned out to be a highly effective "symbolic strategy." Currently, the image of Basque dancers is the most widely recognized symbol of Basque-American identity in Idaho and, perhaps, the American West.[40]

Hormaechea taught the traditional dances to hundreds of Basque-American children. She continued to inspire younger members of the Boise Basque community. Josephine Bilbao, a young advocate of traditional Basque culture, recalled how as a child her parents enrolled her in the classes Jay had begun and how the classes deepened her appreciation of Basque culture. The idea, she said, was that through the movement of dancing you could teach the language. Dancing, she also contended, had a powerful impact on her social life, creating a community atmosphere where friendships could get started.[41]

In starting the dance classes and assuming the role of "dance mistress," Jay Hormaechea assumed the caretaking role ascribed to special women in the Basque Country, called the *serora*. According to Roslyn Frank, the serora's duties fall into two categories: taking care of the church and acting as priestess or mistress of ceremonies for the women of the parish.[42] Jay followed in the footsteps of the serora. By taking care of the traditional dances, she helped preserve the sacred traditions of the Basque-American people.

Juanita "Jay" Uberuaga Hormaechea, eighty-eight, passed away Friday, May 9, 1997.

12

Robert Laxalt
Basque Writer of the American West

RICHARD W. ETULAIN

When Robert Laxalt's *Sweet Promised Land* appeared in 1957, reviewers immediately saluted it as the archetypal story of the Basque sheepherder in the American West. Two generations later, Basques and non-Basques acquainted with the novelized biography of Dominique Laxalt, the author's father, still consider it *the story* of Basques in the New World. Written in the direct, minimalistic style that became Robert Laxalt's trademark, *Sweet Promised Land* dramatically launched Laxalt's literary career, quickly establishing him as the leading literary interpreter of the Amerikanuak, a position he retains nearly forty years later.

Born in 1923 to immigrant parents in Alturas, California, the second child in a family of six, Robert Laxalt passed his infancy on Basque ranches until his family moved to Carson City, Nevada. Although Dominique Laxalt did well as a herder and rancher before 1920, he lost nearly everything in the postwar livestock crash of 1923 that wiped out so many western ranchers and farmers. Once the family relocated in Nevada, Dominique hired out as a herder in the Sierra while his wife, Teresa, operated a boardinghouse in Carson City. For Robert, those boyhood years included frequent trips to the mountains

Robert Laxalt, 1998. (Courtesy of Marilyn Newton, *Reno Gazette-Journal*.)

to visit his father and public schooling in his hometown. In high school, he was active in sports, engaging in a number of matches as an aspiring boxer.[1]

While in high school, Laxalt also dreamed of becoming a writer. Always a voracious reader, especially after an early near-fatal bout with rheumatic fever kept him bedridden and allowed long hours to nourish his book addiction, Robert thought of writing books himself. It was not an ambition he broadcast, however, since small-town westerners sometimes thought of authors as eastern effetes, out of place in their West. But his remarkable English teacher, Grace Bordewich, especially turned Laxalt toward writing. Years later he told an interviewer that she taught him "the richness and the nuances of the English language." In her classes he tried his hand at melodramatic tales that revealed he already knew how to tell a story and to create lively characters.[2]

After graduating from high school in 1940, Laxalt enrolled in Santa Clara University in California. There he found the stiff demands of a Jesuit education, especially the intense courses in philosophy, literally gave him headaches. After World War II broke out, Laxalt left college to join the service, but a heart murmur, which had not kept him out of high school sports, became a barrier to active service. Instead, through his connections with Nevada Senator Pat McCarran, he landed a State Department position in the Belgian Congo, where he unfortunately contracted chronic malaria, amoebic dysentery, and yellow jaundice, and nearly died. After recovering, Laxalt entered the University of Nevada, becoming an English major but also taking courses in philosophy, French, and history. In addition, he worked part time as a journalist and continued as a newspaperman after graduating in 1947. During the next few years Laxalt turned out hundreds of stories as a staff correspondent for United Press International, including "covering probably more executions . . . than anybody in the county." His experiences as a working journalist were invaluable, but he dreamed of being a different kind of a writer.[3]

In the late 1940s and early 1950s Laxalt experimented with several types of writing. Dozens of his brief stories and sketches appeared in Nevada newspapers. Indeed, in early 1948, he signed a contract with the *Las Vegas Evening Review-Journal* to provide "feature stories and histories" for which he would receive "15¢ per column inch." Five years later, twelve of these stories were collected in Laxalt's first book, *The Violent Land*. Focusing on frontier Nevada, often featuring military conflicts with Indians or mining-camp life in booming Virginia City, these stories are more sketches than carefully plotted short stories. Military martinets dominate "Mercy and the Soldier" and "The Hollow," whereas "The Horse Traders" and "The Lieutenant's Uncertainty" describe white–Native American confrontations. The final yarn, "The Gentleman Leaves Town," twice as long as any of the other stories, is a first-person account of an "honest gambler," a gunman and his sidekick, and an innocent young woman trying to launch a stage career.[4] These apprenticeship writings, more similar to Bret Harte's local-color works than to the early regional stories of fellow Nevadan Walter Van Tilburg Clark, are primarily Wild West stories of action and adventure, finger pieces for Laxalt's later fiction.

Meanwhile, Laxalt also tried to place short stories and serials with nationally known fiction magazines. In these efforts, he was less successful than with his home state newspapers, but he also aimed at a much more competitive market. Later, when Laxalt dredged up many of these unpublished stories for a retrospective anthology of his short fiction, he recalled that several of the rejected stories "had run headlong into the taboo-ridden barrier[s] of popular . . . magazines," outlets that desired romantic, dramatic, formula stories. Despite these disappointments, he was able to draw upon his Nevada origins, his small-town and ranch backgrounds, and his service as a roving reporter. As Laxalt confessed later, he felt "fortunate . . . in experiencing things [he] knew well enough to write about." But early in the 1950s, these topics and Laxalt's handling of them did not win acceptance in eastern magazine marts. Although his agent worked assiduously to land the short works with several magazines, from the lordly slicks of the *Saturday Evening Post* and *Collier's* down to the near-pulps, her editorial efforts were often in vain. Several editors spoke of Laxalt's talents, praised his clear and limpid prose, and even encouraged submission of other, later writings, but most of his stories remained unpublished.[5]

These stories, gathered nearly two generations later in *A Lean Year and Other Stories,* illustrate the strengths—and possible shortcomings—of Laxalt's early work. Several of the sixteen stories dramatize a human flaw, a dramatic incident or two, or a violent confrontation, as do the title story "A Lean Year," "The Law Comes to Virginia City," and "The Gun." Others treat Basque herders ("The Herd Stalker"), a sturdy buckaroo ("Old Button"), and men whose excessive pride leads to humiliating falls ("Valley of the Deer," "Guest of Honor," and "Night Ride"). These are primarily narrative sketches. They feature uncomplicated plots, and sometimes they contain unexpected endings. Most often the stories, utilizing frontier ranches and saloons or contemporary Nevada scenes of suburban Reno, prisons, or families under stress, lack complex characters or romance elements. These efforts seem less complex, less love-driven, and less tied to the fictional formulas that magazine editors expected in the early 1950s. On the other hand, they clearly adumbrate the clear, straightforward, and minimalistic style characteristic of nearly all of Laxalt's later writings.

Then, suddenly, Laxalt's career swung into high gear with the publication of *Sweet Promised Land* in 1957.[6] He had already proven he could turn out lively historical sketches, popular local history, and publishable short fiction. Building on these apprentice writings and drawing on his family and personal backgrounds, Laxalt produced a superbly written, evocative account of his father and the archetypal story of the Basque herder in the American West.

In the opening chapter of *Sweet Promised Land,* Laxalt invokes moods that dominate this "shaped" biography of his Basque father. The memorable first two sentences, for example, establish a timeless perspective: "My father was a sheepherder, and his home was the hills. So it began when he was a boy in the misted Pyrenees of France, and so it was to be for the most of his lifetime in the lonely Sierra of Nevada." Picturing his father Dominique's relocation from the Old World to the American West, posing him as a lone sentinel in the hills of both continents, and dramatizing his lifelong work as a sheepherder, Laxalt envelops the reader in the opening paragraph's final phrase: "you could understand why this was what he was meant to be" (9).

The initial chapter also links son and father. Operating as the "I" narrator, as well as the impersonal third-person storyteller, Laxalt pictures his father through his own boyhood reactions at the Laxalt home in Carson City but particularly during his visits to Dominique's sheep camp in the lofty Sierra west of the Nevada capital city. A maturing Robert summarizes his gradual understanding of his father: "I came to realize that the sheep camp was my father's house" (10). More than that, he sees his father saving lambs in a blizzard, reacting with foolhardy belligerence to criticism, and, most important of all (described in a Hemingway-like episode), bravely facing down a mountain lion with only his walking stick and courage as weapons. Through the boy's and young man's eyes, a larger-than-life Basque sheepherder looms up out of the American West.

But what about the troubling matter of organization? Before *Sweet Promised Land* finally took its published form, Laxalt struggled for months—even a few years—with how best to tell his father's story. At first, he planned to focus solely on Dominique's long-delayed return trip to his natal French Basque country. Gradually, mostly as a result of Robert's own changing opinions on the most appealing way to structure his story but also on advice from his agent and Harper and Row editor, he decided to write a fuller biography of his father, using the return trip as the pivot around which to organize the longer story of Dominique's Old World origins, his immigration to the United States, his successes and disappointments as a rancher and sheepman, and his family life as husband and father.[7]

Point of view and organization aside, the story of Dominique, who epitomizes the Basque monomyth, has attracted and held thousands of readers. Laxalt skillfully and invitingly portrays his father as the Everyman immigrant to America, expecting to strike it rich and return to his homeland. But, like most other newcomers, Dominique finds that his resolve to return home falters the longer he stays in his new country. Once he marries and becomes a father, he still dreams of the return but also admits that the United States "has been good for me and many like me" (96). Over the years, Dominique endlessly talks of the return but stubbornly, irrationally puts off all concrete plans for the trip. Robert Laxalt movingly depicts the many ways Dominique evades a decision until finally his family tricks him into the trip.

In these respects, Dominique's life echoes those of hundreds of thousands of other immigrants, but in other areas he clearly represents Basque characteristics. Repeatedly, Laxalt provides revealing glimpses of Dominique the *Euskaldun*. For example, the author writes early on: "And how they were treated was important because they were Basques and their pride was their flaming shield, and they took insult from no man" (46). On other occasions, Laxalt dramatizes his father's courage, stubbornness, and indefatigable energies. Together, these characteristics define the legendary Basque *indarra*, which fortified the Euskaldunak in their centuries-long conflicts in Europe and in their drive to succeed in the New World. At the end of his work, Robert experiences a moment of epiphany when he exclaims, "And then, I did know it" (223), indicating that he has gained a fuller understanding of his Basque father.[8]

Although the reception and sales of *Sweet Promised Land* encouraged Laxalt and his publisher, seven years shot by before he published his next book. Tied to his duties at the University of Nevada, busy with his growing family, and uncertain what ought to be his next long project, Laxalt wobbled toward the new book. At first he thought of finishing a volume of short stories he had planned, and then he spoke of doing one on "a University situation" because it was "fresh and intimate in [his] mind." And then a final sentence in a letter to his agent hinted at a major theme in Laxalt's next book: "It will be a book of characterization and what happens to people when a powerful, partly right and partly wrong, but catalytic figure appears on the scene."[9]

That work was *A Man in the Wheatfield,* Laxalt's most unusual novel.[10] The story of Smale Calder, a collector of rattlesnakes, who moves to a small desert town near the eastern flanks of the Sierra, the novel combines realism and symbolism in a way unique to Laxalt's *oeuvre*. Enigmatic, a loner, and a lover of snakes, Calder immediately becomes the outsider in a Nevada town of first- and second-generation Italians. The town's priest, Father Savio Lazzaroni, driven by an exaggerated sense of evil and the haunting vision of a black-clad mysterious man standing in a wheatfield, concludes that Calder epitomizes evil. Meanwhile, the mayor of the village, Manuel Cafferata, and several of the town's businessmen react to Calder primarily as a new presence threatening their leadership and businesses.

In Laxalt's desert allegory, Smale Calder becomes a mirror image, in which the other characters begin to see—or avoid seeing—their own deeply flawed souls. In the final action, the padre, in a moment of epiphany framed by the burning snake pit near Calder's home, discovers that the shadowy man in the wheatfield wears the priest's face; in that closing scene the father realizes that, not Calder, but he himself represents evil. Only after that illuminating self-discovery does the priest seem able to empathize with others. Until this dramatic event he has been like Nathaniel Hawthorne's Ethan Brand, isolated from people because of his impersonal, self-righteous actions.

Other residents of the town travel parallel journeys of self-understanding. Temptress Tosca Morelli lures young Amado, who plans on the priesthood, into her home where in a moment of passion he attacks her. Understanding herself, Tosca says later: "Calder and me can't help ourselves. He breaks the rule in one way, and I do it in another. He tries to stay away from trouble, and I go looking for it" (130). Another young person, Tony, comprehending the evil in all men, asks the priest, after the cleric's moment of illumination, to pray for Calder. In the closing scene, Father Savio and Tony, joined through wonder and compassion, pray for the dying Calder, with the largest of his snakes, its fangs buried in his face, snuggled near his body.

These closing pages, rich with Christian symbolism, provide striking examples of Laxalt's haunting allegory of a flawed Eden beset with arrogance, sin, and pride but redeemed through partial understanding. When queried about the book's meaning, Laxalt told his publisher: "You are right in seeing it as a parable. But it is my own concept of a parable, grounded in reality with people and ideas in realistic conflict, because to my mind, the perfect parable is not acceptable in the cynical, practical world of now. . . . I saw it as innocence caught up between the opposing forces of spirituality . . . and the practical." [11]

Altogether, *A Man in the Wheatfield* is a clear testament of Laxalt's versatility. As noted western writer and artist Tom Lea confessed, "It was not what I had expected of Robert Laxalt." "Yet," he added, "the new book shows perhaps even more Laxalt's power as a storyteller and his vividness of perception concerning people living in a living landscape." [12] Or, one might have compared Laxalt's perceptive handling of symbolism with his friend Walter Clark's use of elaborate symbols in *The Track of the Cat* and several of his short stories. Most important to Laxalt, however, the novel sold reasonably well, garnered positive reviews, and was named one of the six notable novels of the year.

In scattered references in several previous essays and short stories and particularly in a few sections in *Sweet Promised Land*, Laxalt referred to the history and sociocultural traditions of Old World Basques, but not until *In a Hundred Graves*, published in 1972, did he devote a full book to European Basques.[13] Not surprisingly, the book followed the mosaic-like form that Laxalt had employed so successfully in previous books. Gathering dozens of stories about families, specific individuals, historical events, and general Basque customs, Laxalt pieced together a memorable collection of impressions about his forebears in France.

A short book of less than 150 pages, *In a Hundred Graves* primarily evokes Old World Basque life in the Pyrenees Mountains, which divide Spain and France. Yet standing out from this collection of portraits and episodes is the persona of the narrator, the son of Basque parents who has returned to the land of his ancestors for a brief visit. The book becomes the revealing observations of an American Basque's reactions to the culture of his parents' people.

Laxalt focuses extensively on the *paysan*, the rustic Basque villagers. The stress is on the activities of farmers and shepherds, rarely on those of fishermen and urban workers. In narrowing his purview, Laxalt omits facets of the Basque experience, but his emphases on village life allow him to reveal many cohesive aspects of Basque character and outlook. A cross section of villagers peoples his pages: children, hunters, herdsmen, wives, priests, smugglers, and a variety of outcasts. Probing descriptions of singing and dancing, market-day activities, and church rituals and rites add much to his narrative. Taken together, these finely etched bits of folk life reveal a good deal about the uniquenesses of the Basques.

For more than a century, historians, anthropologists, and other students of cultures have been intrigued with national or racial identities.[14] Like these scholars, within the pages of *In a Hundred Graves*, Laxalt hints at a shadowy Basque character. Basques' tenacious ties to the land and their farmsteads, their inordinate allegiance to the Catholic Church, their mysterious language and unique blood types, and the binding links of extended kinship in their villages—these and other characteristics help to define Basque character. To these qualities Laxalt adds glimpses of Basque taciturnity, their practicalness, their aloofness toward outsiders, and their unbreakable hold on the past.

In a Hundred Graves is not a detailed, analytical account of Old World Basque social and cultural life. Instead, it collects delightful pages of memoir, history, reflection, and insight, with one major theme uniting the individual sections: the old, unique traditions of the Basques and their vigorous adherence—sometimes unconsciously—to them. That unity is made explicit on the final page: "A thousand generations of my ancestors have gone down into this ground. Sometimes when I walk through the aisles of stone, the smell of the ground rises up. It is old and familiar, and I know instantly that this ground is in me. . . . I have been buried here in a hundred little graveyards."

Laxalt's career took an unexpected turn in the mid-1970s. When the American Association for State and Local History (AASLH) began preliminary planning for its States and the Nation Series as a way to celebrate the country's bicentennial in 1976, it decided to select skilled narrative writers rather than local historians to write volumes for each state. Robert Laxalt obviously fulfilled the guidelines the AASLH established for authors of the series books. Clearly identified with his home state of Nevada, a skilled narrative writer, and the author of several books and numerous essays and short stories, Laxalt joined a cast of well-known western writers: David Lavender in California; Marc Simmons, New Mexico; Lawrence Clark Powell, Arizona; Marshall Sprague, Colorado; and John R. Milton, South Dakota. More traditional western historians were assigned to other western states.

From the beginning, Laxalt planned to write a history of Nevada much different from that a professional western historian might have prepared. In the prefatory pages to his completed *Nevada: A Bicentennial History,* Laxalt laid out what he wished to avoid and what he wanted to accomplish in his brief volume.[15] Too much historical writing, he argues, is short on narrative power, long on facts, and generally bereft of personal opinion and authorial presence. But his story of Nevada would be, most of all, a narrative story spiced with his personal opinions.

One might quibble here with some of Laxalt's definitions while agreeing with others. Undoubtedly, he would concur that the works of historians like Bernard DeVoto, Ray Billington, and Robert Utley are exceptions to his generalization that too much western history is fact-filled and dull. He might also admit that most of the bicentennial volumes, even those by academic historians, are primarily extended personal essays, artistically wrought. Conversely, Laxalt is on target in suggesting that too much western historical writing verges toward fact-filled, monographic, deadly dull accumulations of minor facts with little significance or interest. Laxalt's abbreviated story of his home state clearly avoids these traps, veering instead toward a personal, lively, impressionistic study of Nevada.

The form and content of Laxalt's history break noticeably from most historical writing. Rather than begin with the region's first human inhabitants, Laxalt opens his book with an ode to sagebrush, a three-page salute to and evaluation of its smell and its place and influence on Nevada history. Then follow chapters on explorers, rural Nevada, cowboys/buckaroos, sheepmen, mustangers, and miners. Not until Laxalt pushes past midpoint does he devote a few pages to Indians, their life ways, and early conflicts with the first white intruders. Within these and later chapters, the author spices his narrative with several vignettes or pen portraits (e.g., the Donner Party, female ranchers, and the town of Elko). Often prefacing and sometimes dramatizing these specific happenings and places are the voices of numerous Nevadans, especially those outside Reno and Las Vegas.

Not surprisingly, professional historians did not agree with a good deal of what Laxalt said about their craft. Some wondered if he were so addicted to the lively elements of the state's heritage—its boomtowns, prizefights, gambling, and mobsters like Bugsy Siegel—that he overlooked many of the daily and mundane events. They also pointed out that Laxalt devotes little space to the lives of laborers and city folk and that his book skips over cultural topics: schools, churches, literature, music, and art. In his attempt to provide impressions of Nevada, his critics continue, he succumbs to sentimentalism and sensationalism; he takes refuge in rural Nevada and fails to grapple with the underside of urbanization and gambling. What price gambling and its attendant evils? they ask. Next, his detractors add, the vaunted frontier individualism Laxalt so often praises may also have encouraged the uncontrolled gambling and political corruption that has plagued the state. Finally, what about the "rotten borough" epithet that one historian uses to describe the state? [16]

On balance, much of this criticism arises from clashing opinions about the purposes and goals of historical writing. Clearly, Laxalt wants his heart, as much as his head, to spawn his interpretations, and he is convinced that a sense of the Nevada past will likely emerge more readily from an author's and reader's *feelings* than from a collection of monographic facts. On the other hand, most western historians have avoided such a personal narrative approach, which, they contend, too often slides into sensationalism or excessive romanticism.

In the end, no one will miss Laxalt's clear intentions to present a well-told historical story. All his brief chapters—none more than fifteen pages—bulge with anecdotes, lively incidents, pen portraits, and attention-catching quotes. Through these literary devices, as well as through hundreds of well-turned phrases and sentences, Laxalt imports a verve, drive, and immediacy to his prose, allowing it to soar well beyond most writing about the American West. In short, Laxalt's narrative history of Nevada remains what he intended: an impressionistic, loving account of his home state.

Next, Laxalt expanded one of the abbreviated vignettes of *In a Hundred Graves* into a brief book. Barely seventy-five pages of text, *A Cup of Tea in Pamplona* (1985)[17] combines apt descriptions of ethnic culture with a morality tale. In the first half of the novelette, Gregorio, a veteran Basque smuggler in the Pyrenees, looks for a younger man to help him in his clandestine business. Nikolas, whom Gregorio invites to become his partner, occupies center stage in the second half. Undergoing an ordeal that tests his manhood and bravery, Nikolas proves his worth as a leader, even though untoward events bring tragedy to his life.

Laxalt focuses on community, culture, and courage in formulating this cautionary tale tinctured with Basque ethnicity. From the beginning, Laxalt's narrator makes clear the social costs of Gregorio's life of smuggling. Even though smuggling has been an accepted occupation for centuries among Basques, they nonetheless treat Gregorio as a social pariah. Although rich, he and his wife must live on the far edge of respectability. Even his son leaves home to study for the priesthood. "He did it to absolve my sins" (8), Gregorio tells a friend. The son's exit also leaves Gregorio without a partner; he turns to Nikolas to take up the role.

Reluctantly, Gregorio admits that his financial successes have come at great costs. He tries to hint about these costs to Nikolas and his poverty-stricken wife, but as one observer adds ironically, "The prospect of sudden riches can do funny things to a man" (8). Nikolas will understand these costs only after he assumes the burden of leadership, following the death of a relative who breaks the unwritten code of the Basque smugglers. Nikolas comes to understand what Gregorio already knows: Although Basque communities, relatives, and friends wink at the illegality of smuggling, they still isolate themselves from the smugglers. Early on Gregorio defines the contrabanders as men with "good chests and strong legs, a little hunger and an elastic conscience" (9). In the closing pages, Nikolas also comprehends what Gregorio had not explicitly mentioned: Smugglers have traded their nourishing ties to community and culture for riches and financial security. Nikolas enters the road to isolation that Gregorio has already traversed.

Laxalt's morality tale is embedded in the nuances of Old World Basque culture. The Basque characteristics treated throughout *In a Hundred Graves* reappear here: their inordinate desire for respectability, their pride, their jealousies, their ties to tradition. Laxalt also provides brief descriptions of Basque market days, class distinctions, and other peasant practices that enrich the texture of the story. Finally, in a wonderfully drawn adumbrative scene, the flawed performance of a warrior and his comrades' negative reactions to him in a wine glass dance prefigure the tragedy of Nikolas's relative in the mountains when he fails to obey orders. These illuminations of Basque culture are more than fringes on Laxalt's narrative tapestry; they are the warp and woof of this well-told story.

What additional goals did Robert Laxalt as an author still aspire to by the mid-1980s? He had already proven himself a skilled journalist, a notable novelist, a reputable historian, and the leading literary interpreter of the American Basques. What other ambitions still drove him?

For Laxalt, perhaps serendipity reared its head, possibly the *Roots* phenomenon played a role, or maybe the heightened interest in things ethnic during and after the 1960s and 1970s was the key. Probably Laxalt's life-long interest in writing a Basque epic also played around the edges of his mind. Whatever the major impetus, Robert Laxalt turned to his most important fictional project: He would undertake a trilogy of novels about his Basque family's experiences in the Old World and the American West. Even beyond that large goal, and building on these individual and family heritages, he would generalize about the experiences of Euskaldunak as pioneers at the turn of the twentieth century, as settlers in a closing frontier, and as participants in modern Nevada politics. It was a gigantic, risk-taking endeavor.

Every novelist, it is said, must eventually write his or her own life. Laxalt does much of that in his lyrical, coming-of-age story *The Basque Hotel* (1989),[18] the first installment of his Basque trilogy. Dedicated to Grace Bordewich, the high school English teacher who introduced Laxalt to the delights of literature and writing, this superb narrative of a Basque boy becoming a young man is the author's most memorable novel. Undoubtedly based on Laxalt's earlier years, the story is fresh with appealing and revealing insights, all delivered in Laxalt's limpid, descriptive prose.

Set in Carson City in the depression era, *The Basque Hotel* centers on a two-year period in the life of Pete, a young Basque lingering between boyhood and approaching manhood. The first half of the book describes Pete's months in a Basque hotel, but the second half divides between his stay in a new home the family acquires and his unforgettable days in the highland meadows with his father, his uncle, his brothers, and a band of sheep. The novel consists primarily of a series of abbreviated chapters dramatizing single incidents, but together they illuminate Pete's traumatic rites of passage toward adulthood. Laxalt's carefully coordinated plot reinforces his major theme of an adolescent's maturation.

Pete has to sort through a variety of experiences that rush upon him. Early on, while he is still in the protective womb of the Basque hotel, his mother broods over him, he plays soldiers, and he obviously remains a boy. But the author uses a serious illness (which Laxalt himself experienced) and removal from the hotel as turning points in Pete's journey. Although not entirely free from his boyhood, Pete is thrust into an adult world of religious doubts, violence, death, and sex, and his life takes several dramatic turns.

The final scene in *The Basque Hotel* laces together several separate strands of Pete's story that have developed throughout the novel. Hearing the blast of the fire whistle in Carson City, Pete is at first "confused"—"and then he knew"; it was the Basque hotel in which he had spent his boyhood. When the burning building begins to crumble, "a rush of unexpected recollections flooded over Pete, and he closed his eyes against the sight" (122, 123). Pleasant, childish memories evaporate in the inferno.

When bystanders talk about the blaze being "a good fire" because it will help Carson City "join up with *progress*," Pete flees the scene. His mounting alienation reaches a new height when a big-city visitor speaks of the fire as "the most excitement this burg has seen in a long time." Pete wanders away from the conflagration, separating himself from its destruction as well as from what he considers the supercilious attitudes of the onlookers.

Large changes are at work here in Pete, as Laxalt symbolically suggests. One old resident of the hotel, seeing Pete for the first time in several months, says, "[Y]ou growed." Indeed he has, as he himself soon realizes. In a final revealing scene, Pete wanders into a nearby barn where in the opening chapters he and his buddies had played boyish war games. "When he turned to go," Laxalt writes, Pete "saw in the pile of rubble on the floor a wooden lathe broken in the middle. He picked it up and remembered instantly the feel of the whittled handle. He laughed aloud in silence, because he had once imagined it to be a shining sword" (123, 124). Through experience, through traumatic illness, and through self-realization, Pete the Basque boy has assumed young manhood.

As a prequel to *The Basque Hotel, Child of the Holy Ghost* (1992)[19] traces the events that impelled Maitia Garat and Petya, her future husband, out of the Basque Country and drove them to the American Far West. Alternating between the two story lines but placing primary emphasis on Maitia's Old World and Petya's New World years, Laxalt unites the two in a Basque hotel in Reno shortly after World War I. Here, then, are the earliest portions of the longer story that Laxalt tells in his Basque family trilogy.

Pete, the narrator, is a shadowy figure in the novel. Although the story opens with his trip to the French Basque County to study his family's backgrounds as well as "to learn about the ways of the Basques in their ancestral villages" (3), his presence does not dominate the novel. The third-person omniscient narrator, providing personal, cultural, and historical details of Maitia's and Petya's families, carries the story much more than does the "I" storyteller.

Pete soon uncovers a family secret: Maitia was born illegitimate, "a child of the Holy Ghost." As he tracks down his mother's tangled story, Pete discovers how narrow, bigoted, and unrelenting his Basque relatives are, more interested in upholding tradition and honor than in exhibiting understanding or sympathy. Pete says that Americans are much less concerned with the dilemmas of illegitimacy than are their Old World relatives. Inheritance patterns, family honor, and pride of name—all are as closely watched in the old country as an alluring daughter. In describing the French Basque society that spawned Maitia, Laxalt, drawing upon his own mother's story, makes several forays into Basque history and culture, elaborating on ideas and outlooks introduced earlier in *In a Hundred Graves* and *A Cup of Tea in Pamplona.*

Laxalt also provides in the second segment of his trilogy the fullest treatment of the steps by which young Basque men were recruited, packaged, sent from the Basque County to Bordeau and then on to New York City and the American West. Here, the sequence of details is smoothly structured around the stories of Maitia and Petya, especially the unfortunate situation of Maitia's illegitimacy and Petya's chance observation of a murder in the Pyrenees.

A number of supporting characters in *Child of the Holy Ghost* become agents through which Laxalt depicts Basque traditions in southern France. For example, old man Garat, Maitia's grandfather, damns his daughter Jeanne for giving birth to her daughter outside marriage. Driven by his unyielding pride, the unrelenting force of Basque tradition, and his undisguised embarrassment, he drives Jeanne from his home, but eventually his hardened exterior crumbles before his growing love for his granddaughter Maitia, a love that eventually allows him to name her as the inheritor of his land. Another character, Jeanne's intended husband, Labadiste, is austere, businesslike, and perfunctory, accepting Jeanne after her indiscretion but turning away Maitia. Obviously, he is more an entrepreneur and a profit-driven man than husband, lover, and sympathetic person.

Similar reprehensible desires motivate Jean-Baptiste, Jeanne's younger brother, and Viktor, a neighbor. Cold, a calculating gambler, and a drunk bent on gaining the Garat family inheritance, Jean-Baptiste cares little for his sister or family; money drives him. Meanwhile, Viktor seems to desire Maitia as long as he stands to gain the Garat farmstead. Once that inheritance is lost, he disappears more quickly than the sun in the fog-shrouded Pyrenees. Conversely, Laxalt's warm and sympathetic depiction of a demented and earthy neighboring farm worker, Ramon, counterbalances the callous Jean-Baptiste, Viktor, and the town's gossipy postmistress, pliable magistrate, and crooked mayor.

The final two pages of the novel provide a strong sense of closure and vindication. Peter, the "I" narrator, says: "I would not be a proper son of Basques if I did not believe that fate sometimes needs a helping hand to square life's debts" (151). First, Petya's nemesis, the smuggler who threatened his life, is killed, as he himself had murdered a man, by being thrown over a precipice in the Pyrenees. And Peter works out a vengeful speech for his brother Leon to give in Maitia's natal village of Donibane, to which Leon is invited after winning the governorship of Nevada. The speech harpoons the town's residents and Maitia's family for their mistreatment of Pete's grandmother and mother and their robbing Maitia of her inheritance. The Basque sons of the "child of the Holy Ghost" have taken their revenge.

As he did in *Child of the Holy Ghost,* Pete Indart serves as narrator of *The Governor's Mansion* (1994),[20] the third volume of Laxalt's fictional trilogy. Not so much fiction as memoir and political history, this novel deals with Pete's older brother, Leon, and his successful run for the governorship and his unsuccessful pursuit of a U.S. senatorial position. But Pete's identity is even more shadowy here than in the first two novels of the series. Although he tells much of the story, in which he is intimately involved, his character is not easy to fathom.

Indeed, point of view and the context of Laxalt's most recent novel seem to disallow much character development. By organizing most of his plot around two political campaigns, especially the machinations involved in intra- and interparty squabbles, the author severely limits the expansion of his protagonists into round characters; instead they move linearly through the story without demonstrating much growth, change, or surprise. For example, Leon's actions are linked primarily to his campaigning; rather than being dramatized as a thinking, acting, and dynamic political leader, he is depicted as a pragmatic, sometimes cunning politico. His identity as father, husband, and brother gets lost in the political plot.

But these shortcomings can be overemphasized. For instance, one of Laxalt's former colleagues at the University of Nevada, Reno, criticizes the novel for its "confusingly enmeshed" reality and fiction.[21] But when must a novel avoid conflating fact and fiction, when must a novelist avoid linking history and imagined characterizations? If novelists must eschew all rearranging of history or the use of well-known figures under new names, then Leo Tolstoy, Willa Cather, Robert Penn Warren, and Wallace Stegner, among many others, have to be condemned for the open marriages of history and imagination in their historical novels.

In another way, Laxalt displays his abundant skills as novelist. Utilizing an appealing, Hemingwayesque touch, he employs the high, pristine Sierra meadows and hot, dry Las Vegas as the light and dark of the novel's Nevada setting. When Leon and Pete huddle with their political planners in a Las Vegas casino, they are usually plotting shenanigans and even crooked ploys, often ones limned in the grey, threatening atmosphere of their surroundings. But when the two brothers accompany their father to the mountains, they are refreshed through their Basque traditions, cleansed from the wheeling and dealing that even invades their family home in Carson City. The clean, restorative Sierra function as do the Pyrenees in Hemingway's *The Sun Also Rises:* The alpine settings wash away the grey grime of Las Vegas and Paris, respectively. In Laxalt's novel, although his principal characters are forced to hobnob with their materialistic and political cronies in the deserts below, especially in Las Vegas, their hearts and souls remain in the highlands.

The longest of Laxalt's novels and based in part on his earlier *Nevada, The Governor's Mansion* is also the least complex in form and content of all his book-length fiction. Primarily a novel based on politics, it reveals more about Nevada's recent political history than about a group of characters growing and changing. Still, the work tells us much about the leading American Basque family and their important involvements in American politics. Without stressing the ethnic identity of Leon and Peter and their family, the author provides revealing details about the Laxalt clan unavailable elsewhere, and from the perspective of an inside observer.

When an interviewer recently asked Robert Laxalt how he wished to be known, he replied that he hoped that critics would remember him as an American writer who dealt with western and Basque subjects. Quite often, Laxalt *is* mentioned as a well-known American author who treats western and immigration themes.[22] Unfortunately, however, critics have failed to understand his versatility, his significant work in journalism and history, as well as in fiction. Notable changes also mark his writings. For instance, in Laxalt's early short works, men nearly always dominated his scenes, but more recently women have come to center stage, as in *Child of the Holy Ghost.*

Laxalt likewise deserves continuing attention as an important western American novelist. Over time, from his earliest brief sketches and short stories, to *Sweet Promised Land,* and on to the Basque trilogy, he has traced the West from frontier, to region, to postregion, from pioneer to contemporary times. Throughout his career, Laxalt has focused on people-land relationships; that relationship, he contends, is the major theme in his American western writing, as well as in several of his works about Old World Basques. In his most recent work, Laxalt also provides revealing glimpses of the contemporary West, especially in his negative portraits of Las Vegas, but also in persisting ranch and buckaroo cultures. Indeed, his depictions of modern Nevada are illustrative examples of a new urban West that historians are just beginning to chronicle.

Still, despite his desires otherwise, Robert Laxalt is best known as a Basque writer, as an Euskalduna himself, as well as the leading literary interpreter of his ethnic group. When he portrays his father, Dominique, in *Sweet Promised Land* and his family in the Basque trilogy, or when he treats Old World Basque culture in several widely cited essays in *National Geographic, In a Hundred Graves,* and *A Cup of Tea in Pamplona,* he describes an important ethnic culture that spices societies on both sides of the Atlantic. Not only furnishing the most memorable portrait of a Basque sheepherder in the American West, Laxalt also deals with Basque families, particularly his own, involved in activities outside the high mountain pastures and the sagebrush hills.

In supplying rewarding and probing portraits of Basque experiences in the American West, Laxalt joins dozens of other authors who have also written notable fiction about European immigrant groups transplanted to the West. One thinks of Willa Cather's important novels about Eastern European newcomers, Ole Rölvaag and Wallace Stegner on Scandinavians, Frederick Manfred on the Dutch, Ivan Doig on the Scots, and Ruth Suckow on the Germans. Among those treating the Basques in fiction, Laxalt is unsurpassed, although one would do well to compare and contrast his novels with those of Ann Nolan Clark, Frank Bergon, and Laxalt's own daughter, Monique Laxalt Urza. And to his credit, Laxalt avoids ethnic chauvinism. In fact, one wonders how his fellow Basques, especially Old World Euskaldunak, react to some of his unflattering portraits of their bigotry and narrow-mindedness. Enriching his stories with redolent ethnic materials, he eschews the hyped ethnicity that plagues too many recent American novels.[23]

Finally, then, Robert Laxalt is quite simply the most significant of all American Basque writers. He has produced a dozen books, several of which deserve continuing attention. His shorter pieces illustrate the competent writing of a craftsman: *Nevada* and the essays in *National Geographic,* the smoothly wrought work of an artistic historian; *A Man in the Wheatfield,* the fiction of a skilled novelist; the Basque trilogy, the achievement of a notable author; and *Sweet Promised Land,* the apex of a memorable literary career.

13

Robert Erburu and Becoming
a Postmodern Basque

WILLIAM A. DOUGLASS

For students of European immigration in the United States, the common approach is to speak of the "Polish-American," "Italian-American," and "Basque-American" experience. Implicitly, it is the hyphenated collectivity that faces the challenge posed by transposal of an Old World people to a New World setting in which they are then confronted with a series of opportunities, attractions, influences, admonitions, and pressures that favored, facilitated, and even forced their assimilation within the host society and its culture. At one time it seemed that the process was unidirectional, inexorably destined to culminate in the full integration of everyone into the American mainstream. Logically, the perspective predicted the ultimate disappearance of discernible white ethnic groups within the American experience.

Although the assimilation assumption went unchallenged, it was the investigator's task to document the particulars affecting and effecting the differential rates of assimilation of particular groups. Thus, the centuries-long persecution of Jews might translate into a certain self-defensiveness, self-awareness, and group clannishness that slowed the assimilatory process. In nineteenth-century Boston, for example, the terms and attendant stereotypes of the Old World clash between the Irish and the English translated into job, housing, and social discrimination against the former that inhibited their acceptance, at least for a generation or two. Anti-southern- and central-European sentiment clearly segregated or ghettoized Italian and Polish immigrants, at least temporarily. Since the story varied from one group to another, as well as for the same group according to its wider setting (e.g., rural versus urban, East Coast versus American West), it was worth retelling in its many variations. Methodologically, the tale tended to be unimaginative, since it usually turned upon the persistence of certain Old World traits in the New World context as a measure of the degree (or lack thereof) of assimilation of a particular group at a given time.

By the mid-twentieth century it was becoming apparent that the assimilation assumption, the so-called "melting pot" theory, was inadequate to explain the ethnicity maintenance evident in some ethnic groups and resurgent in others. It was Marcus Lee Hansen who underscored the "problem of the third generation," namely that "what the son wishes to forget the grandson wishes to remember."[1] This growing awareness that ethnic identity remained an active agent within the American experience, capable of being recovered or even reinvented, and amenable to change without transformation necessarily implying loss, was further confirmed by the subsequent roots phenomenon and the emergence of the "new ethnicity" among the descendants of Euro-American immigrants.

In positing his third-generation effect Hansen restricted his purview to Americans of European descent. His temporal baseline (i.e., the first or founding generation) regarded those born in Europe who actually emigrated to America. Given the realities of the receiving nation's white dominance and racism, nonwhites were simply ignored. If there was some kind of generation effect operative among Native Americans, blacks, and Asian and Latin American immigrants in the United States (and there clearly was), it did not inform Hansen's thesis.

Hansen had discerned the emerging pattern of ethnic resurgence among Euro-Americans prior to World War II; in the conflict's aftermath several developments coincided to bring them into sharper focus. The outbreak of the Cold War (with its threat of nuclear extermination), as well as the Korean and Vietnam conflicts, quickly challenged American supremacy and invincibility supposedly won on the battlefields but a few years earlier. This, in turn, undermined the seemingly obvious worth of unexamined adherence to a triumphant New World collective identity. The countercultural movement questioned the premises of the consumer society, paralleled by a civil rights movement that forced Americans to examine and acknowledge the huge disparity between rhetoric and reality within American life. In short, the nation's daughters questioned profoundly the values of its mothers (the gendering of the present sentence underscoring yet another powerful rift and social revolution within the national experience). With the "general" under such multipronged attack, it is scarcely surprising that many Americans sought refuge in the "particular."

In short, the new ethnicity, in fine Hansenian fashion, came to represent a kind of "grandmother-knew-best-even-though-she-spoke-with-a-funny-accent" reaction to the parental architects of the national mess. Whether in the form of Black Power, Red Power, or White America's quest for hyphenation, ethnicity equated to authenticity.[2]

As the melting-pot hypothesis (or even thesis) literally melted away before the growing reality that the relationship between immigration and assimilation is as much processual as structural, it has become apparent that ethnicity is an intervening variable not only highly complex and multifaceted but, at least over the short term, multidirectional— seemingly as capable of waxing as of waning.

However, of equal importance is the heightened realization that many of the elements vary according to whether the ethnic group or the individual ethnic actor is under analysis. The former is not merely the sum of its constituent latter, nor are they simply an echo or expression of collective reality. At the same time, it is equally evident that each requires the other, at least partially. Indeed, the complexity of their articulation currently poses the most promising, albeit problematic, challenges to the fields of immigration and ethnic studies alike.

In retrospect Hansen and the new-ethnicity analysts clearly treat this articulation between ethnic group and ethnic actor differently. For the former, ethnic actors are the product of their generation, whereas for the latter, the new ethnicity generates its ethnic actors. For example, Micaela de Leonardo, in her work *The Varieties of the Ethnic Experience*,[3] treats the group experience as the vague parameters within which ethnic actors form their ethnic persona. In this regard, for some second- and third-generation Californians, "Italian American" serves as more of a category than a structure, a field of opportunity rather than a straitjacket, a blank sheet of paper rather than a published text. The present article subscribes to such a view of the role of ethnicity in late-twentieth-century America. Nevertheless, it is equally true that the category is not created *ex nihilo*. That is, it is itself the product of a history and set of boundaries (albeit ones that may shift over time), a situation that Green calls "post-structuralist structure."[4]

At the same time, the formulation of an ethnic persona within the context of the new ethnicity is, for *its* first generation, the conscious decision of adult social actors. We are no longer dealing with an acting out of a received script but rather a seeking out of perceived (or intuited) symbolic meaning. Group structure as individual stricture has little place in the world of new ethnicity in which heritage is more a source of pride and pleasure than a road map for daily existence. In this regard ethnic persona is but one facet of the individual's social persona; ethnic identity cannot be presumed yet can be assumed, and ethnic heritage becomes as much a source of private reverie as of public display. One of the evident consequences is that ethnicity, from an individual's perspective, becomes increasingly less essentialist and genealogical and more the object of serious (as well as playful) play.

In equating the new ethnicity to play I do not mean to trivialize its significance. To the contrary, I mean to suggest that precisely when concepts such as ethnicity are liberated from essentialist assumptions their creative potential is truly unleashed.

At this juncture it might seem like the foregoing overview, none of the elements of which are unique to this essay, is a grandiose and pretentious way to introduce the life story of a single individual—Robert Erburu. However, I implore the reader's patience, since I believe that it provides the essential context for what is to follow. For Robert Erburu is a quintessential example of the new ethnicity, his ethnic persona being, in terms of his own life, the recent rather than remote outcome of a process that began as passive discovery and then became active quest. I intend in the treatment of Robert's life story to conserve as much as possible this sense of discovery, since, to my mind, it is as important to understand the process as its outcome. In this sense I believe that the new ethnicity challenges us to produce new biography.

Forming a Public Persona [5]

In 1948 Robert Erburu, a studious young man from the small town of Ojai, in Ventura County, registered at the University of Southern California (USC). He selected USC despite being wooed by Stanford, largely because of family tradition. His older brother, Lawrence, had studied journalism there, prompting the young Robert to become a Trojans fan. When Lawrence was killed while serving as a marine in World War II, it seemed only natural that Robert would honor his brother's memory in his own choice of colleges. While studying journalism at USC, the young student worked as a sports writer for the school newspaper. In his senior year he was made editor of the *Daily Trojan.*

Upon graduation Robert decided to move to the East Coast to pursue his graduate studies, thinking that a year in New York, or Washington, D.C., would be good experience for a budding journalist, one that might even lead to an opportunity to become a foreign correspondent. However, his faculty adviser at USC convinced him to enroll in law school, arguing that a legal education teaches you to think logically and critically—important skills for an aspiring newspaperman.

Before going off to Harvard Law School, Robert discussed his plans with an elderly attorney and judge in Ventura and was offered a position upon completion of his studies. With law degree in hand and recently married to Lois Stone (of English descent), an education major whom he had met at USC, Robert returned to Los Angeles to study for the California bar exam before moving to Ventura. While in the city he decided to interview with two or three large law firms, including one of the most prestigious—Gibson, Dunn and Crutcher. In the course of that day's discussions he was introduced to a senior partner, Homer Crotty, who asked, "Are you Mariano Erburu's grandson?" It turned out that Crotty's father-in-law's father was Samuel Lloyd, the man from whom Robert's grandfather had once purchased a ranch. A few days later Robert was offered a position with the firm. He called the attorney/judge in Ventura to ask for advice and was told to take the offer, since "you can always come to Ventura, but once you're in Ventura you can never go to Los Angeles."

Robert and a cadre of other young lawyers started out as legal interns in the firm's law library. It was their responsibility to provide the more senior staff with the essential research to try their cases. During his second year Robert was made responsible for the other interns, essentially doling out their work assignments as well as supervising the many law students on summer internships. From there he graduated to the corporate department, where he gained considerable experience in the buying and selling of businesses and the filing of securities registrations.

One of the firm's corporate clients was The Times Mirror Company, publisher of the *Los Angeles Times.* Its corporate attorney specialized in libel and slander law. The company was poised to expand, and it therefore planned to hire its own business counsel, but approached Gibson, Dunn and Crutcher for interim assistance. Given Robert's background in journalism, he was offered the seemingly temporary assignment to serve as Times Mirror's corporate lawyer. However, after about six months he was offered the permanent position. Since he had been with Gibson, Dunn and Crutcher for six years and, typically, promising attorneys were offered a partnership in their seventh year, Robert faced a major personal and professional dilemma. Both Lois and some of the senior partners of his law firm concurred that it was risky to walk away from the sure partnership that was tantamount to a lifetime of security. However, Robert had come to realize that for a practicing private attorney the search for clients was perpetual and that in the lawyer-client relationship the attorney always remained an expendable outsider. The Times Mirror offer was an opportunity to belong to a team and to be part of the excitement of growing with a company committed to aggressive expansion. Robert joined Times Mirror.

At the time the company, although publicly traded, was controlled by the Chandler family. Robert became the assistant secretary and assistant general counsel, and it was intended that he work directly under the company's longstanding counsel. However, within three months the decision was made to reorganize, converting the parent Times Mirror into a holding company poised for aggressive further corporate acquisitions; the *Los Angeles Times* would be its major operating unit. Robert's boss became general counsel for the latter, while, given his corporate law experience, Robert was made general counsel and secretary of the Times Mirror Company. Also, given his background in journalism, he developed a good working relationship with Otis Chandler, the family's heir apparent as publisher of the *Los Angeles Times*. So at the age of thirty, Robert found himself in positions of considerable influence within a company that was poised to make major business strides.

Robert had joined Times Mirror in 1961 and over the next few years was a key player on the negotiating team that made several acquisitions. In 1964 Times Mirror became the first newspaper publisher to be listed on the New York Stock Exchange. That same year Robert was promoted to vice-president of the company and in 1968 was elected to its board of directors. In 1974 he was made president and in 1981 the chief executive officer. From 1986 until his retirement in 1995, he served as chairman of the board. The magnitude of the change at Times Mirror during those years may be appreciated in the growth of its revenues: In 1961 they totaled $100 million; in 1993 they were $3.7 billion.

The details of Robert Erburu's business career, as spectacular as they are, describe but one aspect of his public persona, for he also is a noted civic leader and patron of the arts. It was, of course, only natural that as a prominent executive of the company publishing one of the world's most prestigious newspapers Robert would be called upon to assume civic responsibilities. When still a vice-president, he was approached by the CEO of Security Pacific Bank and asked to become the organizer of the Los Angeles Chamber of Commerce Business Outlook Conference. Robert subsequently served as a board member of the Business Council, the Business Roundtable, the California Business Roundtable, and the Los Angeles World Affairs Council. He was a director of the Los Angeles Area Chamber of Commerce and, from 1974 to 1984, served as a director of the Chamber of Commerce of the United States. Not surprisingly, he became a member of the board of directors of the American Newspaper Publishers Association and served as the organization's chairman (1991–1992). He was appointed to the board of directors of the Federal Reserve Bank of San Francisco and, between 1988 and 1991, served as its chairman, thereby becoming a key player in the formulation of U.S. monetary policy.

With his growing professional visibility Robert was approached frequently to provide leadership to civic and charitable endeavors. He gave of his time generously, serving as trustee of the Brookings Institution, as board member of the YMCA of Metropolitan Los Angeles, as director of the independent Colleges of Southern California, and as member of the Archdiocesan Finance Council of the Catholic Archdiocese of Los Angeles. The breadth of his activities and the esteem in which they were held are reflected in the many individual awards conferred on him. In 1977 he was given the American Jewish Committee's Human Relations Award, and in 1979 he received the Brotherhood Award from the National Conference of Christians and Jews. The Constitutional Rights Foundation's Bill of Rights Award was presented to him in 1983. In 1988 the University of Southern California bestowed upon him the Asa V. Call Achievement Award. In 1989 he and Lois received the Albert Schweitzer Leadership Award from the Hugh O'Brian Youth Foundation. In 1991 he was elected a Fellow of the American Academy of Arts and Sciences.

In all of the foregoing there is profiled the kind of business, civic, and charitable activity that is expected of, and frequently characterizes, America's corporate leaders. There is, however, another dimension to Robert Erburu's public persona that is less predictable—this is, his extraordinary dedication to culture and the arts. In this vein he is beholden to his dear friend and mentor Franklin Murphy. Franklin was, in Robert's words, a true "Renaissance man." In his capacity as

Robert's predecessor as CEO of the Times Mirror, Franklin was a major patron of the arts. He served on many foundation and museum boards and was eventually made chairman of the board of the National Gallery of Art in Washington, D.C.

In one of their many informal conversations Robert asked Franklin to name the world's greatest art museum, expecting to be told that it was the Louvre or some such. Franklin instead replied that you have to distinguish between the large, comprehensive museum and the much smaller one with a choice collection. Franklin cited the Frick Museum in New York as a prime example of the latter. Robert had never heard of it and, in fact, had scarcely visited art museums before. Franklin urged him to go to the Frick Museum on his next trip to New York, which he did. According to Robert, "It was breathtaking. I had never been in a place like that before. I couldn't get enough. So in my many travels I began to schedule brief visits to other museums. Even if I just had an hour I would go to the National Gallery when in London or the Met when in New York."

Art viewing became a passion for Lois as well, so she began to accompany Robert more often in his travels.

In retrospect, Franklin clearly saw in Robert his protégé. According to Robert, "Franklin had his footprints all over Los Angeles and so when he became CEO he took an already public-service-minded company under the Chandlers to an even greater level of community involvement." Franklin urged Robert to engage in foundation work. Up to that point his only such commitment had been to the Huntington Library, an association stemming from his former law firm's role as Henry Huntington's solicitor. Franklin arranged for Robert to become a trustee of the Ahmanson Foundation and member of the board of directors of both the J. Paul Getty Trust and the National Gallery of Art. Robert also agreed to be a board member of the Carrie Estelle Doherty Foundation, the William and Flora Hewlett Foundation, the Fletcher Jones Foundation, the Ralph M. Parsons Foundation, the Times Mirror Foundation, and the Pfaffinger Foundation. At present he serves as the chairman of the board of the J. Paul Getty Trust, one of the most influential players within America's cultural and artistic life.

Since his USC days Robert remains a strong sports fan. In former years, when he had more spare time, he seldom missed a USC football game, and he managed to attend a dozen or more Los Angeles Dodgers baseball games each season. In summing himself up in our interview Robert confided, "My colleagues will tell you that there are two untouchables at the Times Mirror as long as I am CEO. Neither is important from a financial standpoint. One is the *Sporting News,* which I bought from the grandson of the founder, C. C. Johnson Spink, and the other is the art book publisher Harry Abrams, which I didn't buy. While it's not quite true, people think they are my sacred cows."

Forming an Ethnic Persona

Robert was born on September 27, 1930, in Ventura to Kathryn Sarzotti and Michael Erburu. His mother was the daughter of Italian immigrants. Born in Piedmont, she was brought to the United States by her parents when she was two years old. Her father, a peasant farmer in Europe, worked as a ranch hand before buying a small farm near Ventura, where the family raised oranges and lima beans. Kathryn worked on the farm and, after completing two years of high school, took a position as secretary and bookkeeper for a lumber company. At twenty she met Michael, nine years her senior and the son of Mariano Erburu, a Basque immigrant from Aurizberri, Navarre.

Mariano, then, is Robert's active transatlantic link with the Basque Country, although, as we shall see, not his only genealogical one. According to a published biographical sketch,[6] Mariano, born in 1856, entered the United States in 1874. He came from a peasant village in Navarre to Ventura, where he was employed as a sheepherder. Twelve years later he entered the mercantile business with J. Feraud, a Frenchman. In 1900 he sold out to his partner and leased a 3,750-acre ranch from the Lloyd family (which he then purchased in 1903) for the purpose of sheep raising. In 1914 he sold his sheep and concentrated upon feeding cattle (three hundred head) and raising lima beans (60 acres). According to his biographer,

> Mr. Erburu married at Santa Barbara, Miss Juana Orella, and to this union there were born two children: Michael, twenty-five years of age, who attended the public and high schools, graduated from the State Polytechnic School at San Luis Obispo, California, and is now engaged in ranching with his father; and Miss Mercedes, a graduate of the high school, who resides at home. Mr. Erburu is a member of the Union Latin American. He is a republican in politics and a faithful member and generous supporter of the Catholic Church.[7]

Thus we have a "frozen-frame view" of the Erburu family, published in 1917, or before Michael married Kathryn. It is possible, primarily through the recollections of the latter,[8] to flesh out the lives of

Mariano and his wife, Juana—Robert Erburu's paternal grandparents. For reasons that will become apparent, the details form but a sketchy part of Robert's memory.

According to his biographer, Mariano decided to emigrate when he was seventeen since, "[l]ike many other young men of his country . . . he could see nothing of promise in the future for him, and therefore decided to try his fortune elsewhere. Naturally, America attracted him."[9]

This assumption, common at the time (1917), of the power of the American dream as *the* explanation of European emigration to the United States, fails to equate with what Mariano told Kathryn. He left Navarre in order to avoid service in the last Carlist War (1873–1876). His father urged him to leave for the United States, as he didn't want to lose a son to the conflict.

The young Mariano landed in New York, and it is unclear how or why he made his way to Ventura. While herding sheep during his first winter there, he contracted pneumonia. He went to town where he was nursed by a kindly, middle-aged couple from Cuba. The pneumonia evolved into polio, and Mariano's condition became so grave that his benefactors built a wooden coffin that they placed by his sickbed. The patient survived, though he was left without feeling in his feet. Despite this handicap, he went back to sheepherding and eventually came to own a sheep band.

One year the market for sheep was so poor in Ventura that Mariano resolved to trail his lambs along the coast for sale in San Francisco. Just north of Santa Barbara there is a headland that could only be circumvented by traversing the seabed at low tide. Adjacent to it was the Orella ranch, and Mariano asked its owner, Don Bruno, if he could stay overnight while awaiting the next tide. Bruno liked the young man and they became friends. In time Mariano married Bruno's daughter Juana. Shortly after the wedding he departed for his only trip back to Navarre, to visit his ailing widowed father. When he returned to the United States, he brought along two of his nephews to work with him in California.

The Orella ranch, called the Cañada del Corral, was an original Mexican land grant. The Orellas also had a house in Santa Barbara and were members of the "Old California" Hispanic social elite—the so-called "California dons." When Bruno and his wife, Mercedes González Guevara, died they left to each of their eleven surviving children a ranch carved out of the original acreage. Robert Erburu and his sister still own a 300-acre Santa Barbara County property that came down to them as a part of their great-grandparents' patrimony.

Kathryn remembers her mother-in-law, Juana, as a proud if somewhat aloof person who was keenly aware of her high social status. Old Santa Barbara lorded it over upstart Ventura, and when Juana was about to give birth to Michael she insisted upon making the arduous journey to her hometown so that her son would be born there. Juana, despite being a California native, was fluent in Spanish and used it frequently, particularly with her parents. Indeed, her mother was a monolingual Spanish speaker. Kathryn, with her own childhood knowledge of Italian (or, more accurately, the Piedmontese dialect), quickly learned Spanish as a kind of implicit rite of passage for full membership in the Orella/Erburu family. She never spoke English with her mother-in-law.

If we pick up the story in the years after publication of Mariano's biographical sketch, Michael and Kathryn had three children, Barbara, Lawrence, and Robert. Robert was the youngest, and there was a gap of nearly half a generation between him and his older siblings. It was they who grew up in Ventura and within Mariano and Juana's aura.

By the time that Robert was born, Michael was a semiretired property manager of some means, although the grandfather had missed out on the chance of a lifetime. Mariano had failed to buy the mineral rights when he acquired the Lloyd Ranch, and it subsequently became a part of the Ventura oil field, one of California's richest. However, oil was also discovered (in more modest amounts) on the Orella property in Santa Barbara, and Michael managed the family's real estate and stock investments.

Robert was a sickly child, afflicted by severe asthma. Ventura's coastal fog and humidity did not agree with him, so his parents went searching for a better climate. Ojai, just fourteen miles inland, was far drier and more suitable. So Michael and Kathryn settled there with Robert. Barbara and Lawrence, already in school, stayed in Ventura with their grandparents. Every Sunday Robert and his parents traveled to Ventura for family dinner with the Erburus. Thanksgiving was celebrated with Kathryn's parents, who served homemade Italian raviolis along with American turkey and dressing. Christmas was celebrated by both families in Ojai.

Given the split-household arrangement, Robert, already more chronologically distanced than his siblings from his ethnic origins, became physically removed from them as well—at least insofar as family circle intimacy was concerned. The move to Ojai also insulated the young boy from other ethnic influences. There was a Basque contingent in Ventura, and Mariano had frequent visits from some French Basque friends, notably the Uharriet family. Mr. and Mrs. Uharriet visited Mariano and Juana almost daily. The two elderly men would spend hours talking to each other in *Euskara* while downstairs Mrs. Uharriet and Juana conversed in Spanish. At one point there was even a fruitless attempt to arrange marriage between Michael and a Uharriet daughter. And then there was Uncle Alfonso, himself the subject of a biographical sketch in the Gidney, Brooks and Sheridan book.[10]

Alfonso Erburu came to the United States in 1882, when he was seventeen years old. According to his biographer, "His dreams constantly brought to his mind the winning of a worthwhile success in America."[11] However, one suspects that Alfonso's father's vow not to lose another son to the state was still an operative consideration. In the aftermath of the Carlists' defeat, compulsory military service in the Spanish army for the previously exempted Basques was instituted for the first time, and there was a flood of emigration from the rural Basque area of youths approaching draft age.[12] It is scarcely surprising that Alfonso made his way to Ventura, since Mariano was already established there.

Alfonso herded sheep for five years in Ventura County and then went to the northern part of the state, where he became a transhumant operator of his own sheep band. In 1904 Alfonso returned to Ventura County with 3,600 of his own sheep. He sold some and with the remainder went into partnership with the Hobson brothers for four years. He then entered into a sheep-raising partnership with Mariano for another four. In 1912 Alfonso sold his share and bought a fifty-five-acre farm in Ventura County, near Montalvo, where, at the time of his biography, he was cultivating lima beans. According to his biography, "Mr. Erburu is a member of the Union Latin American[13] and of the French Hospital of San Francisco.[14] He is a republican in politics, and adheres to the faith of the Catholic Church. Mr. Erburu is unmarried."[15]

Kathryn relates that when she was a young bride Uncle Alfonso came to her in-laws' house frequently. He never married, having been sorely disappointed in unrequited love, and he was given to returning for part of the year to his natal village. He, therefore, maintained a strong link with his married brother's son, Ildefonso, who continued to operate the family farm in Navarre.

Between them, Alfonso and Mariano had helped three of their nephews come to Ventura, where they had their initial employment as herders with their uncles. Martín cut a dashing figure and became the apple of Juana Orella's eye. He was an accomplished dancer and played the castanets. Martín was very popular with the girls. But he contracted pneumonia and, despite Juana's best efforts, died. She went into full mourning, wearing only black clothing for a considerable time.

Another of the nephews, Mariano, born in 1889, was the godson of Mariano and Juana Orella by proxy. As a young man he worked with his uncle Alfonso until they had a falling out. He eventually settled in Orange County, where he raised oranges. The younger Mariano sent back to Navarre for his bride, and they had two children in California. However, these cousins were not really a part of Robert's ethnic universe, since little ongoing contact exists between these two branches of the Erburu family.

The other nephew, Pedro, remained unmarried and stayed with his uncle Alfonso until reaching retirement age himself. He eventually died in Ventura.

To the extent, then, that the extended Erburu family constituted its own ethnic world, it was focused upon the Ventura branch of the household. Given that he was growing up in Ojai, Robert was but little influenced by it. His recollections of Alfonso are scant, despite the fact that his uncle left him $10,000 in his will[16] (since Robert was his godson).

Ventura had a pervasive California-Hispanic flavor, fostered by long-established families in the area with Mexican and/or Iberian credentials. It also had the Union Latin American, mentioned in both Mariano's and Alfonso's biographical sketches, that brought together Southern European "Latins" of wide-ranging origins—including Mariano's partner, the French storekeeper J. Feraud, and northern Italians like Kathryn's family. The club had its own hall, did charitable work, and sponsored an annual barbecue open to all. But Ventura's ethnic ambiance was considerably more real and relevant for Barbara and Lawrence than for their brother Robert.

Robert's asthmatic condition was life-threatening, and his care became the family's number-one priority. He proved allergic to milk, eggs and, above all, to animal hair and dust. It was clear that Robert could not survive in a livestock environment, and his condition was a key consideration in Michael's decision to abandon ranching.

Whenever Robert suffered an attack it was necessary to place him in an enclosed space and burn the powdered medication Asmador. In this fashion he spent countless hours in the bathroom. Barbara taught him to read by the time he was four, so to pass the time he began to consume the *Encyclopedia Britannica* and other books. To this day he remains a voracious reader.

As he became older the asthma abated, and Robert was able to lead a normal life. He was even able to play on his high school's basketball and tennis teams. His early years in the bathroom academy served him well, however, since his marathon reading honed his comprehension and writing skills. He graduated near the top of his class and went on, as we have seen, to earn a degree in journalism from USC and a law degree from Harvard.

In Robert's recollections his earliest contacts with his Basque roots are largely personified by his grandfather. Mariano would sing nursery rhymes in Euskara to Barbara and Lawrence but not to Robert. By the time that Robert was born Mariano was quite advanced in age and was clearly failing. Yet Robert remembers fondly sitting for long hours with his elderly grandfather. They always interacted in English. Robert vaguely recalls having been told stories about life in Navarre but remembers nothing of their content.

In fact, Robert's real initial insight into Basque ethnicity came through his readings. He was fascinated by world geography and remembers reading enough about Spain to know that it contained part of the Basque homeland. By the time he was in high school he knew that there were many Basques in Argentina. However, to the extent that he felt ethnically linked at all, it was to the southern California Hispanic world and particularly its Old California dimension rather than to an explicitly Basque heritage.

It is equally relevant to consider that he did not become as integrated into an available Italian ethnic world. Indeed, one might have predicted that it would have lent more form and substance to his ethnic persona. After all, his grandparents were alive, and both were Old World–born immigrants from Piedmont. Kathryn's father had a brother in Ventura when he emigrated there himself. Also, there were several other Piedmontese families in the area. Kathryn recalls having had considerable interaction with them while growing up. There were frequent Sunday get-togethers, particularly for the men to play bocce ball and the women bingo. When Kathryn met Michael at a dance at the Armory Hall, she was closely chaperoned, even though she was twenty years of age. In short, Kathryn's ethnic world was much more clearly defined, both linguistically and culturally, than was Michael's.

Yet, to the extent that Robert entered either, it was his father's. As he puts it, "When I went to USC I chose to study Spanish rather than Italian. I guess that says something." However, he does not equate the decision to conscious identification with an ethnic heritage. Given southern Californian (and family) realities, it just seemed like a natural choice. Nevertheless, Robert did not entirely eschew his Italian roots, as we shall see presently.

One obvious line of speculation, of course, is that the skewing of Robert's and his siblings' ethnicity was less a choice than dictated by socioeconomic reality. The Sarzottis' circumstances were certainly more modest than those of the Erburus. Indeed, Kathryn's father would eventually work as a gardener for Mariano. However, there is a further explanation. When Michael and Kathryn married, he was active in the sheep business with his father. Sometime after the Gidney account, the family had acquired seven hundred or eight hundred acres of rangeland near Ventura and sheep bands. Kathryn moved into an extended family household that included her parents-in-law and her unmarried sister-in-law. As she put it, "I didn't have any privacy like you do when you have your own home. But that was the old way of the Spaniards, you know." [17]

Michael and Mariano were running about four thousand sheep. They used their private range near Ventura during the summer and also leased the Chopitea Ranch in nearby Santa Clara Valley (Oxnard), where, after the annual harvest, the sheep grazed the stubble during the winter months. Kathryn recalls that they employed one Mexican herder, but the rest were either Basques or Spaniards. Eventually, the family began to raise cattle, running about two hundred head on the Ventura property before selling out altogether. In short, marriage for Kathryn meant incorporation into Michael's domestic and business spheres rather than vice versa.

At the same time Michael was a tenuous link in the genealogical grid of Erburu ethnicity. Kathryn quickly surpassed him in her knowledge of Spanish. He had graduated from California State Polytechnic College and was thoroughly Americanized in every regard. According to Kathryn he had few Spanish or Basque friends. Ironically, then, she was a more active element in the generational transfer of Basque/Spanish ethnic awareness within the family than was her husband.

In considering Robert's childhood and the shaping of his public persona there is little that would have predicted his subsequent active pursuit of ethnic identity. Rather we have the profile of a successful young professional pursuing career opportunities within the Anglo world and in its terms. By relocating to Los Angeles he had become physically removed from the ethnic influences of family and birthplace (such as they were), and his marriage to Lois scarcely constituted ethnic endogamy. Nevertheless, Robert could never quite eschew or escape his ethnic background altogether. As he puts it, "You can't have a name like Erburu without it raising some questions."

This point requires some consideration, since it regards ethnic uniqueness of a particular sort concerning the Basque experience within American society. Although it might be argued that surnames such as Franklin's "Murphy" or even Kathryn's "Sarzotti" have ethnic implications, their situational consequences arguably differ from those of "Erburu." Irish and Italians simply constitute too large of a tile within the American mosaic for common Irishness or common Italianness to translate readily into a we-versus-they or insider-versus-outsider paradigm. "Erburu," however, possesses the power to elicit the question "What kind of a name is that?" from the uninitiated, a "You're Basque, aren't you?" among the *cognoscenti,* and a "You're a Basque, too!" from fellow ethnics.

Each in its own way is a segue into a range of questions and responses that differ from those demanded of representatives of the larger groups of hyphenated Americans. Thus, to admit that you are a Basque to the uninitiated is to assume the burden of explaining who Basques are (no one expects an Italian-American to expound on Italy or to sum up in a few words the essence of Italian culture). To admit to being Basque to the cognoscenti is to invoke immediately, at least in the American West, the open-range sheep industry (irrespective of one's personal and family history that may or may not have entailed sheep ranching). To admit to being Basque with a fellow ethnic is to elicit "Do you know so-and-so? Have you been to the Chino festival? Where did your grandfather run his sheep?" In short, Basqueness places special burdens upon its carriers, while affording them unique practical, as well as ludic, opportunities.

When Robert was twenty-nine or thirty years old, the *Los Angeles Times* ran an extensive story about the new executive appointments (including his) at the Times Mirror corporation. Robert received a few phone calls from readers who wanted to know if he was Basque. Some callers informed him of an upcoming festival or *pelota* match, and he promised to try to attend, although he never did. And then there was the visit from the *Times*'s Buenos Aires correspondent. He said that he recognized Erburu as being Basque (it was about the time that Admiral Aramburu replaced Perón, so the *-buru* had been a dead giveaway).

The correspondent spoke of his many Basque acquaintances in Argentina, probably seeking some sort of special bonding with this young company officer.

Robert was not insensitive to the bonding potential that his Basque ethnicity might afford him. When he first went on the board of directors of United States Chamber of Commerce he attended a meeting in Washington, D.C., at which Nevada's Senator Paul Laxalt[18] was the keynote speaker. Afterward Robert introduced himself to Laxalt by saying, "Senator, you and I are the only Basques in this room." They have maintained a friendship ever since. Similar was his bonding with Roberto Goizueta, CEO of the Coca-Cola Company. They immediately invoked their common ethnicity when first meeting on the Business Council. Another example is Robert's relationship with John Elorriaga, then CEO of U.S. Bank. Elorriaga, a Basque American from eastern Oregon, provided banking services to the paper mills acquired by the Times Mirror. When he received a Times Mirror annual report, Elorriaga called a contact at the company and asked, "Is your president a Basque? If so, I want to meet him." So the two men first met in a spirit that went beyond their business relationship.

This networking among Basques transcended both Old World and New World internal Basque realities.[19] Thus, it encompassed Erburu, a Navarrese Basque American from southern California, Goizueta, of Bizkaian descent but born in Cuba, Laxalt, a Nevada Basque American of French Basque descent, and Elorriaga, a Pacific Northwest Basque American of Bizkaian descent.

Another consequence of the *Los Angeles Times* article was a congratulatory call to Robert from Mrs. Milton Teague, wife of a prominent Ventura County rancher and the CEO of the Sunkist Corporation. The Teagues lived in Santa Paula (near Ojai) and knew Robert's father Michael. Alfrida Poco Teague was the daughter of a Nevada Basque sheep rancher. She retained a strong interest in her ethnic heritage and knew Robert Laxalt (Paul's brother), author of the book *Sweet Promised Land*,[20] a work that made him literary spokesman of the Basque-American experience.

When, in 1968, the University of Nevada launched a fund-raising drive to support its fledgling Basque Studies Program, Laxalt contacted Alfrida. She, in turn, contacted a few southern California Basques, including Robert Erburu. He decided to make a personal donation, becoming one of the founding Friends of the Basque Studies Program. This meant that Robert became a recipient of the program's semiannual newsletter that kept him informed of the availability of Basque books published by the University of Nevada Press. He ordered many of them, but his many other duties and interests prevented him from reading them in depth. Not surprisingly, the one that he did consume was Rachel Bard's *Navarra, the Durable Kingdom*.[21]

It was about 1975 that Robert and Lois made their first trip to Spain. The *Los Angeles Times* had recently opened a Madrid bureau, and Robert decided to visit it as president of Times Mirror. The secretary of the bureau chief was of Basque descent. She immediately proclaimed Robert to be Basque ("He looks just like my father"). The correspondent took Robert, Lois, and their daughters to a Basque restaurant that evening. When the family returned to their hotel Robert's youngest daughter said, "Father, all the men there looked just like you." Because of this meeting, the Madrid bureau took a special interest in the Basque Country. Thus, the *Los Angeles Times* began to provide more in-depth coverage of Basque issues than other American newspapers. Robert would make a point of clipping articles and sending them to the Basque Studies Program.

In 1976 the United States celebrated its bicentennial, a retrospective exercise that prompted many Americans to question their personal as well as national origins. The quest for family genealogy became a new American pastime. It was at this time that Robert's cousin, Elizabeth Erro Hvolboll,[22] began an Orella family history project.[23] Although Elizabeth and Robert were not particularly close, she began to forward to him the results of her research. They became fast pen pals, and Robert's curiosity about his origins expanded accordingly.

On July 7, 1990 (the feast day of San Fermín, patron of Pamplona), the U.S. descendants of the Orella family gathered in Santa Barbara for a commemorative mass and reunion.[24] For that occasion Elizabeth Hvolboll prepared a genealogy, "Ancestors of Bruno Francisco Orella y Mendizabal," the fruit of her many years of research (and that of others). It notes,

> Orella is a very noble and ancient Basque surname (*solar espacioso* in Spanish) which means spacious estate. The family's first ancestral mansion was in the valley of Araitz in the district of Pamplona in Navarra. Knights of the Orella lineage went to Aragon towards the end of the XI century to take part in the wars of the Reconquest. The family also extended into Valencia, where it inherited country estates in Ruzafa. Miguel and Martin de Orella, brothers, were rec-

ognized as nobles by the Royal Chamber of Pamplona in 1562. Later the family extended to other places in the Navarrese region, as well as to Guipuzcoa, Alava and Vizcaya. It also expanded to the New World where it became established in Chile, Argentina, Mexico and the United States.

Their coat of arms is: On a field of gold, a castle of red guarded by three black wolves, one at each side and another in charge, and, overlapping all, a blue band.

Don Bruno's branch of the family resettled from the Valley of Araitz, first to Berastegi and Zaldibia in Gipuzkoa (for four generations), and then, in the early 1800s, to Muskiz in Bizkaia (near the city of Bilbao). During the Berastegi interlude, the Orellas were united with the Baldas, maternal lineage of Saint Ignatius of Loyola.

In 1993 the Institute Harriluze (located in Algorta, Bizkaia, and dedicated to studies of the Basque emigrant diaspora) prepared an unpublished report entitled "La Familia Orella" (from which much of the foregoing information derives) and situates the decision of several Orella family members to emigrate within the context of nineteenth-century Old World Basque society.

The Harriluze research determined that Bruno's family, even though noble in remote origin, was of modest means when it resettled in the iron-mining district of Muskiz. Bruno was one of nine children. Three sons, including Bruno, emigrated. Eustaquio Antonio became a ship's captain on the Buenos Aires run and amassed a fortune (childless, he endowed the missions of Somorrostro). Juan Benito emigrated to Cuba when he was twenty-four "to engage in commerce."

To date no documentation regarding Bruno's departure from Europe has been discovered. It is family tradition in the European branch of the Orellas, however, that he became a crew member on a brigantine and worked his way to Chile. There he briefly entered the household of a well-to-do Orella, but was scorned by the man's children because of his ordinary or workingman's appearance and ways. He left for California in 1850 following news of the discovery of gold. By 1858 he was employed by Don Leandro González on the latter's Rio Santa Clara land grant. That year Bruno married his patron's daughter, Mercedes González Guevara.

It is through his maternal great-grandmother that Robert Erburu traces his Old California Hispanic ties. One of her paternal great-grandparents was Felipe González, a *mestizo* and soldier who was born in Sinaloa, Mexico. His bride, María Felipa de la Cruz, also from Mexico, was of Indian descent. In 1781 Felipe was among the soldiers who were with the *pobladores* who founded the pueblo of Los Angeles. He was then among the founders of the garrison at Santa Barbara in 1782. Her other paternal great-grandfather was Luis Quintero, a tailor, born in Sonora, who was also an original *poblador* of Los Angeles. He may have been a negro. He was married to María Petra Rubio, of Sonora, who was listed in the census as a *mulata*. Luis and María also relocated to the Santa Barbara presidio.

Mercedes's paternal grandfather was Rafael Gerardo González, a soldier, who was born in Sinaloa prior to his parents' move to Los Angeles and Santa Barbara. He married Tomasa Quintero. According to family legend, Rafael Gerardo whipped some Indian boys when they did a poor job of protecting his crops from the birds. That night the boys' families presented him with poisoned food that killed him. His son Leandro, Mercedes's father, was four years old at the time.

Leandro, born in 1792, also became a soldier at the Santa Barbara presidio. Between 1840 and 1853 he served as administrator and *mayordomo* of Mission Santa Barbara after its secularization. In 1837 he was one of the original recipients (along with seven other retired soldiers) of the El Rio de Santa Clara land grant (48,883 acres) on the Oxnard plain in Ventura County. Bruno Orella worked for Leandro on this property before marrying Mercedes in 1858. His father-in-law died three months later, and one-half of the property passed to his widow, Josefa Guevara, and the other half in equal shares to his six children.

Josefa Guevara, Mercedes's mother, was descended from Blas Verdugo, one of the original Spanish conquistadors in Mexico. She was also descended from Juan Carrillo of the noble Alonzo Carrillo line (Alonzo was the warrior archbishop of Toledo and primate of Spain). Mercedes was also descended from José B. Ladrón de Guevara. Her maternal grandparents were Josef Ignacio Ladrón de Guevara, a soldier born possibly in Queretaro and listed as *español* (i.e., European) in the census, and María Loreta Cota, born in either Sonora or Baja California, who was also an *española*. Mercedes's mother, Josefa, was born in Santa Barbara.

The Ladrón de Guevara connection is of particular interest for present purposes, since it accesses an ancient Navarrese family line, thereby providing Robert Erburu with another Basque genealogical thread. The Ladrón de Guevaras were one of the twelve influential families (*ricos hombres*) in the kingdom of Navarre. They were also known as the Counts of Oñate (an autonomous enclave in the Middle Ages that is now part of the province of Gipuzkoa).[25]

Bruno Orella and Mercedes González continued to live on her share of the Rio Santa Clara land grant for several years after Leandro's death. In 1867 she sold her share to Dwight Hollister, and she and Bruno used the money to buy other land. Shortly thereafter they were in possession of the Rancho Cañada del Corral property north of Santa Barbara. Throughout their lives Bruno and Mercedes purchased and sold several pieces of ranch and city property. They were reasonably well-to-do and provided their children with private schooling (several of the boys attended Santa Clara University).[26]

One of the activities during the Orella family reunion in 1990 was dedication of a commemorative plaque for the Janssens-Orella Adobe House in downtown Santa Barbara. Now a historic landmark, the adobe was built by don Agustin Janssens, a Belgian. It was acquired by Bruno and Mercedes in 1872 as their town home (Rancho Cañada del Corral was more than twenty miles north of Santa Barbara). The day's festivities were attended by a number of dignitaries, including Santa Barbara's mayor, the chairman of its City Landmarks Commission, the auxiliary Catholic bishop of Los Angeles, and the consul general of Spain. Master of ceremonies for the plaque dedication was Robert Erburu. He opened his remarks by stating,

> Buenos días y bienvenidos, in Basque, kaixo!
> On behalf of the Orella family, welcome to the unveiling of a plaque which has been placed on the site of the Janssens-Orella adobe.
>
> I am Robert Francis Erburu, a great-grandson of Bruno Francisco and Mercedes González Orella who lived here with their children in the late 1800s and into the early years of this century.
>
> If my attempt at pronouncing Spanish and Basque hasn't already given me away, let me confess that I speak neither language. It was not the custom in 1930, when I was born, for the generation of my parents to teach their children the languages of their parents—Spanish, Basque, and Italian in my case. Would that it had been otherwise.

Thus Robert's ethnic persona, activities, and sentiments were not limited to his Basqueness. On at least two occasions he was involved in projects that played upon his other ethnic roots. The first involved creation of the Tomás Rivera Center, named after the first Hispanic chancellor of a California university (University of California, Riverside). Franklin Murphy had invited Tomás to join the Times Mirror board of directors out of a desire to diversify its makeup. Tomás was on the board of the Carnegie Foundation and was a strong proponent of creating a public policy institute devoted to Hispanic affairs. At the same time Robert was arguing, as a board member of the Hewlett Foundation, that more should be done to foster relations between the United States and Mexico. The suggestion was well received, but it proved difficult to identify specific university programs to support.

Tomás Rivera initiated negotiations with John McGuire, president of the Claremont Graduate School, to found a Hispanic Public Policy Institute at the Claremont Colleges. Then Tomás died suddenly (at age forty-five), but his death served to galvanize the effort, in part as a memorial. Carnegie made its commitment, and McGuire approached Robert, who committed the Times Mirror Company to support the effort and agreed to approach the Hewlett Foundation as well. Robert's explanation for his involvement was, "It's part of my culture. I see it as another way to return the good fortune that I have had. This is a state in which the Hispanic influence is very great. My ancestors were part Hispanic so it just seemed a very natural thing to do. It gave me great satisfaction."

The second ethnically colored entanglement was the council that provides financial support for the Harvard Center for Renaissance Studies in Florence, Italy, housed in Bernard Berenson's home—the Villa i Tatti. Craig Smythe, then director of the center, wanted Murphy to join the council that he was forming. Franklin demurred on the grounds that he was about to retire and introduced Craig to Robert Erburu instead, while underscoring his protégé's part-Italian ancestry. The center was financially troubled, and Robert ended up cochairing its fund-raising campaign. He remains on the council to this day. In his words, "It is an institution worth preserving if you believe that humanistic study of the Italian Renaissance is something that is a worthwhile endeavor." In short, it is more a commitment to his interest in art and culture than to his Italian background, although there is a sense in which he sees them as inextricably intertwined.

When I interviewed Kathryn she only half-jokingly noted, "Sometimes I have to remind Bobby that he is Italian, too!" In our discussions he emphasized that being Italian is different from being Basque. As we noted earlier, the former does not set one apart as much as the latter. Nevertheless, it is worth mentioning two aspects of Robert's personal history that highlight his Italian heritage. The first is the trip that he took to Italy with Lois and his mother, in which they visited her ancestral village. It is only after retirement in 1996, and despite two earlier trips to Spain, that Robert scheduled travel to the Basque Country.

The second point is his role as grape grower. About 1970 the Orella descendants sold their beachfront property to California for state park consolidation. Robert had a tax incentive to reinvest his proceeds in agricultural land, so he immediately began looking for a vineyard. "Grapes sounded good; I suppose it was the Italian in me." At the time there was a boom in grape-growing in northern California, and in 1971 Robert purchased 114 acres on the Russian River between Healdsburg and Geyserville. He grows grapes there commercially and sells them to such noted wineries as Gallo, Simi, Sebastiani, and Ferrari-Carano.

If Robert's ethnic persona influences his public one, the reverse is also true. Given his prominence in U.S. publishing, business, and cultural circles he is, at times, the object of both requests and accolades articulated in Basque terms. An example of a request stems from his involvement with the University of Nevada's Basque Studies Program.[27] When the University of California, Santa Barbara, recently instituted its José Miguel de Barandiarán Chair of Basque Studies he was invited to the inaugural ceremony and to become involved generally. When a previous commitment precluded his attendance, Basque Cultural Minister Joseba Arregi, in the United States specifically for the ceremony, visited him at the Times Mirror headquarters. Similarly, when Rafael Suso, publisher of the Basque newspaper *Deia,* visited the United States, he made a point of traveling to Los Angeles to meet with Robert.[28] Journalists and television crews from the Basque Country regularly seek interviews with Robert.

There is a sense, then, in which Robert Erburu is not only a Basque but "Mr. Basque," the title stemming far more from his accomplishments and current position than to his descent from Mariano and Bruno. When the Basque government recently organized the American Basque Foundation, which was designed to further the economic interests of the Basque Country (including financing a part of the Basque Country's public debt in the U.S. money markets), Robert was named to its advisory board.[29]

And then there is the accolade. On November 12, 1993, the Society for Basque Studies in America held its annual Basque Hall of Fame dinner in Sparks, Nevada. Robert was one of the four inductees.[30] On the way to the ceremony, reflecting his appreciation of the many subtleties and ironies inherent in being a postmodern ethnic, Robert remarked to Lois mirthfully, "Now we're going to have dinner with some real Basques!"

For Robert Erburu, like most Euro-Americans of the late twentieth century, ethnicity is neither monolithic nor problematic. It is neither a cross to bear nor a stigma to hide. Nor is it an imposition or supposition. For the purist, intent upon totalizing ethnicity and pigeonholing ethnic actors, Robert Erburu's ethnic persona may appear to be a hodgepodge of elements that simply fail to hang together. This view might even question whether he is a serious candidate for "ethnic" status. I would argue, however, that at this point in our history he is an American original. For Robert Erburu's personal history encompasses many of the key themes within American immigration history. His paternal great-grandparents represent the union of the Old World Basque seafarer (Bruno Orella) with the New World synthesis of Spanish colonial, Native American, and possibly black culture (Mercedes González Guevara). Their union also echoed the world of Old California in which a Hispanic social elite claimed pioneer status within an increasingly anglicized society. Mariano Erburu was seeking to escape from a European conflict, thereby invoking the refugee theme prominent in U.S. immigration history, whereas the Sarzottis' decision to emigrate is part of the transatlantic odyssey of Europe's huddled masses in search of economic opportunity. In Bruno/Mariano/Michael there is three-generational involvement in the Basque-American sheepman saga. By facilitating the immigration of relatives and fellow ethnics to be sheepherders on their ranches, they were a part of the primary process whereby a lasting Basque-American presence became established in the American West. The accomplishments of Bruno and Mariano are a part of the discourse on the immigrant's triumph, whereas those of Michael and, above all, Robert underscore the American success story. In Michael's relative indifference toward his ethnic heritage and Robert's adult quest for its authentication there is indeed Hansen's "grandson wishing to remember what the son wished to forget." So, far from being an aberration or exception within the American ethnic process, Robert Erburu is rather its culmination—or at least one of its many possible outcomes.

Additionally, in the reconstruction of the Orella family history (and creation of the Orella Family Association) there is the contemporary

American search for roots. Nor is that quest devoid of its own ludic and mythic properties. There are the evident "Mayflower" and "aristocratic descent" syndromes in which certain ancestors (even knaves) are privileged over the nondescript. Thus, the Orella story highlights such possibilities as descent from the "Thief of Guevara" and the nobles of the Valley of Araitz. There may be common kinship with Saint Ignatius of Loyola.

Filtered through the experience and curiosity of a Robert Erburu, ethnic identity is more processual than structural, partial than total, situational than pervasive, and ludic rather than agonistic.[31] Thus, ethnicity becomes a kind of playland in which, should one choose to enter, elements of the past, present, and future, as well as bits of oneself, can be combined into patterns that are far more personal than public. Like the intriguing potentialities of the kaleidoscope they may, given a twist (either of the actor's hand or of fate), be rearranged into a rich array of new imagery. And, of course, one need not enter Ethnicland at all.

Ethnicity, then, for Euro-Americans[32] has become an active quest in which the individual is the searching agent—or it remains nothing at all. It is this realization, along with skepticism that sufficient numbers of persons care about ethnic heritage to sustain the game, that has prompted some observers to speak in terms of the "twilight of ethnicity" for Euro-Americans.[33] A contrarian view might argue that, given our overly complex and institutionalized world in which the individual feels insignificant, alienated, and the pawn of the "system" (state bureaucracies and mega-corporations), the quest for ethnic persona may actually be increasing in importance as a means whereby "I" can inform "my" sense of personal worth.[34]

In philosophizing about his ethnic persona Robert Erburu notes,

I obviously take pleasure out of this. It's been a positive element in my life, and I think we all like to position ourselves in a way where there's something about us that's special, since we can't all be great concert singers or great basketball players. In the western part of the country, for that matter even in the eastern part, in my experience nobody looks upon Basques in a negative way. Basques are generally thought of as relatively intelligent, hardworking, and successful, and that is certainly the kind of image you want to have if you want to go forward in a business career. And so I guess over the years, in addition to whatever psychic pleasures I've gotten out of my Basque connections for whatever reason, I certainly had positive vibes from a business standpoint. For example, when I became president of the company Franklin Murphy had been on a trip to Spain. He had been through the Basque Country and had duly purchased a beret. So in the board room, in the presence of the board, he put the beret on my head, and everyone thought that was nice. You feel that this is something that is part of your life and background, and that it is positive. You become more interested and feel better about it. Whether it is purely image, I mean myth, really doesn't matter in a way. I mean the Basques are fascinating, and so how can you not find that interesting? There's no particular downside to it and it's kind of fun.

The operative word in the foregoing is *positive,* since, when questioned whether he has ever been challenged to explain or defend ETA, the violent Basque separatist group, Robert replied, "Not really." He added, "Particularly because of my job I wouldn't want to get into Basque politics, I wouldn't like that at all. I would back away from that very quickly." Indeed, he demurred when Euskal Telebista (Basque TV) requested an interview regarding his views on whether northern California should be allowed to form its own separate state.

If, as I would argue, we are not necessarily experiencing Euro-America's "twilight of ethnicity," we are certainly at a critical crossroads. Nor do we possess a clear idea of the future. In this regard the present essay raises as many questions as it answers. Are collective expressions of common ethnicity (e.g., festivals and voluntary associations) destined to wither away as ethnicity becomes entirely individualized? Conversely, can individualized ethnicity persist without at least some collective vehicles of expression? Although Robert Erburu does not attend Basque festivals and is not a member of a Basque club, he is aware of, and approves of, their existence. They are there and, time permitting, one day . . .

Of course, there is also the possibility that as more individuals engage in the personal quest for ethnic authentication they will create the common interests that will then become the bases for new collective expressions of shared ethnicity. It is not farfetched, for example, to posit the evolution of the genealogical interests of several families (such as the Orella Family Association) into a more formalized "Organization of Basque Settlers of the American West."

But then there is the loneliness of the postmodern ethnic, aware that his/her ethnic passion is not necessarily shared by even intimate others. Robert Erburu sums up his isolation in the indifference of both his offspring and forebearers: "There does not seem to be anything like the same feeling [for Basque ethnicity] in my children, and I'm wondering whether twenty years from now they will pick this up the way I have. It did not seem to be a priority with my parents. My parents did not try to make a big deal out of my being either Basque or Italian."

So is Robert torchbearer of a legacy belonging to both former and future generations? Does his flame illuminate the path, or is it just the twilight?

Appendix

Senate Joint Memorial No. 115 / April 6, 1972

A joint memorial to the President of the United States, the Secretary of State of the United States, the President of the Senate and the Speaker of the House of Representatives of the United States in Congress Assembled, the Senators and Representatives representing this State in Congress, the Governors of the fifty States, and the Basque Government in exile in France.

We, your Memorialists, the Senate and the House of Representatives of the state of Idaho assembled in the Second Regular Session of the Forty-first Legislature, do hereby respectfully represent that:

WHEREAS, the history and traditions of this nation rest upon the principle of freedom from oppression and the rights of all citizens to life, liberty and the pursuit of happiness; and

WHEREAS, we believe that democracy and freedom, when denied in one country stand threatened everywhere; therefore, it is our responsibility to bring to the attention of the people of the United States, and, we hope to the people of the entire world that these very freedoms of the Basque people are threatened under the Franco regime in Spain today; and

WHEREAS, the Basque people have a long and glorious history of personal accomplishment and a devotion to the preservation of their national heritage; and

WHEREAS, the sole aim of the Basques, since human time began, has been to bar the world's wars, tribal, racial, religious, imperialistic or civil, from the tiny green mountain land which was their own before history began; and

WHEREAS, no other country in the world holds the traditions of its forefathers so sacred as Euzkadi, as the Basques call their homeland; and

WHEREAS, the Basques have been denied the right to learn their own language, have been jailed, and have been denied human rights by the Franco regime and are virtually threatened in their continued existence; and

WHEREAS, the state of Idaho is known as the North American center of the Basque population, and

WHEREAS, the Basques of North America have carried the traditions of their forefathers as honest and self-reliant peoples, possessing the basic elements of democracy, humanity, charity and mercy; and

WHEREAS, the Basques of North America feel first that they are Americans, and as such they feel for America as the Basques of Euzkadi felt for their country, which is:

Gu Americakarentzat eta America, Jaungoikoarentsat.
which means
We are for America, and America is for God.

WHEREAS, in World War II thousands of American lives were lost in a war which was precipitated from the Spanish Civil War, a war of genocide of the Basques, by the three dictators, Franco, Mussolini, and Hitler; and

WHEREAS, the Basques, who once enjoyed the oldest democratic republic in Europe, fought for the Allies in World War II and

WHEREAS, over 2.4 billion dollars in aid has been given to Franco Spain for economic and military assistance since 1946 by the government of the United States.

NOW, THEREFORE, BE IT RESOLVED by the Legislature of the state of Idaho that we voice our strong belief that as a nation we should reward our friends and not our enemies, and we deplore any free and democratic nation providing assistance to a ruthless, totalitarian government, directly or indirectly.

BE IT FURTHER RESOLVED that we urge all steps be taken to cause the Spanish government to cease and desist the denial of the Universal Declaration of Human Rights of Man and insist that general amnesty for all Basques and Spaniards now imprisoned or exiled for their political and social activities be extended by the Franco government.

BE IT FURTHER RESOLVED that if such steps are not carried out, the President of the United States, the Secretary of State, and Congress of the United States take all necessary steps to withdraw all foreign aid or benefits to the Spanish dictatorship.

BE IT FURTHER RESOLVED that the Secretary of the Senate be, and he is hereby authorized and directed to forward copies of this

Memorial to the President of the United States, the Secretary of State of the United States, the President of the Senate and the Speaker of the House of Representatives of Congress, the Senators and Representatives representing the state of Idaho in the Congress of the United States, the Governors of the fifty states of the United States, and to the Basque government in exile in France.

Notes

Preface

1. We have implemented the official orthography determined by the Academy of the Basque language, as recommended by William Douglass, editor of the Basque Book Series. Since the geographic people of Navarre do not refer to their region as *Nafarroa*, but as the Spanish equivalent of *Navarra*, we have retained the English spelling throughout this volume.

1. Don Fray Juan de Zumárraga: Loyal Basque Vassal and Spanish Churchman

1. Joaquín García Icazbalceta, ed., *Nueva Colección de documentos para la historia de México: Códice Franciscano*, siglo XVI (Mexico City: Editorial Salvador Chávez Hayhoe, 1941), 269. However, see Richard E. Greenleaf, *Zumárraga and the Mexican Inquisition, 1536–1543* (Washington, D.C.: Academy of American Franciscan History, 1961), 34 n, for the statement that Zumárraga was born in "late 1468 or early 1469." For the unresolved problem of Zumárraga's birthdate, see José Mallea-Olaetxe, "Juan Zumárraga, Bishop of Mexico, and the Basques: The Ethnic Connection" (Ph.D. diss., University of Nevada, Reno, 1988), 75–77.

2. Joaquín García Icazbalceta, *Don Fray Juan de Zumárraga, Primer Obispo y Arzobispo de México*, ed. Rafael Aguayo Spencer and Antonio Castro Leal, 4 vols. (Durango, Mexico: Editorial Porrúa, S.A., 1947), 4:206.

3. Fernando Benítez, *The Century after Cortés*, trans. Joan MacLean (Chicago: University of Chicago Press, 1965), 77.

4. J. H. Elliott, *Imperial Spain, 1469–1716* (New York: Meridian Books, New American Library, 1977), 108.

5. John Leddy Phelan, *The Millennial Kingdom of the Franciscans in the New World* (Berkeley: University of California Press, 1970), 47.

6. Richard E. Greenleaf, ed., *Zumárraga and His Family: Letters to Vizcaya, 1536–1548*, trans. Neal Kaveny, O.F.M. (Washington, D.C.: Academy of American Franciscan History, 1979).

7. Mallea-Olaetxe, "Zumárraga and the Basques," 5.

8. Ibid., 332. Julio Caro Baroja has observed that Spaniards of the seventeenth century collectively judged Basques as a distinct people characterized by "a series of well-defined traits reflecting recurrent observation." See Julio Caro Baroja, *Los Vascos: Etnología* (San Sebastián: Biblioteca Vascongada de los Amigos del País, 1949), 357. While all quantitative and qualitative composite pictures lose the individual in arriving at typical characteristics, whether real or imagined, two of six traits associated with Basques fit Zumárraga's personality.

9. García Icazbalceta, *Códice Franciscano*, 263–71; Mariano Cuevas, S.J., *Historia de la iglesia en México*, 5th ed., 5 vols. (Mexico City: Editorial Patria, S.A., 1946–47), 1:267.

10. García Icazbalceta, *Códice Franciscano*, 253.

11. Ibid., 267.

12. Mallea-Olaetxe, "Zumárraga and the Basques," 85, 211–12.

13. García Icazbalceta, *Códice Franciscano*, 270.

In 1514 the town of Tavira de Durango had 637 homes (*fogueras*). If one estimates 4.5 inhabitants per dwelling, the villa of Durango had about 2,866 permanent inhabitants. The scattered houses within its district grouped into twelve *anteiglesias* and outside the towns numbered 736. Vizcaya's total population was about 67,638. See José Angel García de Cortázar, *Vizcaya en el siglo XV: Aspectos económicos y sociales* (Bilbao: Ediciones de la Caja de Ahorros Vizcaína, 1966), 72, 82–83.

14. García Icazbalceta, *Códice Franciscano*, 257–58; Cuevas, *Historia de la iglesia*, 1:268.

15. Greenleaf, *Zumárraga and His Family*, xxvi.

16. García Icazbalceta, *Códice Franciscano*, 267; Greenleaf, *Zumárraga and His Family*, xxii.

17. The custody of Burgos became a province in 1514. Mendieta states that after professing at Aranzatzu, Zumárraga took up his duties in Concepción province so as to live among recollects who wore coarse cloth. In the province of Concepción, he served as guardian and definitor several times and as provincial minister once (1520–23?) (Gerónimo de Mendieta, *Historia eclesiástica indiana*, 4 vols. [Mexico City: Editorial Salvador Chávez Hayhoe, 1945], 4:77). See Greenleaf, *Zumárraga and the Mexican Inquisition*, 34 n, for the statement that Zumárraga "joined the Order at Abrojo."

18. Manuel Giménez Fernández, *Bartolomé de Las Casas*, 2 vols. (Seville: La Escuela de Estudios Hispano-Americanos, 1953–60), 2:53–54.

19. Marcel Bataillon, *Erasmo y España: Estudios sobre la historia espiritual del siglo XVI* (México–Buenos Aires: Fondo de Cultura Económica, 1966), 822–23.

20. Ignacio Aldecoa, *El país vasco* (Barcelona: Editorial Noguer, S.A., 1962), 45–47.

21. Marcelino Menéndez y Pelayo, *Historia de los heterodoxos españoles*, 7 vols. (Madrid: Librería General de Victoriano Suárez, 1911–32), 3:383–84, 298–99; Julio Caro Baroja, *The World of the Witches*, trans. O. N. V. Glendinning, 4th ed. (Chicago: University of Chicago Press, 1973), 103, 144–45.

22. Mallea-Olaetxe, "Zumárraga and the Basques," 69–75.

23. Roger Bigelow Merriman, *The Rise of the Spanish Empire in the Old World and the New*, 4 vols. (New York: Macmillan, 1918–34), 3:161–62; Mendieta, *Historia eclesiástica indiana*, 4:77.

24. Mendieta, *Historia eclesiástica indiana*, 4:94.

25. Ibid., 4:77; Hugh Redwald Trevor-Roper, *The European Witch-Craze of the Sixteenth and Seventeenth Centuries and Other Essays* (New York: Harper Torchbooks, 1969), 91, 96; Julio Caro Baroja, *El Señor Inquisidor y otras vidas por oficio* (Madrid: Alianza Editorial, 1968), 107.

26. Mendieta, *Historia eclesiástica indiana*, 4:77; Trevor-Roper, *European Witch-Craze*, 112; Caro Baroja, *World of the Witches*, 155, 179, 187. Salazar noted that there were at least 1,672 cases of perjury and false witness in the trial of the alleged witches of Zugarramurdi.

27. García Icazbalceta, *Juan de Zumárraga*, 1:18–19, 2:20–22.

28. Ralph H. Vigil, "A Reappraisal of the Expedition of Pánfilo de Narváez to Mexico in 1520," *Revista de historia de América* 77–78 (January–December 1974): 101–25; Lesley Byrd Simpson, *The Encomienda in New Spain: The Beginnings of Spanish Mexico* (Berkeley: University of California Press, 1966), 56–64.

29. Hernán Cortés, *Letters from Mexico*, trans. and ed. A. R. Pagden, intro. by John Huxtable Elliott (New York: Grossman Publishers, 1971), 88.

30. Robert Ricard, *The Spiritual Conquest of Mexico: An Essay on the Apostolate and the Evangelizing Methods of the Mendicant Orders in New Spain, 1523–1572* (Berkeley: University of California Press, 1996), 4–5.

31. García Icazbalceta, *Juan de Zumárraga*, 2:171; France V. Scholes, "The Spanish Conqueror as a Business Man," offprint from *New Mexico Quarterly* 28 (spring 1958): 1–29; *Postrera voluntad y testamento de Hernando Cortés, Marqués del Valle*, ed. with intro. and notes by G. R. G. Conway (Mexico City: Editorial Pedro Robredo, 1940), 47.

32. Fidel de Chauvet, O.F.M., "Fray Juan de Zumárraga, Protector of the Indians," *The Americas* 5 (1949): 283–95.

33. Ernesto Schäfer, *El consejo real y supremo de las Indias*, 2 vols. (Seville: Escuela de Estudios Hispano-Americanos de Sevilla, 1935–47), 2:4; García Icazbalceta, *Juan de Zumárraga*, 2:185–94.

34. García Icazbalceta, *Juan de Zumárraga*, 2:185.

35. Ibid., 184–85.

36. Ibid., 188, 216–17.

37. Ibid., 224.

38. Donald E. Chipman, *Nuño de Guzmán and the Province of Pánuco in*

New Spain, 1518–1533 (Glendale, Calif.: Arthur H. Clark Company, 1967), 230.

39. *Colección de documentos inéditos relativos al descubrimiento, conquista y colonización de las posesiones en América y Oceanía,* 42 vols. (Madrid: Imprenta de Manuel B. de Quiros, 1864–84), 41:2.

40. Joaquín García Icazbalceta, ed., *Colección de documentos para la historia de México,* 2 vols. (Mexico City: Editoria Porrúa, 1971), 2:248–64.

41. García Icazbalceta, *Juan de Zumárraga,* 2:281–83.

42. Ibid., 2:236.

43. Chauvet, "Fray Juan de Zumárraga," 291.

44. Vasco de Puga, *Provisiones, cédulas, intrucciones para el gobierno de la Nueva España* (Madrid: Ediciones Cultural Hispánica, 1945), 65; Simpson, *The Encomienda in New Spain,* 89.

45. Carlos Castañeda, "Fray Juan de Zumárraga and Indian Policy in New Spain," *The Americas* 5 (1949): 296–310; Puga, *Provisiones,* 85v.

46. Benítez, *The Century after Cortés,* 77; Greenleaf, *Zumárraga and the Mexican Inquisition,* 41.

47. Benjamin Keen, *The Aztec Image in Western Thought* (New Brunswick, N.J.: Rutgers University Press, 1971), 74.

48. Gabriel Méndez Plancarte, *Humanismo mexicano del siglo XVI* (Mexico City: Universidad Nacional Autónoma de México, 1946), 27–52. The selection chosen is Zumárraga's *Doctrina breve muy provechosa de las cosas que pertenecen a la fé católica y a nuestra cristianidad en estilo llano para commún inteligencia,* printed in Mexico by Juan Cromberger, 1544. For the educational work of the friars and Zumárraga's educational leadership, see Joaquín García Icazbalceta, *Education in Mexico City during the Sixteenth Century,* trans. Walter J. O'Donnell, Preliminary Studies of the Texas Catholic Historical Society, distributed under the auspices of the Texas Knights of Columbus Historical Commission, I (April 1931); and Pius J. Barth, "Franciscan Education and the Social Order in Spanish North America, 1502–1821" (Ph.D. diss., University of Chicago, 1945), 63–73.

49. Plancarte, *Humanismo mexicano,* 31–34.

50. Simpson, *The Encomienda in New Spain,* 136.

51. García Icazbalceta, *Juan de Zumárraga,* 2:234–35.

52. Silvio A. Zavala, *La encomienda indiana* (Madrid: Centro de Estudios Históricos, 1935), 88–95; Juan Friede, "Las Casas and Indigenism in the Sixteenth Century," in *Bartolomé de Las Casas in History: Toward an Understanding of the Man and His Work,* ed. Juan Friede and Benjamin Keen (DeKalb: Northern Illinois University Press, 1971), 127–234.

53. For example, Mexico City had some 8,000 Spaniards in 1529, but "the number of encomiendas in the Valley as of the mid-1530s stood at thirty, with an estimated 180,000 Indian tributaries" (Charles Gibson, *The Aztecs under Spanish Rule: A History of the Indians of the Valley of Mexico, 1519–1810*

[Stanford, Calif.: Stanford University Press, 1964], 61). Angel Rosenblat notes that "Bishop Zumárraga said in 1529 that there were 8,000 Spaniards in Mexico City" (Rosenblat, *La población indigena y el mestizaje en América,* 2 vols. [Buenos Aires: Editorial Nova, 1954], 1:245).

54. Simpson, *The Encomienda in New Spain,* 134.

55. García Icazbalceta, *Juan de Zumárraga,* 2:269.

56. Alberto María Carreño, *Fray Domingo de Betanzos, fundador en la Nueva España de la venerable Orden Dominicana* (Mexico City: Imprenta Victoria, S.A., 1924–34), 73–74; Stafford Poole, C. M., *Pedro Moya de Contreras: Catholic Reform and Royal Power in New Spain, 1571–1591* (Berkeley: University of California Press, 1987), 128–29.

57. García Icazbalceta, *Juan de Zumárraga,* 2:269–70.

58. Ibid., 3:130.

59. Ricard, *Spiritual Conquest of Mexico,* 225.

60. Poole, *Pedro Moya de Contreras,* 128.

61. García Icazbalceta, *Juan de Zumárraga,* 1:272–73, 3:90–94, 281–82.

62. Richard E. Greenleaf, *The Mexican Inquisition of the Sixteenth Century* (Albuquerque: University of New Mexico Press, 1969), 70.

63. Ibid., 74; Jacques Lafaye, *Quetzalcóatl and Guadalupe: The Formation of Mexican National Consciousness, 1531–1813,* with a foreword by Octavio Paz, trans. Benjamin Keen (Chicago: University of Chicago Press, 1976), 19.

64. García Icazbalceta, *Juan de Zumárraga,* 4:170–72.

65. Mendieta, *Historia eclesiástica indiana,* 4:29–30. For "the strange and mysterious duality of Pedro Moya de Contrera," see Poole, *Pedro Moya de Contreras.*

66. Ibid., 4:82.

67. García Icazbalceta, *Juan de Zumárraga,* 1:200–201; 3:241–47.

68. Ibid., 3:234. This appears to be an echo of Aristotle's *Nicomachean Ethics* and *Politics:* "equality according to proportion" in a socially, politically, and economically unequal society ruled by virtue for "the common good of all."

69. Bartolomé de Las Casas, *Brevissima relación de la destruición de las Indias,* with Bernardo Vargas Machuca, *Refutación de Las Casas* (Paris: Librería de la Viuda de C. Bouret, n.d.), 24.

70. Alonso de Zorita, *Life and Labor in Ancient Mexico: The Brief and Summary Relation of the Lords of New Spain,* trans. and with an intro. by Benjamin Keen (Norman: University of Oklahoma Press, 1994), 219–20.

71. Ralph H. Vigil, *Alonso de Zorita: Royal Judge and Christian Humanist, 1512–1585* (Norman: University of Oklahoma Press, 1987), 169–71.

72. Alberto María Carreño, "The Books of don Fray Juan de Zumárraga," *The Americas* 5 (1949): 311–30.

73. Lafaye, *Quetzalcóatl and Guadalupe,* 3.

74. Ibid., 18–21.

2. A Borderlands Basque: The Career of Don Juan de Oñate

1. Antonio Arribas, *The Iberians* (New York: Frederick A. Praeger, 1964), 22.

2. Alberto y Arturo García Carraffa, *Diccionario heráldico y genealógico de apellidos españoles y americanos,* 88 vols. (Madrid: Neuva Imprinta Radio, 1919–50), 70:182–83.

3. Donald T. Garate, "Juan de Oñate *Prueba de Caballero,*" 1625: A Look at His Ancestral Heritage." *Colonial Latin American Historical Review,* 7, no. 2 (Spring 1998): 129–73.

4. Donald Chipman, "The Oñate-Moctezuma-Zaldívar Families of Northern New Spain," *New Mexico Historical Review* 52 (October 1977): 300–301.

5. That Juan de Oñate was a twin was first suggested by Lansing B. Bloom in a letter written from the Archive of the Indies in Seville, Spain, and printed in *New Mexico Historical Review* 14 (January 1939): 115–20. Confirmation was finally supplied by publication of a 1567 document in Jorge Palomino y Cañedo, ed., *Miscelánea Oñacina: Cristóbal de Oñate y sus hijos* (Guadalajara: Unidad Editorial, 1987), 181.

6. Marc Simmons, "In the Footsteps of Oñate," *New Mexico Magazine* 70 (July 1992): 106.

7. Palomino y Cañedo, *Miscelánea Oñacina,* 175–76.

8. Oñate's contract is translated in George P. Hammond and Agapito Rey, eds. and trans., *Don Juan de Oñate, Colonizer of New Mexico, 1595–1628,* 2 vols. (Albuquerque: University of New Mexico Press, 1953), 1:42–57. This work contains most of the major documents pertaining to the founding of New Mexico.

9. Luís Weckmann, *The Medieval Heritage of Mexico* (New York: Fordham University Press, 1992), 76–77.

10. Marc Simmons, *The Last Conquistador: Juan de Oñate and the Settling of the Far Southwest* (Norman: University of Oklahoma Press, 1991), 115.

11. For a first-hand account of the Acoma battle, see Gaspar Pérez de Villagrá, *Historia de la Nueva México, 1610* (Albuquerque: University of New Mexico Press, 1992), 267–74.

12. On the end of the Oñate regime, see George P. Hammond, *Don Juan de Oñate and the Founding of New Mexico* (Santa Fe: El Palacio Press, 1927), 170–86.

13. Eric Beerman, "The Death of an Old Conquistador: New Light on Juan de Oñate," *New Mexico Historical Review* 54 (October 1979): 305–19.

14. Beverly Becker, "Around the Plaza," *El Palacio* 100 (winter 1994–95): 14–16.

3. Anza: A Basque Legacy on New Spain's Northern Frontier

1. This story is pieced together from original documents in archives in the United States, Mexico, and Spain, which if footnoted properly might require

more room than the story itself. In the interest of space, only the major epics in the lives of the Anzas will be footnoted. An account of the senior Anza's death is recorded in Archivo General de las Indias (AGI) in Seville, Audiencia de Guadalajara 88, fol. 564.

2. Information on Hernani and the Anza family of Gipuzkoa was gleaned from Gernikako Batzarretxaren Artxiboa (GBA) in Gernika, núm. 1593, fols. 1–805; Bizkaiko Eleizaren Histori Artxiboa Seminario Ikastetxea in Derio, Books of baptisms, marriages, and deaths for parishes in Bizkaia; Elizbarrutiko Artxiboa in Donostia, Books of baptisms, marriages, and deaths for parishes in Gipuzkoa; Gipuzkoako Artxibategi Orokora (GAO) in Tolosa, caja SS212, exp. 02; Gipuzkoako Protokoloen Artxiboa in Oñate, Judicial records relative to Antonio de Anza; and Archivo Municipal de la Villa de Hernani, Obras, negociados, y relaciones.

3. El Archivo de Hidalgo del Parral (AHP), Autos de visita, fols. 26–26v.

4. AHP, Autos de visita, año 1718, fols. 17, 19, 22.

5. Anza's *prueba de nobleza* is located in GAO, caja SS212, exp. 02.

6. The controversy between the Basques and Álvarez Tuñón is told in AHP, año 1720, fols. 491–521; Archivo Histórico de Hacienda (AHH) in Mexico City, legajo 278, exps. 11, 28, 29, 31, 33, 35, 38, 41, 43, 48; and Biblioteca Nacional de México (BNM) in Mexico City, Departmento de Manuscritos, Estampas, e Iconographias, núm. 21/699, año 1722.02.08. A secondary source that covers the conflict strictly from a nonethnic viewpoint is Fay Jackson Smith, *Captain of the Phantom Presidio: A History of the Presidio of Fronteras, Sonora, New Spain, 1686–1735* (Spokane: Arthur H. Clark Co., 1993). Donald T. Garate, "Vizcaínos, Jesuits, and Álvarez Tuñón: An Ethnic View of a Frontier Controversy," *Journal of the Society of Basque Studies in America* 16 (1996): 70–71, covers the subject from an ethnic view.

7. Anza family documentation in Sonora (here and later in the story) comes from University of Arizona, Tucson (AZU), Special Collections Microfilm 811, Parish records of Sonora; AGI, Guadalajara 169, exp. 536, núm. 436, partida 4; GBA, núm. 1593, fols. 1–805; University of Texas, El Paso, Manuscript Collection, Bautismos, casamientos, informes militares, 1723–80; and Tumacacori National Historical Park (TUMA) Microfilm Collection, Rolls 2, 4, 25, Parish records of Tumacacori, Santa María de Suamca, and Guevavi.

8. AGI, Guadalajara 67, exp. 3, núm. 29.

9. Ibid.

10. AGI, Guadalajara 67, exp. 3, núm. 13.

11. This period in the life of Anza and his associates comes from AGI, Guadalajara 67, exp. 3, núms. 13, 29.

12. Materials relative to the Campos incident and Anza's Jesuit relations are in Archivo General de la Nación (AGN) in Mexico City, Historia 333, fols. 1–82.

13. For an excellent treatise on the meaning of *Arizonak* and the naming of Arizona, see William A. Douglass, "On the Naming of Arizona," *Names* 27

(December 1979): 217–34. See also Donald T. Garate, "Who Named Arizona: The Basque Connection," *Journal of Arizona History* (spring 1999).

14. The *planchas de plata* documents are located in AGI, Guadalajara 185, fols. 1–132v.

15. AGI, Guadalajara 185, fols. 8–9.

16. For the Arisivi incident, see AGN, Reales Cédulas, vol. 59, fols. 216–19v.

17. For information on Anza's and Vildósola's activities during the Pima rebellion, see AGI, Guadalajara, núm. 69, and AGN, Provincias Internas 47.

18. For information on the Seri and Apache situations and campaigns, see AGN, Provincias Internas 47, fols. 263–64, Provincias Internas 86, fols. 63, 105v, 107, 122, 133–40, 145, 153, 251, 251v, Provincias Internas 250, fols. 334–35v, and AHH, leg. 17, exp. 69, fols. 1–18.

19. TUMA 25, fols. 59, 68.

20. Anza's baptism and marriage in AGN, Provincias Internas 87, fols. 389–403, and AGI, Guadalajara 169, exp. 536, núm. 436, partida 4.

21. AGI, Guadalajara 169, exp. 536, núm. 436, partida 4; AZU núm. 811; TUMA 4, 25.

22. Concerning the Jesuit expulsion and its immediate aftermath, see AGN, Provincias Internas 47, fols. 206–207v, and BNM, núms. 58/736, fols. 5–7v, and 236/912, fols. 11–17v.

23. The letters and two diaries that describe this phase of the campaign are in AGN, Provincias Internas 47, fols. 312–15v, and BNM, 255/933, año 1769.02.24.

24. Seri War documents in AGI, Guadalajara; AGN, Provincias Internas 81; and BNM 63/741, 67/745, 69/47, 259/936, 268/946.

25. This epic story is told in Herbert E. Bolton, *Anza's California Expeditions*, 5 vols. (Berkeley: University of California Press, 1930), Donald T. Garate, *Captain Juan Bautista de Anza: Correspondence on Various Subjects, 1775* (San Leandro: Los Californianos Antepasados VIII, 1995), Garate, "Basque Ethnic Connections and the Expeditions of Juan Bautista de Anza to Alta California," *Colonial Latin American Historical Review* 4 (1995), and Garate, *Juan Bautista de Anza National Historic Trail* (Tucson: Southwest Parks and Monuments Association, 1994). See also Donald T. Garate, *Anza's Return from Alta California* (San Leandro: Los Californianos Antepasados IX, 1998).

26. Much of the story of Anza's New Mexico years is told in Alfred Barnaby Thomas, *Forgotten Frontiers: A Study of the Spanish Indian Policy of Don Juan Bautista de Anza, Governor of New Mexico, 1777–1787* (Norman: University of Oklahoma Press, 1932), and Ronald E. Kessler, *Anza's 1779 Comanche Campaign: Diary of Governor Juan Bautista de Anza* (Monte Vista, Colo.: Ronald E. Kessler, 1994). Other documentation is found in BNM 84/762, fols. 1–8v; AGN, Provincias Internas 250, fols. 410–42; and Archives

Division of the State of New Mexico Records Center, Spanish Archives of New Mexico, 1621–1821.

27. The story of Anza's final days and his death are told in AGN, Provincias Internas 83, fols. 39–48v, Provincias Internas 235, fols. 10–12v, 37, Provincias Internas 250, fols. 410–42; and AGI, Guadalajara 169, exp. 536, núm. 436, partida 4. The original death entry is recorded in the parish record at Arizpe, Sonora.

4. Pedro and Bernardo Altube: Basque Brothers of California and Nevada

1. Archivos Parroquiales de la Villa de Oñati (Paroquial Archives of the Town of Oñati), records of baptism, marriage, and death, Oñati, Gipuzkoa, Spain, 1650–1880.

2. Ibid.

3. Ibid.

4. Iñaki Zumalde, *Pedro de Altube (Palo Alto) y los Pastores Vascos en los Estados Unidos* (San Sebastián: Real Sociedad Bascongada de los Amigos del Pais, 1980), 16.

5. Ibid. That he took this route to California with Basque companions has been reiterated time and again by each line of descendants, but no documents record his actual journey.

6. William A. Douglass and Jon Bilbao, *Amerikanuak: Basques in the New World* (Reno: University of Nevada Press, 1975), 204.

7. William Perkins, *Three Years in California: William Perkins' Journal of Life at Sonora (1849–1852),* introduction and annotations by Dale L. Morgan and James R. Scobie (Berkeley: University of California Press, 1964), 300–301.

8. Edna B. Patterson, Louise A. Ulph, and Victor Goodwin, *Nevada's Northeast Frontier* (Sparks, Nev.: Western Printing and Publishing, 1969), 390.

9. Book of Deeds, 1840–60, Buenos Aires, Argentina, 1851. Copy in the care of George Alvisio-Altube of Hamilton, New York.

10. Douglass and Bilbao, *Amerikanuak,* 415.

11. Interviews with family members have confirmed that Pedro did go to the gold mines and became "quite rich" very quickly; the consensus is that he turned to other business ventures within a year or two after arriving in California.

12. Robert Glass Cleland, *The Cattle on a Thousand Hills* (San Marino, Calif.: Huntington Library, 1949), 139–40.

13. José Antonio Aguila, interview by Ralph Leroy Milliken, n.d., "San Juan Book," 2:359, in Ralph Leroy Milliken Museum, Los Banos, Calif.

14. Earle E. Williams, *El Camino Viejo* (Concord, Calif.: n.p., 1970).

15. Aguila interview.

16. Juanita Loinaz Hillberg and Kathleen Loinaz Mumma, granddaughters of Pablo and Catalina Loinaz, interviews by Carol Hovey, Novato and Mill Valley, Calif., May 1985.

17. Aguila interview. The spelling of Salvador's last name was done phonetically by the interviewer. There were never any records that provided the "correct" spelling of the surname *Ihitzaque* until a memoir of the Loinaz family was located. Their family records also state that there were two brothers in the family, one named Salvador.

18. Marie Elena Altube Verdugo, published interview in "Day by Day" (unidentified) newspaper column by Dick Emerson, Calexico, Calif., n.d. [1960s?], clipping in author's possession.

19. Douglass and Bilbao, *Amerikanuak*, 414–15.

20. Deeds, 1850–70, Contra Costa Historical Society, Pleasant Hill, Calif.

21. Tax Assessment Book, 1859, San Mateo County Courthouse, San Mateo, Calif.

22. Federal Bureau of the Census, 1860, Contra Costa County, Calif.

23. *People* vs. *Charles Garat,* Criminal Record (E13 Garat) 1858, Contra Costa Historical Society, Pleasant Hill, Calif. In 1858, Carlos Garat was found guilty of malicious mischief for cutting the manes and tails off of twenty of the Sunols' horses. Garat appealed the case and was ultimately found not guilty by a jury.

24. Alameda County land map, 1884, Alameda County Courthouse, Alameda, Calif.

25. Book of Deeds, 1850–80, Calaveras Historical Society, Angel's Camp, Calif.

26. Ibid.

27. Book of Deeds, 1855–70, Santa Barbara County Courthouse, Santa Barbara, Calif.

28. Douglass and Bilbao, *Amerikanuak,* 214.

29. Deeds, Santa Barbara County, 1859–66; San Francisco city directories, 1863–66, listings for Altube, Dolheguy, Louis Peres & Co.

30. Deeds, Contra Costa County, 1863–64.

31. Edward Treadwell, *The Cattle King* (New York: Macmillan, 1931), 54–59.

32. Wallace Smith, *Garden of the Sun* (Los Angeles: Lymanhouse, 1939), 196, 197 (illustration).

33. Joseph Arburua, interview, 1950, Basque Studies Collection, University of Nevada, Reno, Library. Arburua's property was adjacent to land owned by Henry Miller.

34. Treadwell, *Cattle King,* 54–59.

35. Arburua interview.

36. Notes to Arburua interview.

37. Ibid.; Book of Deeds, 1860–70, Merced County Courthouse, Merced,

Calif., and Book of Deeds, 1860–70, San Benito County Courthouse, Hollister, Calif.

38. Deeds, Merced County, 1860–1910.

39. Tax assessment records, 1870, Los Angeles County Courthouse, Los Angeles, Calif.

40. Arburua interview notes.

41. Mrs. John B. Garat, interview by author, Lafayette, Calif., June 1984.

42. Roger R. and Nancy L. Olmstead, Allen Pastron, and Jack Prichett, *Rincon de las Salinas y Potrero Viejo: The Vanished Corner* (San Francisco Clean Water Management Program, November 1981), 67.

43. San Francisco city directories, 1866–80, listings for Altubes, Peres, Louis Peres & Co.

44. Lester W. Mills, "Sagebrush Saga," *Elko (Nevada) Free Press,* January 18, 1889, p. 2.

45. Book of Deeds, 1870–75, Elko County Courthouse, Elko, Nev., June 1873, August 1874.

46. *Independence Valley (Nevada) Press,* March 31, 1874.

47. Stanley Paher, *Nevada: Ghost Towns and Mining Camps* (Las Vegas: Nevada Publishing, 1970), 202.

48. Deeds, Elko County, May and November 1878.

49. Book of Deeds, 1860–1904, San Francisco County Courthouse, San Francisco, Calif.; Deeds, Alameda County, 1875–80.

50. Declaration of water rights, 1880–1910, Elko County Courthouse, Elko, Nev., August 1889, May 1905; Deeds, Elko County, 1873–1905.

51. Henry Brown, untitled manuscript, 1884, Bancroft Library, Berkeley, Calif.

52. Arlene Evans, untitled manuscript, 1965, Basque Studies Collection, University of Nevada, Reno, Library.

53. Patterson, Ulph, and Goodwin, *Nevada's Frontier,* 388.

54. Ibid.

55. Federal Bureau of the Census, 1900, Elko County, Nev.

56. Corrine Loinaz, "Memoirs of My Early Years," n.d., Basque Studies Collection, University of Nevada, Reno, Library.

57. Loinaz interviews.

58. Loinaz, "Memoirs." The families of Etcheverry, Gastambide, Idiart, and Ihitzague are all from the same valley, Aldude, in the French Basses Pyrenees.

59. These photographs (and albums) are in the possession of Elena Talbott of Los Banos, Calif. The picture of Lucretia Altube is the only "visible" proof of her existence.

60. Loinaz, "Memoirs."

61. Baptism, marriage, and death records, 1856 through 1920, Notre Dames des Victories (French Church), and 1875 through 1925, Nuestra Señora de Guadalupe (Spanish Church), San Francisco, Calif.

62. Family records of the Altube and Garat families, documented by marriage records of the French Church and Spanish Church, San Francisco, Calif.

63. Baptism and death records, ibid.

64. Marriage records, ibid.

65. James Guinn, *Historical and Biographical Record of Monterey and San Benito Counties* (Los Angeles, 1910), 362–64. Albert Trescony of Monterey County always hired Basque workers through Aguirre. Trescony's only son, Jules, married the Aguirres' only daughter, Kate, in 1875.

66. Juan Miguel Aguirre had been in business in San Francisco as early as 1851, selling water. At $1 a bucket, he made at least $30 a day. He established his Basque Hotel and the first handball court in San Francisco by 1865.

67. San Francisco city directories, 1869–94, listings for Aguirres, Altubes, and Garats.

68. Miguel and Polonia Goldarecena (Silveria and Odel's parents) owned property in Calaveras County until the mid-1860s, then moved to Los Angeles and to San Francisco by the 1880s. Miguel was in the Spanish consulate. Peter and Silveria Garat's only child married Pedro and Marie Altube's granddaughter, Marie Lucretia Ormart.

69. Baptism and marriage records, French Church.

70. Arburua interview notes.

71. Joseph Arburua, "Rancho Panocha, de San Juan y los Carrizalitos," n.d., Basque Studies Collection, University of Nevada, Reno, Library.

72. Twenty-eight letters, written in Spanish or French, dating from June 25, 1870, to January 10, 1893, are still in the possession of Altube descendants.

73. Family letters dated April 13, 1871, and July 24, 1882.

74. Baptism and death records, French and Spanish Churches.

75. Family letter dated November 27, 1875.

76. Family letter dated July 24, 1878.

77. Baptism and marriage records, French Church.

78. San Francisco city directories, 1869–94, listings for Altubes and Gesvret.

79. Marie Elena Altube Verdugo, interview by author, July 1983, Calexico, Calif.

80. San Francisco city directories, 1887–89, listings for Spanish Benevolence Society. Arrillaga, who taught the Altube daughters piano, was organist for the Spanish Church for forty years.

81. Verdugo interview. Peter Altube and Marie Elena Altube Verdugo shared many anecdotal stories of their father's and their aunts' families' experiences on the Spanish Ranch, many occurring during the summer roundups or horse races between the ranches.

82. Corrine Loinaz and her Loinaz nieces all shared the same stories about the pressure on Jules and Amelia to marry and keep the Spanish Ranch "intact." Jules was highly respected and very successful in his management of the ranch.

83. Patterson, Ulph, and Goodwin, *Nevada's Frontier,* 391.

84. Ibid., 389.

85. Book of Deeds, February 29, June 13, July 8, 1901, San Francisco County Courthouse, San Francisco, Calif.

86. Described by Marie Elena Altube Verdugo, an Altube granddaughter who was born in the house and lived there until she was fourteen years old (Verdugo interview).

87. *Elko (Nevada) Daily Free Press,* February 13, 1960, p. 3.

88. Birth records, 1905, Elko County Courthouse, Elko, Nev. Twin grandsons, Pedro Joaquin and Bernardo Jules, were born at the ranch with the help of a Basque midwife on May 5, 1905.

89. Probate records, 1905, case 1929, San Francisco County Courthouse, San Francisco, Calif.

90. Deeds, Elko County, Nev., 30:123–31, 217–24; 34:115–18.

5. John B. Archabal (1873–1945): A Portrait of an Immigrant Success Story

1. James H. Hawley, *History of Idaho: The Gem of the Mountains* (Chicago: S. J. Clarke Publishing Co., 1920), 101–2. See also Sol Silen, *La Historia de los Vascongados en el Oeste de los Estados Unidos* (New York: Las Novedades, Inc., 1917), 52–53.

2. Patrick Bieter, "John Archabal and the American Basques" (Unpublished paper, May 1956), 12–13.

3. Joe Eiguren, interview with author, January 27, 1992, Boise, Idaho; Mike Hanley, *Owyhee Trails: The West's Forgotten Corner* (Caldwell, Idaho: Caxton Press, 1973), 268; *Caldwell Tribune,* July 17, 1909, p. 4.

4. Cathy Achabal, "John B. Archabal: Basque Sheep King of Idaho and Oregon," *Jaialdi '95 International Festival Program* (Boise: Euzkaldunak, Inc., 1995), 82–83; see also Bieter, "Archabal and the American Basques," 13–14.

5. Idaho Wool Growers Association, "History of Idaho's Sheep Industry and Sheep and Lambs: On Farm January 1, Number and Value, Idaho, 1867–1979," 6–8.

6. Ramon Ysursa, interview by author, January 5, 1996, Boise, Idaho; see also Achabal, "Archabal: Basque Sheep King," 82–83.

7. Cyprian Bradley and Edward J. Kelly, *History of the Diocese of Boise* (Caldwell, Idaho: Caxton Printers, 1953), 376.

8. Eloise Garmendia Bieter, interview by author, July 15, 1995, Boise, Idaho.

9. Marjorie Archabal, interview by author, July 30, 1995, Boise, Idaho.

10. Dan Archabal, interview by author, August, 2, 1995, Boise, Idaho.

11. Hawley, *History of Idaho,* 101–2.

12. Dan and Marjorie Archabal interviews.

13. *Idaho Statesman,* October 7, 1925.

14. Achabal, "Archabal: Basque Sheep King," 82–83.

15. Dan and Marjorie Archabal interviews.

16. Charles Hummel, interview by author, August 5, 1995, Boise, Idaho.

17. Ysursa interview; see also *Denver Post*, December 21, 1947, p. 5; Janette Guthmann, "Basque People of the Northwest" *National Wool Grower* 35, no. 14 (December 1945): 13.

18. *Idaho Statesman*, December 24, 1939, December 24, 1943.

19. Marjorie Archabal recalled that it was the only time she really felt out of place in the Archabal home. Basque was spoken the entire evening and she felt looked down upon by the visiting dignitaries (Marjorie Archabal interview).

20. *Idaho Statesman*, July 31, 1937.

21. Ibid., November 25, 1940.

22. Ibid., December 17, 1942.

23. Dan Archabal interview.

24. *Idaho Statesman*, October 2, 1945.

25. *Idaho Statesman*, December 23, 1945.

8. Santi's Story

1. The *baserri,* or farmstead, was the typical, traditional unit of production in the rural districts of the Basque Country. Its average size is about twenty-five acres of woodland, pasture, and arable fields. The typical farming family engaged in a mixed agricultural economy with a combination of livestock raising (milk cows, sheep, and pigs) and some grain (corn and wheat), and row (vegetables) cropping and fruit growing (primarily apples). While there was some production for the market, much of the emphasis was upon household self-sufficiency. Most of the Basque men who emigrated to the United States to herd sheep were raised on a baserri.

2. William A. Douglass and Jon Bilbao, *Amerikanuak: Basques in the New World* (Reno: University of Nevada Press, 1975), 310–18.

3. In 1962 Gregorio returned to the United States to work for another year in Idaho. By then his sons were all living elsewhere. As soon as he qualified for Social Security benefits, in 1963, Gregorio retired definitively to the Basque Country.

4. The National Monument to the Basque Sheepherder, inaugurated in Reno, Nevada, in 1989, includes a large metal sculpture by Basque artist Nestor Basterrechea. It was founded in Mexico City. Because of international regulations, it had to be transferred to an American trucking firm at the U.S.-Mexican border. Luis donated his services to the monument project—sending one of his trucks to Texas to transport the sculpture to Nevada.

5. It was that summer that I met Santiago. I was a graduate student in anthropology and was scheduled to leave in September to begin field research in a Basque village. I was working as a laborer for Helms to earn some extra

money. Santiago and I were on the same crew. He didn't really believe me when I told him about my plans, but he humored my queries. I learned my first Basque words digging trenches by his side. Two years later we ran into each other again in Mariano's Bar in Aulestia, the Bizkaian town where I was conducting my research. Gerrikaitz-Munitibar was the next town over, and he was courting a local woman.

6. Agriculture is on the decline in rural Bizkaia. For much of the latter half of the twentieth century it has become common practice to plant pine trees on former grain fields and meadows. The pines grow quickly and provide a commercial crop. Once the farm is no longer an agricultural production unit, there is little justification for passing it on intact to a single heir. It is now often the practice to divide stands of timber more or less equally among all of the children of the next generation (William A. Douglass, *Echalar and Murelaga: Opportunity and Rural Exodus in Two Spanish Basque Villages* [London: Christopher Hurst, 1975; New York: St. Martin's Press, 1975], 170–71). This was the case with Goikola. However, with all four of the Basterrechea brothers well-situated in the United States and their sister and brother-in-law residing on Goikola, the brothers have all deeded over their shares in Goikola's timber to Gloria.

7. William A. Douglass, "The Vanishing Basque Sheepherder," *The American West* 17, no. 4 (1980): 30–31, 59–61.

8. William A. Douglass, "Euskal-Amerikar Nortasuna," *Jakin* 90 (1995): 11–29.

9. Lyda Esain: A Hotelera's Story

1. Basque Americans frequently use the term *hoteleros* for the hotel-keeping couple, with *hotelero* used for a male and *hotelera* for a female.

2. This Martinto-Esain family history is based upon interviews, conducted by the author, with Lyda Martinto Esain in Fresno, Calif., on February 18, 1987, April 24, 1987, and April 10, 1996.

3. Wallace W. Morgan, *History of Kern County, California, with Biographical Sketches* (Los Angeles: Historical Record Company, 1914), 1350–51.

4. The only nineteenth-century Basque-language newspaper in the United States, the *California'ko Eskual Herria* (Basques of California), included a feature article entitled "Jean Martinto Builds a Ball Court at His Hotel," May (*Maitza*) 15, 1897, lib. 2, no. 37:2. Los Angeles, Calif.

5. *Ostatu* is the Basque word for an inn and—along with hotel—is often used as a name for the Basque boardinghouses found in the North American landscape.

6. For more on Tehachapi's Basque colony, see Jeronima Echeverria, "*California'ko Ostatuak*: A History of California's Basque Hotels" (Ph.D. dissertation, University of North Texas, Denton, Tex., 1988), 112–17.

7. Between 1900 and 1930, two or three Basque families in San Pedro opened their homes to Basque seafarers as boardinghouses. One—the Uruburu home on Fifth Avenue—flourished during the years the Martintos were there (Raymond Uruburu, interview with the author, Wonder Valley, Calif., March 11, 1995).

8. Mary Grace Paquette, *Basques to Bakersfield* (Bakersfield: Kern County Historical Society, 1982), 51.

9. *Lomo* is a salt-cured pork and *chorizo* is a type of sausage.

10. Sanborn Fire Insurance Maps, Fresno, Calif., 1933, vol. 1, map W, 71, Fresno County Library, Fresno, Calif.

11. As Felix was fond of saying, "One hand washes the other one clean." Lyda's aunt and Marie's sister, Mrs. Yturri, had another boardinghouse by the Santa Fe railroad tracks, and Felix visited regularly.

12. For a history of Basque boardinghouses, see Jeronima Echeverria, *Home Away from Home: A History of Basque Boardinghouses* (Reno: University of Nevada Press, 1999).

13. *Etxe aita* is Basque for father of the house and *etxe ama,* mother of the house.

14. Although one newspaper account spells the family surname *Uriquiri,* local Basques use *Urquidi* (John Croner, "Independent Basque Sheepmen Brought Unique Lifestyles," *Daily Argus Observer* [Ontario, Ore.], June 5, 1983).

15. Ibid.

16. Josephine Echanis Keim, as quoted by John Croner, ibid., 3C.

17. Patrick J. Bieter, "Letemendi's Boarding House: A Basque Cultural Institution in Idaho," *Idaho Yesterdays* 37 (spring 1993): 6–7.

18. Gretchen Holbert, "Elko's Overland Hotel," *Northeastern Nevada Historical Quarterly* 5 (winter 1975): 14.

19. Robert Laxalt, *Sweet Promised Land* (New York: Harper Brothers, 1957; reprint, Reno, University of Nevada Press, 1996), *The Basque Hotel* (Reno: University of Nevada Press, 1989), *Child of the Holy Ghost* (Reno: University of Nevada Press, 1992), and Monique (Laxalt) Urza, *The Deep Blue Memory* (Reno: University of Nevada Press, 1993). Also note in this volume Richard Etulain's chapter on Robert Laxalt, whose early years were shaped by growing up at the French Hotel.

20. Charlotte Crawford, "The Position of Women in a Basque Fishing Community," in *Anglo-American Contributions to Basque Studies: Essays in Honor of Jon Bilbao,* ed. William A. Douglass, Richard W. Etulain, and William H. Jacobsen Jr. (Reno: Desert Research Institute, 1977), 145–52.

21. In the 1980s Gretchen Holbert and Mateo Osa interviewed dozens of Nevada's hoteleras. Tapes of these interviews are housed at the University of Nevada, Reno, Getchell Library, Basque Studies Program. Paquita Garatea's master's thesis ("*Burns'eko Extekoandreak:* Basque Women Boarding House Keepers of Burns, Oregon" [Portland State University, 1990]) deals with the

women of the Burns boardinghouses. And, finally, Nancy Zubiri's *A Basque Travel Guide: Families, Feasts, and Festivals* (Reno: University of Nevada Press, 1998) includes commentary from a number of hoteleras in the American West.

22. Dominic Sorcabal, interview by author, Huntington Beach, Calif., May 1, 1987.

23. William and Albert Beterbide, interviews by author, Alturas, Calif., May 22, 1987.

24. For further discussion, see Echeverria, *"California'ko,"* 186–203.

25. Garatea, *"Burns'eko,"* 34–36.

26. Ibid., and Lucy Alboitiz Garatea, interview by author, Boise, Idaho, March 22, 1989.

27. Catherine Goyenetche, interview by author, San Francisco, Calif., May 13, 1987.

28. Elena Celayeta Talbott, interview by author, Los Banos, Calif., March 10, 1987, and Sodie Arbios, *Memories of My Life: An Oral History of a California Sheepman* (Stockton: Techni-Graphics Printing, 1980), 20–33.

29. Gretchen Holbert Osa, "The Overland: The Last Basque Hotel," in *Essays in Basque Social Anthropology and History,* Basque Studies Occasional Papers Series, no. 4, ed. William A. Douglass (Reno: Basque Studies Program, 1989), 322.

30. Donna Gabaccia, *From the Other Side: Women, Gender, and Immigrant Life in the United States, 1820–1990* (Bloomington: Indiana University Press, 1994), xi.

31. Teresa del Valle, "The Current Status of the Anthropology of Women: Models and Paradigms," in *Essays in Basque Social Anthropology and History,* ed. Douglass, 129–48; Jacqueline Urla, "Reinventing Basque Society: Cultural Difference and the Quest for Modernity, 1918–1936," ibid., 149–76; and Roslyn Frank, "The Religious Role of Women in Basque Culture," in *Anglo-American Contributions to Basque Studies,* ed. Douglass, Etulain, and Jacobsen, 153–62.

32. Deborah Fink, *Open Country, Iowa: Rural Women, Tradition, and Change* (Albany: State University of New York Press, 1986), 3, 234–40. Glenda Riley, *The Female Frontier: A Comparative View of Women on the Prairie and the Plains* (Lawrence: University Press of Kansas, 1988), 14–41, and Deborah Fink, *Agrarian Women: Wives and Mothers in Rural Nebraska, 1880–1940* (Chapel Hill: University of North Carolina Press, 1992), 189–96, provide food for thought in this area as well.

33. Iban Bilbao and Chantal Equilaz, *Diaspora Vasca,* vol. 1, *Vascos llegados al puerto de Nueva York, 1897–1902* (Vitoria: Gasteiz, 1981), and Marie Pierre Arrizabalaga, "A Statistical Study of Basque Immigration into California, Nevada, Idaho, and Wyoming between 1900 and 1910" (master's thesis, University of Nevada, Reno, 1986), 35–128.

34. Echeverria, *"California'ko,"* 186–204.

10. Pete Cenarrusa: Idaho's Champion of Basque Culture

1. Robert P. Clark, *The Basques: The Franco Years and Beyond* (Reno: University of Nevada Press, 1979), 182.

2. All biographic data was taken from information supplied by Pete Cenarrusa in two five-hour interviews by author, in Cenarrusa's office, Idaho State Capitol, January 3, 10, 1996.

3. Tom Sanford to Senator William Borah, 1927, in Pete Cenarrusa's papers.

4. Freda Cenarrusa, interview by author, Boise, Idaho, January 12, 1996.

5. Ibid.

6. Perry Swisher, interview by author, Moon's Cafe, Boise, Idaho, January 11, 1996.

7. Ibid.

8. Cenarrusa interviews.

9. Clark, *The Basques,* 182.

10. Ibid., 183.

11. Ibid., 184.

12. All letters cited herein can be found in the Cenarrusa Papers, in Pete Cenarrusa's possession.

13. *New York Times,* December 27, 1970.

14. Ibid.

15. *Idaho Statesman,* December 20, 1970.

16. Ibid., December 21, 1970.

17. Ibid., December 20, 1970.

18. *New York Times,* December 27, 1970.

19. Letter to William P. Rogers, Secretary of State.

20. Clark, *The Basques,* 186.

21. *El Diario (Bilbao) Vasco,* August 1971.

22. *Congressional Record,* April 6, 1972. See Appendix herein for text of the memorial.

23. Swisher interview.

24. Former Gov. Cecil D. Andrus, interview by author, January 22, 1996.

25. Inaki Zubizarreta, letter to Cenarrusa, April 1972.

26. Ibid.

27. Martin Ugalde, letter to Inaki Zubizarreta, June 1972.

28. Zubizarreta to Cenarrusa, May 1972.

29. Transcription in Cenarrusa Papers.

11. Juanita "Jay" Uberuaga Hormaechea and the Boise Heritage School of Basque Dancing

1. Elizabeth Robinson, "Neither Slave Nor Tyrant," *Scenic Idaho* 6 (winter 1951).

2. Jack Beardwood, "Second Generation Basques Typically American Youths," *Capital News*, n.d., June 1937, clipping in the Hormaechea Papers, Basque Museum and Cultural Center, Boise, Idaho.

3. Earl N. Pomeroy, "Basques: Highway Brings in New Customs," *Sunday Oregonian*, August 25, 1946.

4. Judith Lynne Hanna, *Dance, Sex, and Gender* (Chicago: University of Chicago Press, 1988), xiii.

5. Biographical details, commentary, and opinions from Jay Hormaechea, unless otherwise noted, derive from the author's numerous conversations with her beginning fall 1991 and ending spring 1996, but particularly three personal interviews by the author in Jay's home, Boise, Idaho, on November 16, 1991, April 3, 1992, and July 4, 1992.

6. Robert Laxalt's account of one woman's ill-treatment in the old country as a result of her birth out of wedlock is relevant to Jay's experience. See Robert Laxalt, *Child of the Holy Ghost* (Reno: University of Nevada Press, 1992).

7. Flavia Maria McCullough, *The Basques in the Northwest* (San Francisco: R and E Research Associates, 1974). Originally, "The Basques in the Northwest" (master's thesis, Portland State University, 1945).

8. "Sheepman and Biscayans," *Caldwell (Idaho) Tribune*, July 17, 1909.

9. Jerónima Echeverría, "California's Basque Hotels and Their *Hoteleros*," in *Essays in Basque Social Anthropology and History*, Basque Studies Program Occasional Papers Series, no. 4, ed. William A. Douglass (Reno: University of Nevada Press, 1989), 297–316, 309.

10. Robinson, "Neither Slave Nor Tyrant," 8.

11. Program book, *Ballets Basques De Biarritz* (New York: Lou Dunetz and Paul Lovett Publishers, 1957), 8; the Hormaechea Papers.

12. Rodney Gallop, *A Book of the Basques* (Reno: University of Nevada Press, 1970), 178.

13. For an account of the important role that dancing played in the life of young boys in the old country, see Eleanor Lisner, *The Romance of the Basque Country and the Pyrenees* (New York: Dodd, Mead & Company, 1928), 163–64.

14. Joanne Aldrich, telephone interview by author, Richmond, Calif., June 4, 1992.

15. For a list of individuals who provided Jay with support, see Bernice Brusen, *Basques from the Pyrenees to the Rockies* (Portland, Ore.: Dynagraphics, 1985), 19. Among the musicians who played for Jay were Domingo Ansotegui (tambourine), Valen Lee Letemendi (accordion), Ramon Echevarrea (guitar), Angeles Bicandi (accordion), Jimmy Jausoro (accordion), Joe Anacabe (tambourine), and Joe Ansotequi (tambourine).

16. Albert Erquiaga, interview by author, Boise, Idaho, August 13, 1992. As one of the original organizers of the Boise Oinkari dance troop and NABO (North American Basque Organizations), Erquiaga was a key source of information. Incorporated in 1974, NABO currently represents twenty-four clubs

from Idaho, Utah, Wyoming, California, Oregon, and Nevada. Erquiaga was its first president.

17. Barbara Dana, "Traditions of Basque Dances Preserved by Boise Teacher," *Idaho Statesman* (Boise), June 6, 1948.

18. Dabney Taylor, "Western Basques: People of An Ancient Race," *Spokesman-Review* (Spokane, Wash.), October 17, 1948.

19. Boise Music Week File, 1919–1952, Idaho Historical Society, Boise, Idaho.

20. "'Song of Basque' to be Presented," *Idaho Statesman,* May 9, 1949.

21. Betty Penson, "Thousands Throng to Greatest Basque Spectacle," *Idaho Statesman,* May 10, 1949.

22. "Song of the Basque To Show Again Next Friday," *Idaho Statesman,* May 13, 1949.

23. "Basque Music, Dances Draw Crowd of 5000," *Idaho Statesman,* May 15, 1950.

24. "Boise Music Week Festival To Continue Tradition," *Idaho Statesman,* May 15, 1954.

25. "Music Reigns as Queen at Boise Fete," *Christian Science Monitor,* June 3, 1950.

26. William A. Douglass, "Inventing an Ethnic Identity: The First Basque Festival," in *Basques of the Pacific Northwest,* ed. Richard W. Etulain (Pocatello: Idaho State University Press, 1991), 79–85.

27. Chamber of Commerce letter, 1953, in Hormaechea Papers.

28. Adelia Garro Simplot, interview by author, Boise, Idaho, April 3, 1992. Adelia Garro married one of J. R. Simplot's sons. J. R. Simplot, known as the "Potato King," is an Idaho agribusiness magnate and one of the richest men in the world.

29. Albert Erquiaga, interview by author, Boise, Idaho, August 13, 1992.

30. John Bieter, interview by author, Boise, Idaho, January 20, 1992.

31. Joseph V. Eiguren, *Kaspar* (Boise: Basque Museum and Cultural Center, 1988), 179.

32. For an account of "Sabino De Arana Y Goiri and the Creation of Basque Nationalist Ideology," see Stanley G. Payne, *Basque Nationalism* (Reno: University of Nevada Press, 1975), 61–86.

33. Merle Wells, interview by author, Boise, Idaho, May 27, 1993.

34. Albert Erquiaga, interview by author, Boise, Idaho, August 13, 1992.

35. Brusen, *Basques from the Pyrenees to the Rockies,* 15.

36. "Jay Hormaechea," *Journal of the Society of Basque Studies* 10, special tenth-anniversary issue (1990): 132.

37. Bethine Church, "Citation for Cultural Achievement Honoring Jay Hormaechea by the Basque Museum and Cultural Center," copy courtesy Jay Hormaechea.

38. "Portrait of a Distinguished Citizen," *Idaho Statesman,* April 4, 1993.

39. Trisha Clausen Zubizarreta, "Juanita's *Abarketak,*" in *Chorizos,*

Beans, and Other Things: A Poetic Look at the Basque Culture (Boise, Idaho: Lagun Txiki Press, 1987), 14.

40. For a discussion of symbolic strategies in the creation and maintenance of group organization, see Abner Cohen, *Two-Dimensional Man: An Essay on the Anthropology of Power and Symbolism in Complex Society* (Berkeley: University of California Press, 1974), 65–89.

41. Josephine Bilbao, interview by author, Boise, Idaho, January 26, 1994.

42. Roslyn M. Frank, "The Religious Role of the Woman in Basque Culture," in *Anglo-American Contributions to Basque Studies: Essays in Honor of Jon Bilbao,* ed. William A. Douglass, Richard W. Etulain, and William H. Jacobsen Jr. (Reno: Desert Research Institute, 1977), 153.

12. Robert Laxalt: Basque Writer of the American West

1. Much of the biographical detail and all of Robert Laxalt's personal opinions expressed in this essay, unless otherwise noted, derive from the author's extended personal interview with Laxalt and his wife, Joyce, in their Carson City home on January 5, 1996. Brief sections of this article first appeared as reviews of Laxalt's books in *Journal of Ethnic Studies, High Roller,* and *Nevada Historical Society Quarterly.* See also "Dominique Laxalt: Basque Sheepherder," *Nevada Historical Society Quarterly* 26 (winter 1983): 298–301.

2. *Dedication of the Grace Bordewich School, September 25, 1974,* pamphlet in Robert Laxalt Papers, 85-9, box 4, Getchell Library, University of Nevada, Reno. Grace Bordewich to Robert [Laxalt], March 7, 1965, Laxalt Papers, box 8. Several of Laxalt's earliest creative writings are available in his papers. Laxalt once told a writer: "The Basques regard the arts as a sort of lazy man's occupation. . . . They believe if you can't work, you dance. If you can't dance, you sing. If you can't do any of these . . . , you write" (Hank Nuwer, "Last of a Hardy Breed," *Dynamic Years* [November–December 1979]: 10).

3. Joan D. Morrow, "The Shepherder's Son," *Reno* 2 (February 1980): 22–24; Senator Pat McCarran to "My dear Bob [Laxalt]," January 17, 1945, Laxalt Papers.

4. A. E. Cahlan of the *Las Vegas Evening Review-Journal* to Robert Laxalt, February 10, 1948, Laxalt Papers, box 4. Robert Laxalt, *The Violent Land: Tales the Old Timers Tell* (Reno: Nevada Publishing Co., 1953).

5. Robert Laxalt, *The Lean Year and Other Stories* (Reno: University of Nevada Press, 1994), xii. Laxalt's attempts to publish in eastern literary magazines are chronicled in correspondence with his agents Emilie Jacobson and Naomi Burton of Curtis Brown, Ltd., in 1953 and 1954 in the Laxalt Papers, box 4.

6. Robert Laxalt, *Sweet Promised Land* (New York: Harper and Row, 1957; reprint, Reno: University of Nevada Press, 1996).

7. For revealing evidences of Laxalt's struggle to find a satisfactory form for

Sweet Promised Land, see numerous letters in the early to mid-1950s between Laxalt, his agent Naomi Burton, and Elizabeth Lawrence of his eventual publisher, Harper and Brothers/Harper and Row, in the Laxalt Papers.

8. The place of *Sweet Promised Land* in literature written about the American Basques is discussed in Richard W. Etulain, "The Basques in Western American Literature," in *Anglo-American Contributions to Basque Studies: Essays in Honor of Jon Bilbao,* ed. William A. Douglass, Richard W. Etulain, and William H. Jacobsen Jr. (Reno: Desert Research Institute, 1977), 7–18.

9. Laxalt to Naomi Burton, Curtis Brown, January 20, 1957, Laxalt Papers, box 4.

10. Robert Laxalt, *A Man in the Wheatfield* (New York: Harper and Row, 1964; reprint, Reno: University of Nevada Press, 1987).

11. Robert Laxalt to Elizabeth Lawrence of Harper and Row, September 27, 1963, Laxalt Papers, box 1; Roger Smith, "'A Man in the Wheatfield' is news again," *Nevada Arts, Reno Gazette,* August 26, 1979.

12. Tom Lea to "Miss Lawrence," May 9, 1964, copy in Laxalt Papers, box 1.

13. Robert Laxalt, *In a Hundred Graves* (Reno: University of Nevada Press, 1972). Vignettes by Laxalt similar to those contained in *In a Hundred Graves* accompany the well-known photographs of William Albert Allard in *A Time We Knew: Images of Yesterday in the Basque Homeland* (Reno: University of Nevada Press, 1990).

14. The now-classic account of Basques throughout the Old and New Worlds is William A. Douglass and Jon Bilbao, *Amerikanuak: Basques in the New World* (Reno: University of Nevada Press, 1975).

15. Robert Laxalt, *Nevada: A Bicentennial History* (New York: Norton, 1977). Laxalt tried out some of the themes of this book in his earlier brief volume, *Nevada* (New York: Coward-McCann, 1970), and in several essays in *National Geographic.*

16. For a revealing cross section of reactions to Laxalt's *Nevada,* see the three professional readers' reports on file in Laxalt Papers, box 1.

17. Robert Laxalt, *A Cup of Tea in Pamplona* (Reno: University of Nevada Press, 1985).

18. Robert Laxalt, *The Basque Hotel* (Reno: University of Nevada Press, 1989).

19. Robert Laxalt, *Child of the Holy Ghost* (Reno: University of Nevada Press, 1992).

20. Robert Laxalt, *The Governor's Mansion* (Reno: University of Nevada Press, 1994).

21. Jerome E. Edwards, review of Robert Laxalt's *The Governor's Mansion, Nevada Historical Society Quarterly* 38 (spring 1995): 57.

22. Laxalt's roles as a western writer and as a literary interpreter of the Basques are treated in Etulain, "The Basques in Western American Literature"; in Wilbur S. Shepperson, *Restless Strangers: Nevada's Immigrants and Their*

Interpreters (Reno: University of Nevada Press, 1970); and in Levi Peterson, Introduction to "The Rocky Mountains," and Gerald Haslam, Introduction to "Earth Tones: Ethnic Expression in American Literature," in *A Literary History of the American West*, ed. J. Golden Taylor, Thomas J. Lyon et al. (Fort Worth: Texas Christian University Press, 1987), 841, 1033.

23. General trends in twentieth-century western American literature, including recent emphases on ethnic fiction, are traced in Richard W. Etulain, *Re-imagining the Modern American West: A Century of Fiction, History, and Art* (Tucson: University of Arizona Press, 1996).

13. Robert Erburu and Becoming a Postmodern Basque

1. Marcus Lee Hansen, *The Problem of the Third Generation Immigrant* (Rock Island, Ill.: Swedish Immigration Center and the Augustana Library, 1987), 15. The text of this publication was a speech first given in 1937.

2. It is clear, however, that "authenticity" itself assumed new meaning, since the past was as much reconstructed and then reconciled with twentieth-century life as it was rediscovered in order to be reincorporated into our family existence (see Edward Bruner, "Abraham Lincoln as Authentic Reproduction: A Critique of Postmodernism," *American Anthropologist* 96, no. 2 [1994]: 397–415). In this regard ethnic pride, in its present guise, is an exercise in appreciating the humbleness of our origins and the subsequent travails traversed (for Euro-Americans the great metaphor being the Atlantic Crossing) in order to underscore our individual and group successes (i.e., the immigrant as an Horatio Alger character).

3. Micaela de Leonardo, *The Varieties of the Ethnic Experience: Kinship, Class, and Gender among California Italian-Americans* (Ithaca: Cornell University Press, 1984).

4. Nancy L. Green, "The Comparative Method and Poststructural Structuralism—New Perspectives for Migration Studies," *Journal of American Ethnic History* 13, no. 4 (1994): 3–22.

5. This section is based upon interviews with Robert Erburu conducted January 13–14, 1994, Los Angeles, Calif.

6. C. M. Gidney, Benjamin Brooks, and Edwin M. Sheridan, *History of Santa Barbara, San Luis Obispo, and Ventura Counties, California* (Chicago: D. Lewis Publishing Co., 1917), 2:712–13.

7. Ibid., 713.

8. I interviewed Kathryn on March 19, 1994, when she was ninety-four years old, in Ojai, Calif.

9. Gidney, *History*, 712.

10. Ibid., 618–19.

11. Ibid., 618.

12. William A. Douglass and Jon Bilbao, *Amerikanuak: Basques in the New World* (Reno: University of Nevada Press, 1975), 123–26.

13. Articles of Incorporation of the Union Latina Americana Estado de California were filed with the State of California on January 19, 1907. Mariano Erburu was the first signator. When the organization was dissolved on December 2, 1948, Alfonso Erburu was the first signator as its president and Mariano was one of the forty-nine signators electing for dissolution (documents in the Santa Barbara Historical Association archive).

14. The French Hospital, supported by subscription, was the medical facility used by northern Californian Basques, including those from Spain. Alfonso's membership would suggest that his California ramblings indeed took him north of Bakersfield. One of Bruno Orella's sons, Fermín Orella, M.D., was a member of the staff of the French Hospital.

15. Gidney, *History*, 619.

16. Alfonso had promised his estate to Ildefonso. His two brothers in California decided to contest the will, and Ildefonso actually came to California from Navarre to defend his inheritance. The three brothers reached some kind of a settlement. Robert's father studiously avoided the whole affair.

17. Indeed, it was the classic stem family household pattern common in rural northern Navarre and other parts of the Basque Country. What Kathryn failed to note was that in rural Piedmont the patrilineally extended, joint-family household, in which several married sons co-reside with their parents, is common.

18. Paul Laxalt was a former governor of Nevada as well. His term overlapped with Ronald Reagan's stint as governor of California, and they developed a close personal and working relationship. Laxalt was one of the first to promote Reagan's run at the U.S. presidency. At one time he headed the Reagan election campaign, and he subsequently served as national chairman of the Republican Party as well.

19. Within the Basque Country of Europe there is marked political division between Navarre and the Basque provinces of Spain. Navarre forms its own autonomous region, while Bizkaia, Gipuzkoa, and Araba constitute the Autonomous Community of Euskadi. The French-Spanish frontier divides the Basque Country into two additional political spheres of influence. The history of Basque settlement in the American West has divided Basque Americans into two discernible colonies. In Idaho and Oregon Bizkaians predominate, whereas in California, parts of Nevada, Utah, Wyoming, and Montana, Navarrese and French Basques are in the majority.

20. Robert Laxalt, *Sweet Promised Land* (New York: Harper, 1957; reprint, Reno: University of Nevada Press, 1996).

21. Rachel Bard, *Navarra, the Durable Kingdom* (Reno: University of Nevada Press, 1982).

22. Elizabeth is descended from Miguel Erro, a man who, like Mariano Erburu, was from Navarre. Miguel entered the United States in 1875 at age sixteen. He herded sheep in Ventura County and in 1888 was married to Josefa Orella, Juana's sister. When Bruno died in 1901, Josefa (like Juana) inherited

a 607-acre portion of the Orella ranch that she and her husband then used for cattle raising (Michael James Phillips, *History of Santa Barbara County, California* [Chicago: S. J. Clarke Publishing Company, 1927], 2:250, 253).

23. What follows regarding the history of the Orella and González families is derived from unpublished (and uncatalogued) correspondence and documentation and a collection of Orella family newsletters and memorabilia, archived with the Basque Studies Program library, Gretchell Library, University of Nevada, Reno.

24. There is an Orella Family Association with an annual (Christmas) newsletter edited by Tracey Orella, Elizabeth Hvolboll, and Michael Haines Orella, which serves as an informational forum for Orella descendants while also providing them with the results of new genealogical investigation into their origins.

25. Legend has it that the name was acquired when, during a campaign against the Moors in the ninth century, the king and queen of Navarre fell mortally wounded. A young knight named Guevara happened upon the dying queen and saw a tiny arm protruding from her body. He plucked an infant from the dying mother. Twelve years later he presented the royal heir to the Navarrese court and was given the honorific title of Ladrón (Thief) de Guevara.

26. Earlier we noted that Kathryn Sarzotti recalled that her mother-in-law (Bruno and Mercedes's daughter) Juana was given to putting on social airs. This should be qualified by the fact that both Bruno and Mercedes were rather poorly educated. He was literate but not particularly erudite whereas she used an X to sign her name. There is also an echo within the family of the longstanding struggle within Latin American society between *peninsulares* (Old World–born Spanish nationals) and *criollos* (New World–born persons of largely European descent) for social superiority. Although Bruno worked for Leandro González upon his arrival in California, he, as a peninsular, frequented Santa Barbara's Old World–born De la Guerra family household, arguably Santa Barbara's most prominent. After Bruno married Mercedes, of mixed ancestry albeit the daughter of a land grantee, Bruno was no longer welcomed by the De la Guerras.

27. As his interest in his Basque heritage increased, so did his commitment to the Basque Studies Program. About 1980 I received a most extraordinary letter from Robert in which he noted that we hadn't asked him for a donation since our 1968 request, and didn't we need help?! He has been a major benefactor of the Basque Studies Program ever since.

28. Suso was accompanied by reporter Koldo San Sebastian, a key player at Harriluze (Institute for the Study of the Basque Diaspora). Upon his return to Europe, San Sebastian initiated a study of the European origins of the Erburu and Orella families that led to a lengthy report sent to the Orella Family Association. They had it translated into English and have employed parts of it in their annual newsletter.

29. His fellow board members include Cecil Andrus (former governor of Idaho), James McClure (U.S. senator from Idaho), John Elorriaga (former CEO of US Bank), and Thomas Krens (director of the Guggenheim Museum). The honorary chairman is José Antonio Ardanza, president of the Autonomous Basque Community.

30. Along with John Elorriaga, the Prudencio Unanue family, of Navarrese and Cuban descent and founder of Goya Foods, a major Hispanic foods producer in the United States, and Linda White, coauthor of a Basque-English dictionary.

31. Fischer underscores the agonistic dimensions in autobiography written by minority ethnics who have experienced discrimination (Michael M. J. Fischer, "Ethnicity and the Post-Modern Arts of Memory," *Writing Culture: The Poetics and Politics of Ethnography*, ed. James Clifford and George E. Marcus [Berkeley: University of California Press, 1984]). It may, indeed, be symptomatic of their plight that if the agony of their ethnic odyssey is to be told at all the telling becomes autobiographical. Conversely, it may only be possible to relate the ethnic persona of a Robert Erburu in biographical fashion simply because it is more likely to strike the analyst than the actor as relevant and revealing. Were Robert Erburu to pen an autobiographical text it would, no doubt, give very different weighting than does the present one to the elements of his life story. I would argue that in considering Robert Erburu's ethnic persona we are, therefore, accessing the least developed and understood galaxy of America's ethnic universe. It is not that white ethnics failed to experience discrimination or to recount it. We have many such accounts by immigrants and their offspring (the works of Jerre Mangione, *Monte Allegro: A Memoir of Italian American Life* [New York: Columbia University Press, 1981], and *An Ethnic at Large: A Memoir of America in the Thirties and Forties* [Philadelphia: University of Pennsylvania Press, 1983], are a prime example of the latter). What we truly lack, for the most part, are the ethnic narrations of the grandsons and granddaughters. For the Basque case, however, there is the notable exception provided by Monique Urza's *A Deep Blue Memory* (Reno: University of Nevada Press, 1993).

I would further argue that the two approaches—the autobiographical/minority and the biographical/majority—ultimately converge and then merge into a common enterprise. In this regard, Fischer's words are quite applicable to Robert Erburu's case. Fischer tells us:

> The recreation of ethnicity in each generation, accomplished through dream- and transfer-like processes, as much as through cognitive language, leads to efforts to recover, fill in, act out, unravel, and reveal. Though the compulsions, repressions and searches are individual, the resolution (finding peace, strength, purpose, vision) is a revelation of cultural artifice. Not only does this revelation help delegitimize and place in perspective the hegemonic power of repressive political or majority discourses, it sensitizes us

to important wider cultural dynamics in the post-religious, post-immigrant, technological and secular societies of the late twentieth century. In these societies processes of immigration and cultural interaction have not slowed; quite the contrary. There is increasingly a diversity of cultural tapestry that is not—as many have assumed—being homogenized into blandness. The great challenge is whether this richness can be turned into a resource for intellectual and cultural reinvigoration. (231)

32. For nonwhite populations within American society, the odyssey toward, and even the possibility of, full assimilation (that is, acceptance) is obviously different, colored as it is by racism. But then that is another story that is beyond the scope of the present treatment.

33. Richard D. Alba, "The Twilight of Ethnicity among Americans of European Ancestry: The Case of the Italians," *Ethnicity and Race in the U.S.A.: Toward the Twenty-First Century*, ed. Richard D. Alba (London: Routledge and Kegan Paul, 1985), 134–58.

34. Herbert J. Gans, "Symbolic Ethnicity: The Future of Ethnic Groups and Cultures in America," *Ethnic and Racial Studies* 2 (January 1979): 1–20.

Selected Readings

Bibliographies and General Reference Works

Aulestia, Gorka. *Basque-English Dictionary.* Reno: University of Nevada Press, 1989. This is a standard dictionary for scholars and lay readers wishing to translate Basque words and phrases into English.

Aulestia, Gorka, and Linda White. *English-Basque Dictionary.* Reno: University of Nevada Press, 1990. Readers interested in English equivalents to Basque words and terms should begin with this extensive dictionary.

Bilbao, Jon, ed. *Eusko Bibliografía.* San Sebastián, Spain: Editorial Auñamendi, 1970. This multivolume bibliography and its supplements are the preeminent bibliography of Basque studies.

Douglass, William A., and Jon Bilbao. *Amerikanuak: Basques in the New World.* Reno: University of Nevada Press, 1975. After nearly a quarter century, this well-researched, comprehensive historical overview remains the best source on this subject.

Douglass, William A., and Richard W. Etulain, eds. *Basque Americans: A Guide to Information Sources.* Detroit: Gale Research Company, 1981. This volume includes annotations to more than four hundred items on Old World and New World Basques.

Autobiographies and Biographies

Laxalt, Robert. *Sweet Promised Land.* New York: Harper, 1957; 40th anniversary ed., Reno: University of Nevada Press, 1997. This novelized biography of the author's immigrant father is still the first book one should read about Basque sheepherding in the American West.

Paris, Beltran (as told to William A. Douglass). *Beltran: Basque Sheepman of the American West.* Reno: University of Nevada Press, 1979. Douglass uses the life of this immigrant Basque to Nevada to trace archetypal herder and sheepman experiences in the twentieth-century American West.

Simmons, Marc. *The Last Conquistador: Juan de Oñate and the Settling of the Far Southwest*. Norman: University of Oklahoma Press, 1991. This brief, very readable biography traces the life of the Basque pioneer of New Mexico.

Novels

Clark, Ann Nolan. *Year Walk*. New York: Viking Press, 1975. This adolescent novel authentically and convincingly treats a young Basque's herding experiences in the American West.

Laxalt, Robert. *The Basque Hotel*. Reno: University of Nevada Press, 1989. The first installment of Laxalt's Basque trilogy of fiction, this novel lovingly evokes a Basque young man's coming of age. The other two novels in the trilogy are *Child of the Holy Ghost* (1992) and *The Governor's Mansion* (1994), both published by the University of Nevada Press.

Urza, Monique. *The Deep Blue Memory*. Reno: University of Nevada Press, 1993. This superb first novel details Basque immigrant and second-generation family experiences in the American Far West, especially from a woman's perspective.

Other Works

Busca Isusi, José María. *Traditional Basque Cooking: History and Preparation*. Reno: University of Nevada Press, 1987. Of the several good Basque cookbooks, this one best integrates food history with superb recipes.

Collins, Roger. *The Basques*. London: Basil Blackwell, 1986. This excellent history book covers the struggles of Old World Basques in establishing their identity and self-determination for the past two thousand years.

Douglass, William A., ed. *Essays in Basque Social Anthropology and History*. Reno: Occasional Papers of the Basque Studies Program, 1989. This volume contains fourteen essays by noted scholars in the fields of Basque anthropology, history, folklore, and immigration studies.

Echeverria, Jeronima. *Home Away from Home: A History of Basque Boardinghouses*. Reno: University of Nevada Press, 1999. The author revealingly examines one of the major Basque institutions in the American West.

Etulain, Richard W., ed. *Basques of the Pacific Northwest*. Pocatello: Idaho State University Press, 1991. This anthology gathers fifteen essays that illustrate, over time, varied Basque experiences in the Pacific Northwest.

Gallop, Rodney. *A Book of the Basques*. London: Macmillan, 1930; reprint, Reno: University of Nevada Press, 1970. The author provides a comprehensive history of Old World Basques by examining their complex language, folklore, ancient dances and sports, art, and architecture.

Lane, Richard H., and William A. Douglass. *Basque Sheepherders of the American West: A Photographic Documentary*. Reno: University of Nevada Press, 1985. The most valuable of the photographic treatments of

Basque sheepherders in the American West, this attractive volume contains dozens of revealing photographs and readable text in English, Basque, Spanish, and French.

Zubiri, Nancy. *A Travel Guide to Basque America: Families, Feasts, and Festivals.* Reno: University of Nevada Press, 1998. This smoothly written travel guide contains hundreds of pages of information of interest to general and academic readers.

Contributors

J. PATRICK BIETER was professor emeritus of social studies education at Boise State University. He was married to Eloise Garmendia, whose family first sparked his interest in Basque history and culture. He has written of the Basques in Idaho and was instrumental in creating a program in the Basque Country for the study of Basque language and culture.

JOHN BIETER is a doctoral student in American history at Boston College. He received a B.A. in social science from the University of St. Thomas, St. Paul, Minnesota, and a M.A. in history from Boise State University. Bieter lived and studied for two years in the Basque Country and has lectured on the history of the Basques through the Idaho Humanities Council.

ANGELINE KEARNS BLAIN is an adjunct professor of sociology at Boise State University and a social historian who resides in Boise. She specializes in the study of women's contributions to culture in social and historical contexts. Her publications include a book, *Tactical Textiles: A Genealogy of the Boise Peace Quilt, 1981–1988* (1994), and numerous articles on women's issues.

ROBERT BOYD is a history teacher in the Bend–La Pine School District and curator of western heritage at the High Desert Museum in Bend, Oregon, with responsibility for producing exhibits that intrepet the region's exploration and settlement. In recent years, his exhibits have included *Gum San: Land of the Golden Mountain,* focusing on the Chinese experience, and *Amerikanuak! Basques in the High Desert.*

WILLIAM A. DOUGLASS is professor of anthropology and coordinator of the Basque Studies Program at the University of Nevada, Reno. He studies Basque and Italian emigration. His previous books include *Echalar and Murelaga: Opportunity and Rural Exodus in Two Spanish Basque Villages* (1975),

Amerikanuak: Basques in the New World (coauthor, 1975), *Emigration in a South Italian Hill Town* (1984), *Basque Sheepherders of the American West* (coauthor, 1985), and *From Italy to Ingham: Italians in North Queensland* (1995).

JERONIMA ECHEVERRIA is professor of history and associate dean of the School of Social Sciences at California State University, Fresno. Her parents were Bizkaian and Navarrese Basques who migrated to Southern California and became sheep ranchers. She has written several articles on Basque settlement in the American West and authored *Home Away from Home: A History of Basque Boarding Houses* (1999).

RICHARD W. ETULAIN is professor of history and director of the Center for the American West at the University of New Mexico. A specialist in the history and culture of the modern American West, he has authored or edited more than thirty books, including *Anglo-American Contributions to Basque Studies* (coeditor, 1977), *Basque Americans* (coeditor, 1981), and *Basques of the Pacific Northwest* (1991). His most recent works are *Re-examining the Modern American West: A Century of Fiction, History, and Art* (1996) and *Telling Western Stories: From Buffalo Bill to Larry McMurty* (1999).

DONALD T. GARATE is chief of interpretation and a historian at Tumacacori National Historical Park in southern Arizona. His published works include *Red Rock to Ravendale: Memories of a Northern California Community* (1975), *Termo to Madeline: Northern California's Last Frontier* (1982), *The Zion Tunnel: From Slickrock to Switchback* (1989), *The Juan Bautista de Anza National Historic Trail* (1994), and *Captain Juan Bautista de Anza: Correspondence on Various Subjects* (1995). For the past six years he has specialized in research and documentation of the Basque influence on the Spanish frontier, conducting research in archives in the United States, Mexico, and Spain, and has published several articles on these subjects.

CAROL W. HOVEY is a theater arts teacher at Livermore (California) High School, is the theater manager for Livermore's Performing Arts Theatre, and is the great-great-great-granddaughter of Pedro Altube. She has been researching her Basque ancestry for many years and, in 1995, fulfilled a lifelong dream by visiting Zugastegui—the Altube family *caserio* in Oñati.

MARC SIMMONS is an independent historian and author living in Cerrillos, New Mexico. His special interests include the Spanish colonial Southwest and the Santa Fe Trail. He is cofounder and past president of the Santa Fe Trail Association. Among his thirty books are *New Mexico: An Interpretive History* (1977) and *The Last Conquistador: Don Juan de Oñate and the Settling of the Far Southwest* (1991).

RENE TIHISTA is a psychiatric social worker, consultant, and trainer specializing in stress management and conflict resolution training for corporations, health-care facilities, and professional groups. He and his wife, Mary H. Dempy, cofounded Focal Point Programs in 1977 and have written two books on the stress personalities model, a behavioral model they developed: *Stress Personalities: A Look inside Our Selves* (1991) and *Dear Job Stressed: Relief for the Overworked, Overwrought, and Overwhelmed* (1996).

RALPH H. VIGIL is professor of history at the University of Nebraska, Lincoln. His special interests include colonial Latin America and the Spanish-Mexican Southwest. Among his various works are *Alonso de Zorita: Royal Judge and Christian Humanist, 1512–1585* (1987).

Index

Note that boldface page numbers indicate an extended treatment of the subject

Rivera, Tomás, 250–51
Roman Catholics, 3–18, 24, 25,
41–42, 63, 88. *See also* Catholic;
Inquisition; Priests; Spanish
Catholic Church; *and under
names of individual orders*

Sabala, Gregoria, 162
Sacramento, Calif., 59, 60
Saint-Jean-Pied-de-Port, 122–23
Salazar, Catalina de, 21
Salazar, Gonzalo de, 10, 11
Samuelson, Don, 172, 179, 181–82,
183
San Francisco, Calif., 56, 63
San Gabriel, N.Mex., 27, 28, 29
San Joaquin Valley, Calif., 61, 65,
66–67, 156
San Juan Indians, 25
San Sebastián, Spain, 149
Sanford, Tom, 173, 174
Santa Barbara, Calif., 65, 239–40,
249–50
Santa Fe, N.Mex., 30, 53, 54
Santa Nella (Sentinella), Calif., 61,
63
Santo Domingo pueblo, 24
Saracondi Boardinghouse, 194
Sasoeta family, 32
Segesser, Felipe, 44, 47
Senate Joint Memorial No. 115,
257–59
Seri Indians, 34, 46, 50–51
Serora, 210–11
Serving girls, 155, 162, 164
Seven Cities of Gold, 21
Shearing, 129–31
Sheepherders and sheepherding,
84–85, 86, 95, 98–99, 101,
108–10, 111–13, 114–40, 151,
169, 173–74, 215–16, 239. *See
also* Livestock raising; *and under
individual herders*
Sheepherders' Ball, 91, 95, 200

Sheepmen, 84, 86, 89–90, 92,
95–96, 241, 244, 245. *See also*
Altube, Pedro; Altube, Bernardo;
Archabal, John B.
Shoshone, Idaho, 174
Simplot, Adelia Garro, 207
Sinaloa, Mexico, 32
Slaughterhouses, 64–65, 68–69,
75–76
Slavery, 14, 15, 17
Smale Calder (fictional character),
217–18
Smugglers, 122–23, 222–23
Society of Basque Studies in Amer-
ica, 209
Socorros Mutuos, 91
Soldiers, 31, 35, 37, 39, 44, 46–48,
53
Song of the Basque (1949), 193,
204–6
Sonora, Mexico, 31, 39–40, 42
South America, 57, 62. *See also
under individual countries*
Spain, xiii, 21, 30, 75, 87. *See also
under individual provinces and
other locations*
Spanish, 3, 55
Spanish Catholic Church, 29. *See
also* Roman Catholics
Spanish Civil War, 92, 141, 143,
175–76, 182
Spanish colonial system, 17
Spanish Ranch, 57, 69, 70, 78
Sparks, Nev., 207
Stegner, Wallace, 227, 229
Stockman's hotel, 145
Stories and storytelling, 218, 223,
225, 231
Sweet Promised Land (Laxalt), xiii,
212, 215–17, 218, 228, 229

Taylor, John G., 77
Taylor Grazing Act, 92
Teague, Alfrida Poco, 246

Copyrights